D0569678

THE 50% AMERICAN

JK
1759
R46
.2005
WITHDRAWN

THE 50% AMERICAN

IMMIGRATION AND NATIONAL IDENTITY IN AN AGE OF TERROR

STANLEY A. RENSHON

GEORGETOWN UNIVERSITY PRESS
Washington, D.C.

Georgetown University Press, Washington, D.C.
© 2005 by Stanley A. Renshon. All rights reserved.
Printed in the United States of America
10   9   8   7   6   5   4   3   2   1   2005

This book is printed on acid-free paper meeting the requirements of the
American National Standard for Permanence in Paper for Printed Library Materials.

As of January 1, 2007, 13-digit ISBNs will replace the current 10-digit system.

Cloth: 978-1-58901-067-3

Library of Congress Cataloging-in-Publication Data

Renshon, Stanley Allen.
    The 50% American : immigration and national identity in an age of terror /
Stanley A. Renshon.
        p.   cm.
    Includes bibliographical references and index.
    ISBN 1-58901-067-1 (cloth : alk. paper)
    1. Americanization.   2. United States—Emigration and immigration—
Government policy.   3. National characteristics, American.   4. Immigrants—
United States—Social conditions.   I. Title: Fifty percent American.   II. Title.
JK1759.R46   2005
323.6'0973—dc22

                                                                    2005008371

For my son Jonathan,
Smart, thoughtful, sensitive, and so accomplished. . . .
A true scholar in progress. . . .
With great love and affection

Are we a "we," one people or several? If we are a "we," what distinguishes us from "thems" who are not us? Race, religion, ethnicity, values, culture, wealth, politics, or what? Is the United States . . . a "universal nation," based on values common to all humanity and in principle embracing all peoples? Or are we a Western nation with our identity defined by our European heritage and institutions? Or are we unique with a distinctive civilization of our own, as proponents of "American exceptionalism" have argued throughout our history? Are we basically a political community whose identity exists only in a social contract embodied in the Declaration of Independence and other founding documents? Are we multicultural, bicultural, or unicultural, a mosaic or a melting pot? Do we have any meaningful identity as a nation that transcends our subnational ethnic, religious, racial identities?

—Samuel Huntington

CONTENTS

vii

LIST OF TABLES

ACKNOWLEDGMENTS

THIS BOOK ON AMERICAN NATIONAL IDENTITY IS FRAMED BY MY
training first as a political scientist and later as a clinical psychologist and psychoanalyst. It draws on a number of diverse theoretical areas, primarily within the American experience: immigration, identity, history, politics, policy, and political theory.

No author can legitimately claim exhaustive knowledge of the substantive domains that this book covers. I certainly do not. The knowledge that I am able to bring to bear on these issues has been greatly aided by those that have supported my work and those from whom I have learned a great deal.

My work on immigration and diversity was greatly facilitated by two fellowships from the Center for Immigration Studies, most recently as Richard E. Estrada Fellow. I would like to thank its director, Mark Krikorian, for those opportunities to reflect and study. My work on race relations, identity, and issues of diversity was facilitated by a fellowship from the Institute of Race Relations, Boston University. My work on presidential leadership in the context of immigration theory and questions of amnesty, integration, and national security was facilitated by a fellowship from the Center for Public Leadership, John F. Kennedy School of Government, Harvard University, during the 2002–3 academic year. My work on political leadership in divided societies was also aided by two research grants from the City University of New York's Faculty Award Program. I am appreciative to the anonymous reviewers of both grants for their helpful comments. My work on President Bill Clinton's "One America" initiative was aided by a research grant from the Horowitz Foundation for Public Policy.

Some aspects of this work were presented at a Conference on Morality and Politics in the fall of 2002 at Bowling Green State University, and I would like to thank my fellow attendees there for their helpful comments: David Coop, George P. Fletcher, John J. Haldine, Russell Hardin, Harvey Klehr, James B. Murphy, John Tomasi, and Robert Weissberg.

Further aspects of this work were presented at the Gerst Conference on America's Ambivalent Egalitarianism: Facts and Perceptions, Duke University, in the spring of 2003. I would like to thank my fellow participants Michael Allen Gillespie, Jennifer Hochschild, Catherine Zuckert, and Michael Moses for their useful observations.

I taught a seminar on American National Identity at the City University Graduate Center in the fall of 2004 while I was finishing the revisions to this book and benefited enormously from that class and its discussions. My thanks to Meryem Ataselim, Joe Dallarda, Gregory Donovan, Bobbi Gentry, Jeremiah Minh Greenblatt, Tony Monchinski, Amy Perlow, and Matt Polazzo.

Those who read or who offered their observations on these issues in correspondence or discussions immeasurably helped my work on this book. I would like to thank Amitai Etzioni, Nathan Glazer, Eugene Goldstein, Meredith Krause, Mark Krikorian, Peter Schuck, Peter Skerry, Peter Spiro, and Stephan Thernstrom for their helpful comments. Mae M. Chung of *Newsday* graciously shared her data with me on New York City immigration and dual citizenship. Charles Bahmueller of the Center for Civic Education shared his valued perspective on the center's Guidelines for American History Standards.

I owe a special word of appreciation to Noah M. J. Pickus, a true scholar—informed, thoughtful, balanced, and insightful. The author and this book were greatly helped by the many conversations we shared on our mutual interests.

Two anonymous readers of the manuscript provided pages of detailed observations and thoughtful questions. I am very appreciative of the time and interest they took in this work.

My research assistant, Rebecca Blanton, has been a tremendous help throughout this project. Whether the task was tracking down papers, citations, or people, she did her job very competently and quickly. Every researcher should be so blessed.

Again it is my pleasure to acknowledge the help of my literary representative, Andrew Blauner.

Richard Brown, the director of Georgetown University Press, has welcomed this book and its author. Over several years and over a number of conversations, we have developed a very good working relationship that I deeply appreciate. The entire staff of Georgetown University Press provided excellent services.

No appreciation would be complete without acknowledging my family, whose presence and love allow me the freedom to do the work I love. My wife, Judith, has been a warm, supportive, and loving partner for twenty-eight years. I am a fortunate man indeed. My children, David and Jonathan, have been a continuing source of pleasure and pride over many years. For that I am truly blessed. I love them all.

This book is dedicated to my son Jonathan, whose interests in these issues have paralleled mine. He took a course in nationalism at the same time I started writing this book, and I owe much of my attention to the debates on liberal nationalism and its variants to our discussions. I appreciated the substance of those conversations, and of course it was a father's great pleasure to have them.

PROLOGUE

CONDUCT A SMALL EXPERIMENT. ASK YOUR FRIENDS AND COLLEAGUES how many countries permit their citizens to be citizens of more than one country. Frame your question by asking whether it might be a few, less than a dozen, several dozen, or even more. Aside from puzzled looks, my bet is that the most frequent answer will be a few or less than a dozen.

Then continue the experiment by asking more specifically how many countries allow their citizens to do all the following: become a citizen of one or more countries, swear allegiance to a foreign state, vote in foreign elections, run for office in another country while at the same time being a citizen in good standing of their home country, be elected or appointed to office in another country and serve while still a citizen in good standing of their home country, join another country's armed forces while a citizen of their home country, or fight in another country's army even if that country was hostile to the interests of their home country. Chances are, the looks you receive will range from suspicion to disbelief.

Press them to give you a number, and almost without fail, it will be either very small or none. Then ask if they are aware that the United States is the only country in the world to allow its citizens, whether natural or naturalized, to do all these things.

The facts that form the basis of this experiment are the subject of this book.

INTRODUCTION

AMERICA REMAINS A BEACON FOR IMMIGRANTS. THEY COME TO THE United States by the hundreds of thousands each year, from different cultural, religious, psychological, and political traditions. As a result, the United States now has a more diverse population than at any time in its history.

This new diversity raises old questions. In a nation like the United States comprising many ethnic, racial, religious, and political groups, what exactly binds us together as a people? What, if anything, can be done to help further the national attachments of those who arrive or are already here? This is the critical, hidden core of the immigration debate.

Contemporary immigration takes place in an age in which immigrants can and often do retain emotional, political, and economic ties to their "home countries." Moreover, their home countries increasingly encourage and actively urge them to do so. In the meantime, there has been little discussion about the implications of these developments for America's civic life and its national community. Is it possible to honor the understandable wish to retain some of these ties with the necessity of truly integrating large numbers of immigrants into our society? Is it possible to do so without threatening the immigrants' or American national identity?

The traditional answer to this question is this: The American Creed will unite us. Theorists on both the left and the right generally agree that a belief in justice and democracy, also known as the Creed, will be our salvation. I think this view is profoundly mistaken. People are not united primarily by abstractions operating at the stratospheric level—not unless they are connected to something that carries a deeper emotional power. The critical issue facing this country is not a matter of allegiance to abstract values, as laudable as they might be, but of attachment.

The same mistake is being made in other Western democracies facing similar issues. European Union officials urge that new immigrants from countries and cultures with different traditions learn the language of their new country and "adhere to European Values."[1] In Amsterdam, "all new arrivals are now obliged to attend 'integration classes,' In return for promises that immigrants

xvii

would be treated as equal citizens, the state demanded 'respect for the prevailing standards, values and customs.'"[2] Whether lip service to European values or "prevailing standards, values and customs" will help to truly integrate these alienated groups and forge a real emotional connection with their new countries is doubtful. Mohammed Bouyeri, who was charged with the brutal murder of Theo van Gogh, was born in the Netherlands, was well educated, spoke fluent Dutch, and "seemed well integrated in society."[3] A survey of Muslim immigrants and coverts after the terrorist attacks of July 7, 2005, found that one in four sympathized with the terrorists, and that six percent, which is more than 100,000 people, thought them to be "fully justified."[4] The assumption that the Creed will save us misses the very critical psychological foundation, emotional attachment, which underlies our culture and hence our politics.

I agree with Samuel Huntington that our Anglo-Protestant culture is central to American national identity, although I widen the scope of those traits and view them primarily through the lens of national psychology. Where we part company, however, is on the role of religion.

Huntington's controversial answer to the question of what unites us is our Anglo-Protestant culture and our bedrock Christianity.[5] I believe he is only partially correct. We were and are primarily a Christian nation, but we need not be religious in order to be united. Moderate religions, of whatever persuasion, fit in well with the ethos of the American national community.

The glue that holds this country together is a much maligned, wholly misunderstood psychological force: patriotism. Far from being the "last resort of scoundrels"—as Dr. Johnson wrote, speaking of "false patriotism"—it is the indispensable foundation of our attachments to each other and the institutions that form our national community.[6] It is critically important that we understand what patriotism really is, and the role it plays in American public life. We cannot ask much of immigrants if we do not understand it ourselves.

It is possible, of course, to have the rights of a citizen but feel little emotional attachment to the country that provides them. In that case, citizenship is primarily instrumental, sought for the advantages it confers. Yet a community requires more than instrumental membership and a "what's-in-it-for-me" calculus to function and prosper. Emotional attachments provide a community with the psychological resources to weather disappointments and disagreements, and they help to maintain a community's resolve in the face of historic dangers. Emotional attachment and identification are the mechanisms that underlie sacrifice, empathy, and service.[7] Citizenship without emotional attachment is the civic equivalent of a one-night stand.

Contentious issues regarding national integration and identity have been gathering force for the last forty-plus years of American history, and we have not made much progress in resolving them. As if that were not difficult enough, we must now contend with these problems in the context of catastrophic terrorism. The term is a simple one with profound implications. Since September 11, 2001, it has been abundantly clear that there are groups with the will, the desire, and—if they can acquire the means to do so—the intention to unleash chemical, biological, or nuclear weapons against their sworn enemies—primarily the United States.

The question of national identity recently posed by Huntington—"Who are we?"—must now be considered alongside of the question of whether we will survive intact. The nature of our attachments to each other and the country we share—American national identity—has always been extremely important in maintaining the attachments that underlie this union. In an age of terrorism, it is profoundly so.

The rise of catastrophic terrorism takes place in a context of increasing globalization. The essence of globalization is the extraordinary worldwide fluidity of information, markets, and people. This raises questions not so much about the future of the nation-state but of its basis. States are, and will continue to be, the primary sources and institutional base of global trends. Money and people may flow across state boundaries—but they still need banks and passports, respectively, to do so.

Yet globalization in the form of unprecedented international migration, which flows primarily from east to west and from south to north, has raised basic questions of inclusion, identification, and accommodation for liberal democracies (which are the destinations of most of these migrants). At the same time, the rise of catastrophic terrorism is associated with regions and countries that contribute substantially to the immigration flow to Western liberal democracies. This raises the ante considerably for countries like the United States. It must reconcile its generally liberal traditions and the call to be more "welcoming"—a deceptively inviting term whose exact meaning and consequences are rarely discussed—with the need to maintain and develop an American national community.

The purpose of this book is to develop a theory and understanding of American national community and identity that goes beyond the misplaced preoccupation with the American Creed. My starting point is the issue of dual citizenship. Multiple citizenship is an increasingly prevalent form of modern political life. This is an important but poorly understood development, and its implications for the United States as a republic and a people have not been explored to any great extent. In the United States, 80 percent of the immigrants who arrived in this country from 1961 to 2003 were from countries that allow dual citizenship. That translates to more than 26 million dual-citizenship immigrants, which does not include their children, illegal immigrants, or Americans who can also claim dual-citizenship status. Those categories combined might easily translate to 40-plus million people, and rising.

Immigration advocates remind us that Americans live in an interdependent world and urge us to accept plural national attachments. However, though technology may make us more interconnected, we are not necessarily in touch with each other. Robert Putnam and a host of national civic commissions have both documented and lamented the decline of American community. When it comes to civic and national attachments, Americans continue to bowl alone.

The concerns regarding national attachments are by no means confined to immigrants; in fact, quite the contrary. Although the issue of multiple citizenships in the United States arises in the context of unprecedented immigration, the larger concerns addressed in this analysis are shared by citizens and immigrants alike.

Any study examining the implications of multiple citizenship and multiple attachments for the American national community is likely to be controversial. Analyses of the trends associated with that process and their implications for the American national community and identity are not "anti-immigrant" or "nativist"—although I can easily envision some making that argument. I hope the issues discussed here will be examined in the same spirit in which they are presented—as a set of important questions for the United States as a national community that deserves attention and reflection.

The title of this book is meant to raise the issue of conflicted attachments—between two (or more) countries, ways of life, the understandings that underlie them, and the psychological and political implications that flow from such multiple national attachments. It does *not* suggest that all people who claim the status of dual citizenship are by definition suspect as citizens or as Americans. They are not.

The issues of national attachment and identity are psychologically complex. People organize their attachments in diverse ways. Sometimes these attachments operate harmoniously; at other times they are in direct conflict; and sometimes they introduce a subtle presumption in favor of, or against, one element of that identity—and the person does not even see an overt conflict. Indeed, psychological avoidance is one of the most frequent and effective ways to reduce such a conflict. Regretfully, that does not mean the conflict disappears or that it does not have an adverse effect.

Trying to reconcile two different nationalities, cultures, and psychologies is no easy matter. Yet that is precisely what tens of millions of Americans must now attempt to do. The subject of this book is whether that reconciliation is possible and, if it is, how we may assist immigrants while keeping the needs of the American national community in view.

Notes

1. Constant Brand, "EU Officials Implore New Immigrants to Learn 'European Values,'" Associated Press, November 19, 2004.

2. Andrew Higgins, "Rude Awaking," *Wall Street Journal*, November 22, 2004.

3. Higgins, "Rude Awaking."

4. Anthony King, "One in Four Muslims Sympathises with Motives of Terrorists," *New Telegraph*, July 23, 2005. The specific YouGov poll numbers are given in a sidebar of that article.

5. Samuel P. Huntington, *Who Are We? The Challenges to American National Identity* (New York: Simon & Schuster, 2004).

6. See chapter 3, note 29, for a fuller explanation of Dr. Johnson's views on the crucial importance of patriotism.

7. This view runs contrary to that of Fein, who argues that "dual allegiances do not imminently threaten the fabric of the United States. But they fuel a yawning indifference to American customs and civic spirit indispensable to national vitality." Bruce Fein, "Dual Citizenship Folly," *Washington Times*, March 1, 2005.

American Democracy and the Dilemmas of Dual Citizenship

AMERICANS LIVE IN A PARADOXICAL COUNTRY. WE EXALT CITIZEN-ship but require little of our citizens. We believe that every person deserves his or her own identity and also that, paradoxically, the sum of fiercely held ethnic and racial loyalties will produce a common American one. And we believe that we can integrate the tens of millions of new immigrants who have come to our country by encouraging their emotional, political, and economic ties to their "home" countries.

The paradoxes that face America are not confined to our national identity. Americans live in a country whose wealth and power are unparalleled. Yet we also live in a country vulnerable to murderous hatred on a catastrophic scale. We know there are people and groups with the will and intent to unleash terrorism—whether nuclear, biological, or chemical. They lack only the means, which they are frantically trying to acquire.

As a result of the terrorist attacks of September 11, 2001, the sharp line between domestic and international security concerns has substantially blurred. At the same time, debates about immigration have been recast. The sense of American national community, the presumption that we are all Americans regardless of our differences, has become a national security problem as well as a matter of civic concern. Immigrant integration—the process of helping newcomers fit into American life—as well as the emotional attachment of America's increasingly diverse ethnic groups to the American national community have taken on new urgency in an age of catastrophic terrorism.

National identity has a structural dimension for both a country and a people. The question for this country is how well the different elements that constitute the core foundations of American society—our psychology, our emotional attachments to our country, our values and ideals, and the institutions that reflect and encourage ties to them—fit together. The question of national community is different. It asks how and how much members of that society are attached to it, and to each other. National attachment is a psychological barometer that reflects the degree to which individuals are emotionally connected to the primary elements of their country. Strong emotional attachments are not only critical to the American civic process but also help provide the glue that keeps the country together and serve as the basis for united action in tough times.

In the last four-plus decades, the national attachments of those recently arrived and those already here have been increasingly subject to powerful centrifugal forces. These challenges to an American national identity come from two directions: one domestic, and the other global. The elements that constitute the first are found in several powerful trends, such as multiculturalism, cultural conflict, civic disconnectedness, and avoidant tolerance—the preference to get along by going along, even if one does not agree.

These elements are connected. In fact, cultural conflict has helped stimulate civic *disconnectedness*, and both have made avoidant tolerance more attractive as a personal and institutional stance. All four of these trends have substantial implications for the attachment to, and functioning of, the American national community.

The same is true for those challenges to an American national identity associated with global trends—interdependence, information flows, and population mobility. The challenges here are to be found in the rise of transnational attachments, transnational organizations, and transnational ideals—all of which define international cosmopolitanism.

The challenge that these domestic and global trends pose for American national identity and attachment is captured by the premise of advocates on both sides of the domestic global divide. Multiculturalists and international cosmopolitans are united in their view that less is better—in this case, less *American* national attachment. Serious multiculturalists view the ethnic or racial group, not the nation, as the primary and preferred anchor of American individual and national group identity. They propose that attachment to this country is best achieved by emphasizing the strong differences between groups. Although not often thought of in this way, multiculturalism is a form of ethnic dual citizenship with attachment and allegiance to the group trumping any national attachment.

International cosmopolitans view national attachments as insular and an impediment to ever-widening circles of inclusion, democracy, and rights. Like their multicultural domestic counterparts, they also believe that less attachment to national identities is preferable. They, too, offer a form of group identification as the preferable alternative. However, they emphasize transnational attachments—of which dual citizenship is a prominent embodiment.

One fundamental and critical question that arises in connection with dual citizenship is that of conflicted attachments. The issue of conflicted attachments begins with a fact: Persons who grow up and spend their formative years in a country develop strong emotional connections to it. These early attachments take several forms. They are reflected in ways of seeing and understanding the world, the use of language and the cultural frames embedded in it, and the web of relationships and experiences that provide the internal skeleton upon which later external experience is built. The question therefore arises of whether, given the importance of their national attachments to many people, it is possible to put aside those older attachments and give primary weight to new ones.

What, exactly, is dual citizenship?[1] At its most basic level, dual citizenship involves the simultaneous holding of more than one citizenship or nationality. In many culturally homogenous countries, nationality and citizenship coincide, yet they are not synonymous. "Citizenship" is a legal term and refers to the rights and responsibilities that become attached to a person by virtue of their having been born into, or having become, a recognized or certified member of a state community.

"Nationality" is a psychological term that refers to the emotional ties and core understandings about the world and common experience that bind members of a group together. Common community identifications develop through several, or more, of the following elements: language, racial identifications, ethnicity, culture, geography, historical experience, and identification with common institutions and practices.

In culturally homogenous countries, nationality and citizenship coincide; in the United States, they increasingly do not.[2] Or, as a *Harvard Law Review* editorial puts it: "An individual's national identity is not necessarily the same as the passport she holds."[3] This is precisely the issue raised by multiple citizenships.

Dual citizenship allows a person to have many, or in some cases all, of the rights and responsibilities that adhere to citizenship in each of the several countries in which he or she is a citizen—regardless of their actual physical residence in a country; the geographical proximity of the "home" to the chosen country; or the nature of their economic, cultural, or political ties to the new country.[4] The idea seems counterintuitive. How could a person owe allegiance or fully adhere to the responsibilities of citizenship in several or more countries at the same time? In the United States, the legal answer is: Easily.[5]

The United States does not formally recognize dual citizenship, but neither does it take any stand politically or legally against it. Many people are surprised to learn, as I suggest in the prologue, that there are no U.S. policies or laws that prohibit an American citizen from obtaining a second or even a third citizenship, swearing allegiance to a foreign state, voting in another country's election, serving in the armed forces (even in combat positions, and even if the state is a hostile one), running for office and (if successful) serving as an adviser to a foreign government—all while still an American citizen. Informed constitutional judgment suggests that Congress could legislatively address any of these or other issues arising out of these multiple, perhaps, conflicting responsibilities.[6] Yet, to date, it has chosen not to do so.

September 11 has made Americans more aware of their common fate. It has also brought a renewed focus on issues of national integration, attachment, and immigration. The national security implications of national attachment are very real, but the relationship of national attachment and integration for the political and cultural well-being of this country rivals that critical focus.

The consequences of allowing or encouraging the acquisition of multiple citizenships by immigrants and citizens in the United States has rarely been discussed outside of a small group of law school professors and postmodern political theorists, but they deserve serious attention. Some have endorsed the desirability of allowing new immigrants and American citizens to pursue their associations with their countries of origin. Some go further and advocate the acquisition and consolidation of active attachments to other countries as a means of overcoming what they view as the parochialism of American national identity. But the psychological implications and political consequences of having large groups of Americans holding multiple citizenships are rarely, if ever, seriously considered.

This issue reaches the very heart of what it means to be an American and a citizen. It also holds enormous implications for the integrity of American civic and cultural traditions. Is it possible to be fully engaged and be knowledgeable citizens of several countries? Is it possible to follow two or more very different cultural traditions? Is it possible to have two, possibly conflicting, core identifications and attachments? And assuming such things are possible, are they desirable?

Dual Citizenship in America: Many Routes

How does an immigrant or an American become a dual citizen? Aleinikoff notes that a person in the United States may acquire multiple citizenships in any one of four ways.[7] To his list, I will add two new dual-citizenship routes.

First, he or she may be born in the United States to immigrant parents. All children born in the United States are U.S. citizens, regardless of the status of their parents (*jus soli*). Second, a person may be born outside the United States to one parent who is a U.S. citizen and another who is not (*jus sanguinis*). A child born to an American citizen and a British citizen in the United

Kingdom, for example, would be a citizen of both countries. Third, a person can become a naturalized citizen in the United States, and that act is ignored by his or her country of origin. In that case, the person remains a national of his or her home country even though he or she has taken an oath of allegiance to another country, or even served in a high political office in that country.[8]

There are many reasons why countries may wish to ignore the fact that their nationals have become citizens elsewhere,[9] but in doing so they mirror U.S. practice. Those naturalized in this country take an oath of citizenship that asks them to renounce their former citizenship/nationality ties. This has become controversial to those for whom the dilution of national attachments is a preference. Yet failure to take action consistent with the renunciation carries no penalties, and other countries can, and often do, simply ignore the U.S. oath of allegiance.

Fourth, a person can become a naturalized citizen of the United States and in doing so lose their citizenship in the country of origin—but he or she can regain it at any time and still retain U.S. citizenship. This is de facto dual citizenship, which occurs when a national from another country that does not recognize dual citizenship nonetheless makes easy provision for its nationals to return home and rejoin that community. Ordinarily, this form does not allow for the exercise of formal political rights in the immigrant's country of origin. But to the extent that repatriation is the person's ultimate goal, it may very well effect attachments to a new country.[10]

These four traditional routes to dual citizenship are now joined by two new ones. The United States, which has no policy on dual citizenship, contains many citizens whose countries of origin have dual-citizenship agreements with third, fourth, and even fifth countries. For example, Spain has dual-nationality agreements with eleven Latin American countries.[11] Guatemala has the same with other Central American nations.[12] France has specialized citizenship arrangements with some of its former colonial territories like Algeria. The common citizenship status of all individuals whose countries are part of the European Union is another example of these multiple linked citizenships.[13]

The proliferation of multiple citizenships and special bilateral or multilateral citizenship agreements has national security implications as well. A number of former colonial powers have such agreements with their former colonies—some of which have proved fertile ground for extremist sentiment and recruiting. Countries such as France and the United Kingdom have admitted many of their former colonial subjects to live in their country as citizens. The integration of large numbers of such immigrants into British and French society, respectively, has become a matter of urgent civic and security concern in both countries, as the recent terrorist bombings in London make very clear.[14] Meanwhile, these underintegrated groups have created substantial pools of potential terrorist recruits—ones that are not so easily recognized by carrying a passport from a country on the American terror-watch list.

Zacarias Moussaoui, now on trial in U.S. federal court on terrorism charges from the September 11 attacks, was a citizen of France. He could have entered the United States without a visa because France is part of the visa waiver program that allows citizens of certain countries to enter the United States for up to ninety days without a visa. In Israel, two British citizens, Assif Muhammad Hanif and Omar Khan Sharif, were admitted on tourist visas, and they launched suicide bomb attacks against Israeli civilians. These are examples of how national security and multiple nationalities are becoming increasingly interconnected.

Last, and this is relevant to America's circumstances, many people here retain their nationality if their parents, especially their fathers, were nationals—even if their home countries make no provision for dual nationality. So, for example, the African country of Senegal does not recognize dual citizenship. However, any child whose father and a grandfather were Sierra Leoneans of African Negro descent, regardless of the child's country of birth, is considered a national of Senegal.[15] The same circumstances are true for U.S. immigrants from forty-two other countries.[16] Their home countries consider them nationals. Many of them have provisions that require their nationals born abroad to choose their citizenship at some age, usually eighteen or twenty-one years. Yet there is absolutely no vehicle in the United States to ascertain whether one of its citizens has indeed made a choice to retain his or her "home" nationality or not. They are, in effect, hidden dual citizens.

Multiple-Citizenship Countries: A Large, Fast-Growing Group

A 1996 survey conducted by a Hispanic advocacy group found that seven of seventeen (41 percent) Latin American countries allowed some form of multiple citizenship. Only four years later, fourteen out of seventeen Latin American countries in that survey (84 percent) were allowing multiple citizenship and another, Honduras, had a bill to do so pending before its legislature.[17]

A list of countries allowing or encouraging multiple citizenships is listed in the appendix. Drawing on several helpful,[18] but sometimes inconsistent,[19] lists in conjunction with my own inquiries,[20] I have established that currently 151 countries, including the United States, allow some form of multiple citizenship in one of the six ways I have outlined above. It is a number that is likely to grow as the relatively few remaining countries that now do not allow dual citizenship recognize the advantages of maintaining and even encouraging the attachments of their emigrants to their place of origin. On the basis of these numbers, dual citizenship is not simply a wave of the future—rather, it is a tidal surge of the present. But the consequences for the United States are not necessarily salutary.

In the past, many countries have called upon their nationals residing in America to further their preferences of the "home country."[21] What is different now, however, is the absolute numbers of such individuals, and the increasingly sophisticated and aggressive efforts on the part of home countries to influence their American nationals. Mexico, for example, has taken a number of steps to evade or weaken U.S. immigration laws and to recruit its nationals for Mexican policy preferences. And it is not alone in doing so.[22]

This is not a criticism of the home country's self-interest. It is merely a statement of fact. It is entirely understandable that countries would prefer to have their nationals organized in their new country, especially if that country is the United States, while retaining and even expanding their attachments to their old one. Yet the interests of home countries and the United States are not always the same.

Why should Americans care how many other countries allow their nationals to hold multiple citizenship, their motivation for doing so, or the specific ways in which dual citizenship affects the American national community? To answer these questions, one useful place to begin is with the rates and nature of immigration to the United States following Congress's 1965 landmark changes in immigration law. No single number, of course, can do justice to the complex array of changes that this law has promoted. However, some perspective can be gained from the most recent Census Bureau figures.

The latest census figures show that the number of legal and illegal immigrants living in the United States has almost tripled since 1970, rising from 9.6 million to 34.2 million today.[23] That number has climbed over 14 million since the 1990 census. Before that, the foreign-born population had expanded from 9.6 million in 1970, the lowest total in the twentieth century, to 14.1 million in 1980 and to 19.8 million in 1990. Between 2000 and 2004, a time of economic downturn in the United States, nearly 6.1 million immigrants, both legal and illegal, arrived in the United States.[24]

These figures represent the largest absolute number of foreign-born population in U.S. history.[25] The percentage of foreign-born living in the United States was higher once in the twentieth century, in 1911, but in absolute numbers the 1911 figures amounted to about 13.5 million people, a figure that is 8 million less than the 21 million foreign-born living in the United States today, and that number is rising. Approximately 1.2 million immigrants, both legal and illegal, now settle in the United States every year, and they have been doing so for decades.[26] The number of immigrants for the last years of the decade stretching from 1990, coupled with the total number of immigrants in the previous decade, add up to the largest consecutive two-decade influx of immigrants in the history of the United States.

September 11 has not resulted in any decrease of these numbers.[27] Camarota, using estimates derived from the Census Bureau's Current Population Survey taken in March 2002, finds that more than 3.3 million legal and illegal immigrants have come to the United States since the last figures reported in the 2000 census. Overall, he estimates that about 1.5 million legal and illegal immigrants have arrived here every one and a half years since 1970.

These absolute numbers, percentages, and historical comparisons of American immigration provide one view of the changes that have taken place and continue to do so in the United States. The regional and national sources of this immigrant stream provides another. Among the foreign-born population, 50.7 percent were born in Latin America, 27.1 percent were born in Asia, 16.1 percent were born in Europe, and the remaining 6.2 percent were from other parts of the world.

The foreign-born population from Central America and Mexico accounted for two-thirds of the foreign-born population from Latin America and for one-third of the total foreign-born population.[28] In 2000, of the 14.5 million foreign-born residents, one out of every two foreign-born residents was from Latin America.

Mexico by itself accounted for 7.8 million of the foreign-born in 2000, up from 800,000 in 1970.[29] By 2004, Mexico accounted for 31 percent of all immigrants.[30] Cuba, the Dominican Republic, and El Salvador have at least 500,000 of their fellow nationals in the United States. All these countries, plus the other Latin American nations that make up the Latin American contribution to U.S. immigration figures, are from countries that encourage dual citizenship.

As I noted above, a substantial portion of these immigrants come from Mexico, a country with a contiguous border with the United States, or from countries from which it is relatively easy to reach the United States. Further, the Mexican government has become increasingly aggressive in solidifying and further developing the ties of its nationals in the United States to their "home" country. These developments underlie Huntington's concern that the United States stands in danger of developing a "de facto splitting between a predominately Spanish-speaking America and English-speaking America" and a subsequent loss of American national identity.[31]

These numbers are not in themselves either positive or negative. Yet they have many consequences for American culture and political life. They raise in a very direct way a key question for this book. How well is the United States able to integrate such large numbers of new immigrants every year into its national community? The troubling answer, for a variety of reasons, is not very well.

This is not the conventional view. Those who disagree might point to the large number of immigrants who report in response to census questions that they speak English "well." They might also point to the intergenerational educational advancement of immigrants and their children. And they might well point to increasing home ownership among immigrants. All these data, it might be said, show the success of immigrant assimilation.

Yet, here are some questions about all these measures and one serious drawback to them all: None of them addresses the degree to which immigrants are or are not emotionally connected to the country. It is quite possible to own a house and not be very attached to the country in which it is located. Or consider the issue of immigrant remittances to their "home" countries. The data presented in chapter 8 show that these numbers are substantial, running into the tens of billions. These funds are extremely important to foreign governments, and they have enormous incentives to ensure these funds continue and grow. This can be accomplished most easily by sending more immigrants to the United States, whether legal or not, and by ensuring that they retain emotional ties to their "home country." A recent major study by the Inter-American Development Bank of remittances sent by immigrants living in the United States is titled *Sending Money Home*. Home, apparently, is not the United States.[32]

Instead of measuring instrumental advancement like immigrant home ownership, it might be more to the point to measure behavior that actually reflects emotional attachment and commitment. Consider remittances: We might well construct a three-tiered model in which sending money "home" represents the lowest level of American community attachment. The second tier would be contributing to the well-being of one's fellow nationals in the United States. And the third level would be substantial contributions to general community-wide American organizations like the American Cancer Society.

Some Dual-Citizenship Numbers

Because the United States does not keep any records on the dual-citizenship status either of its citizens or of arriving immigrants, exact numbers are not possible. Nonetheless, it is possible to make some estimates. Consider, for example, the relationship between the countries that provide the vast pool of immigrants to the United States and the multiple-citizenship status of those they send us. Table 1.1 presents a list of the top twenty high immigrant-sending countries drawn from the Immigration and Naturalization Service's (INS') official figures for 1994 to 2003.[33] Those countries that allow their nationals to hold multiple-citizenship status are highlighted in the table in bold type. In 2003, seventeen of the top twenty immigrant-sending countries (87 percent) allowed some form of dual citizenship. One of the remaining three countries, South Korea is actively considering adopting such legislation.

TABLE 1.1

Dual Citizenship Status of Top Twenty Immigrant-Sending Countries, 1994–2003

Country of Birth	2003 Number (%)	2002 Number (%)	2001 Number (%)	2000 Number (%)	1999 Number (%)	1998 Number (%)	1997 Number (%)	1996 Number (%)	1995 Number (%)	1994 Number (%)
1. Mexico	115,864 (16.4)	219,380 (20.6)	206,426 (19.4)	173,919 (20.5)	147,573 (22.8)	131,575 (20.1)	146,865 (18.4)	163,572 (17.9)	89,932 (12.5)	111,395 (13.8)
2. China	40,659 (5.7)	55,974 (5.3)	50,821 (4.8)	45,652 (5.4)	32,202 (5.0)	36,884 (5.6)	41,147 (5.2)	41,728 (4.6)	35,463 (4.9)	53,985 (6.7)
3. India	50,372 (7.1)	66,864 (6.3)	65,916 (6.2)	42,046 (4.9)	30,237 (4.7)	36,482 (5.6)	38,071 (4.8)	44,859 (4.9)	37,748 (4.8)	34,921 (4.3)
4. Philippines	45,397 (6.4)	48,674 (4.5)	50,870 (4.8)	42,474 (5.0)	31,026 (4.8)	34,446 (5.2)	49,117 (6.2)	55,876 (6.1)	50,984 (7.1)	53,535 (6.7)
5. Dominican Republic	26,205 (3.7)	22,474 (2.1)	21,256 (2.0)	17,536 (2.1)	17,864 (2.8)	20,387 (3.1)	27,053 (3.4)	39,604 (4.3)	38,512 (5.3)	51,189 (6.4)
6. Vietnam	22,133 (3.1)	32,425 (3.0)	34,648 (3.3)	26,747 (3.1)	20,393 (3.2)	17,649 (2.7)	38,519 (4.8)	42,067 (4.6)	41,752 (5.8)	41,345 (5.1)
7. Cuba	9,304 (1.3)	27,520 (2.6)	26,073 (2.4)	20,831 (2.5)	14,132 (2.2)	17,375 (2.6)	33,587 (2.6)	26,466 (2.9)	17,937 (2.5)	14,727 (1.8)
8. Jamaica	13,384 (1.9)	15,099 (1.4)	14,567 (1.4)	16,000 (1.9)	14,733 (2.3)	15,146 (2.3)	17,840 (2.2)	19,089 (2.1)	16,398 (2.3)	14,349 (1.8)
9. El Salvador	28,296 (4.0)	30,539 (2.9)	31,054 (2.9)	22,578 (2.7)	14,606 (2.3)	14,590 (2.2)	17,969 (2.3)	17,903 (2.0)	11,744 (1.6)	17,644 (2.2)
10. South[a] Korea	12,512 (1.7)	19,933 (1.9)	20,114 (1.9)	15,830 (1.9)	12,840 (2.0)	12,268 (2.2)	14,329 (1.8)	18,185 (2.0)	16,047 (2.2)	16,011 (2.0)
11. Haiti	12,314 (1.7)	22,535 (2.1)	19,189 (1.8)	22,364 (2.6)	16,532 (2.6)	13,499 (2.0)	15,057 (1.9)	18,386 (2.0)	14,021 (1.9)	13,333 (1.7)
12. Pakistan	9,444 (1.3)	16,448 (1.5)	13,743 (1.3)	14,535 (1.7)	13,496 (2.1)	13,094 (2.0)	12,969 (1.6)	12,519 (1.4)	9,774 (1.4)	8,698 (1.1)

13. Columbia	14,777 (2.1)	16,333 (1.5)	18,488 (1.7)	14,498 (1.7)	9,966 (1.5)	11,836 (1.8)	13,004 (1.6)	14,283 (1.6)	10,838 (1.5)	10,847 (1.3)
14a. **Russia**	13,951 (2.0)	20,413 (1.9)	20,833 (2.0)	17,110 (2.0)	12,347 (1.9)	11,529 (1.7)	16,632 (2.1)	19,668 (2.1)	14,560 (2.0)	15,249 (1.9)
14b. **Ukraine**	11,666 (1.7)	20,975 (2.0)	21,217 (2.0)	15,810 (1.9)	10,123 (1.6)	N.R.	15,696 (2.0)	21,079 (2.3)	17,432 (2.4)	21,010 (2.6)
15. Canada	11,446 (1.6)	30,203 (2.8)	27,299 (2.6)	16,210 (1.9)	8,864 (1.4)	10,190 (1.5)	11,609 (1.5)	15,825 (1.7)	12,932 (1.8)	16,068 (2.0)
16. Peru	9,444 (1.3)	11,131 (1.0)	11,999 (1.1)	N.R.	8,438 (1.3)	10,154 (1.3)	10,853 (1.4)	12,871 (1.4)	8,066 (1.1)	9,177 (1.1)
17. **United Kingdom**	9,601 (1.4)	20,258 (1.9)	18,057 (1.7)	13,385 (1.6)	7,690 (1.2)	9,011 (1.4)	10,651 (1.3)	13,624 (1.3)	12,427 (1.7)	16,326 (2.0)
18. Bangladesh	4,625 (.66)	7,171 (0.67)	5,492 (0.5)	N.R.	6,046 (1.2)	8,621 (1.3)	N.R.	N.R.	N.R.	N.R.
19. Poland	10,526 (1.5)	12,355 (1.2)	13,304 (1.2)	10,114 (1.2)	8,798 (1.4)	8,469 (1.3)	12,038 (1.3)	15,772 (1.7)	13,824 (1.9)	28,048 (3.5)
20. Iran	7,251 (1.0)	7,730 (0.73)	8,063 (0.8)	N.R.	7,203 (1.4)	7,883 (1.2)	9,642 (1.2)	11,084 (1.2)	9,201 (1.3)	11,422 (1.4)
Total top twenty immigrant-sending countries	479,171	724,434	699,429	547,639	414,083	441,088	552,648	582,393	479,592	559,279
Dual-citizenship top twenty immigrant-sending countries	416,696	621,007	603,421	465,326	354,909	374,561	463,585	496,014	410,115	474,556
Percent of dual citizenship	86.9	85.7	86.2	84.2	85.7	81.5	83.8	85.1	85.5	84.8
Other immigration[b]						217,419	245,822	291,440	243,869	245,134
Total immigration	705,827	1,063,732	1,064,318	849,807	646,568	660,477	798,378	915,900	720,461	804,416

Note: Dual-citizenship countries are in bold. N.R. = not reported.

[a] The U.S. Immigration and Naturalization Service does not distinguish between North Korea and South Korea.

[b] Data are provided on other immigration from dual-citizenship countries that are not reflected in the top twenty countries.

The numbers for specific years are even more graphic. In 1998, of the 441,088 immigrants admitted that year from the top twenty immigrant-sending countries, 374,561 (84.5 percent) were from dual-citizenship-allowing countries. In 1997, of the 552,648 immigrants from the top twenty immigrant-sending countries, 496,014 (83.5 percent) were from dual-citizenship-allowing countries. The figures for 1996, 1995, and 1994 are comparable, with dual-citizenship-allowing countries accounting for 86, 85, and 84 percent, respectively. Overall, of the 5.48 million immigrants from the top twenty immigrant-sending countries from 1994 to 2003, 4.7 million (85 percent) were from dual-citizenship-allowing countries.

Recall, too, that while seventeen of the top twenty immigrant-sending countries are multiple-citizenship-allowing countries, that number represents only a small percentage of the total number left (133) of dual-citizenship-allowing countries (not including the United States). And, of course, many of these remaining 133 multiple-citizenship-allowing countries send the United States many thousands of immigrants. It is possible that these figures are not really representative because they cover only the top twenty or because they cover a limited period of time. A wider frame of focus coupled with a longer period of historical analysis effectively suggests that this is not the case. A historical perspective on all current dual- and multiple-citizenship-sending countries is found in table 1.2.

Table 1.2 presents data on immigration to the United States by nationals from all dual-citizenship-allowing countries for the four decades beginning in 1960 and for 2001 through 2003. Figures in bold at the bottom represent the total contribution of dual- and multiple-citizenship-allowing countries for that same period and their percentage of the total for that period.

Data for some countries in some periods is not available. Therefore, the figures presented in table 1.2 most likely slightly underestimate the number of dual-citizen immigrants. However, even so, they clearly show the extent to which immigrants to the United States are disproportionally from countries that allow or encourage dual and/or multiple citizenship and the retention of ties to their countries of origin. And they do give some indication of the actual numbers of such persons.

A few summary figures may be helpful. Of the 26-plus million immigrants legally admitted into this country between 1961 and 2003, over 22 million, or about 82 percent, are from dual- and multiple-citizenship-allowing countries. In the decade 1961–70, that percentage was 84; in 1971–80 it was 82; in 1981–90 it was 84; in 1991–2000 it was 76; and in 2001–2003 it was 85, 84, and 86 percent, respectively.

There are several ways to get a fuller appreciation of these figures.[34] If you examine the home countries of immigrants that contributed 500,000 or more persons to America's foreign-born population in 2000, ten out of thirteen (76

(text continues on p. 20)

TABLE 1.2

Dual-Citizenship Countries Listed in Alphabetic Order, 1961–2003:
Immigrants Admitted to the United States by Region and Country of Birth

Country	1961–70	1971–80	1981–90	1991–2000	2001	2002	2003	TOTAL
Total	3,221,677	4,493,314	7,338,062	9,095,417	1,064,318	1,063,732	705,827	26,982,347
Albania	N.A.	N.A.	N.A.	22,042	4,363	3,768	3,363	33,536
Antigua and Barbuda	N.A.	N.A.	12,900	3,967	463	382	301	18,013
Argentina	42,100	25,100	25,700	26,644	3,328	3,685	3,157	129,714
Angola	N.A.	N.A.	N.A.	N.A.	95	92	59	246
Austria	N.A.	49,721	18,340	15,500	1,004	2,657	297	87,519
Australia	9,900	14,300	13,900	16,256	2,830	2,576	1,847	61,609
Bahamas	N.A.	N.A.	7,300	5,681	931	811	426	15,149
Bangladesh	N.A.	N.A.	15,200	43,266	7,171	5,492	4,625	75,754
Barbados	9,400	20,900	17,400	8,007	910	817	517	57,951
Belgium	918	6,023	7,727	9,816	818	782	458	26,542
Belize	N.A.	N.A.	18,100	6,729	939	974	591	27,333
Belarus	N.A.	N.A.	N.A.	28,990	2,909	2,928	1,860	36,687
Benin	N.A.	N.A.	N.A.	326	67	137	76	606
Bolivia	N.A.	N.A.	12,300	14,171	1,826	1,670	1,382	31,349
Botswana	N.A.	N.A.	N.A.	N.A.	24	30	27	81
Brazil	20,500	13,700	23,700	44,144	9,505	9,474	6,357	127,380
Brunei Darussalam	N.A.	N.A.	N.A.	N.A.	1,383	1,359	1,194	3,936
Bulgaria	N.A.	N.A.	N.A.	22,530	4,411	3,616	3,380	33,937
Burkina Faso	N.A.	N.A.	N.A.	169	68	64	60	361
Cambodia	1,200	8,400	116,600	15,295	2,473	2,809	2,271	149,048
Cameroon	N.A.	N.A.	N.A.	N.A.	795	985	927	2,707

(continues)

TABLE 1.2 Continued

Country	1961–70	1971–80	1981–90	1991–2000	2001	2002	2003	TOTAL
Canada	286,700	114,800	119,200	191,987	21,933	19,519	11,446	765,585
Cape Verde	N.A.	N.A.	N.A.	8,209	872	880	1,746	11,704
Central African Republic	N.A.	N.A.	N.A.	N.A.	N.A.	N.A.	N.A.	N.A.
Chile	11,500	17,600	23,400	14,082	1,947	1,858	1,323	71,710
Colombia	70,300	77,600	124,400	128,499	16,730	18,845	14,777	451,151
Congo (former Zaire)	N.A.	N.A.	N.A.	N.A.	N.A.	N.A.	N.A.	N.A.
Costa Rica	17,400	12,100	15,500	11,363	1,744	1,602	1,253	60,962
Côte d'Ivoire	N.A.	N.A.	N.A.	N.A.	605	630	485	1,720
Croatia	N.A.	N.A.	N.A.	5,208	2,862	3,805	1,162	13,037
Cyprus	N.A.	N.A.	N.A.	1,606	218	162	127	2,113
Cyprus (North)	N.A.	N.A.	N.A.	N.A.	N.A.	N.A.	N.A.	N.A.
Denmark	N.A.	5,370	6,079	556	741	655	436	13,837
Dominica	N.A.	N.A.	N.A.	4,553	93	148	204	4,998
Dominican Rep	94,100	148,000	251,800	335,251	21,313	22,604	26,205	899,273
Ecuador	37,000	50,200	56,000	76,592	9,706	10,602	7,083	247,183
Egypt	17,200	25,500	31,400	41,110	5,128	4,875	3,355	128,568
Eritrea	N.A.	N.A.	N.A.	N.A.	544	561	556	1,661
El Salvador	15,000	34,400	214,600	215,798	31,272	31,168	28,296	570,534
Fiji	N.A.	N.A.	N.A.	12,360	1,457	1,211	1,099	16,127
Finland	N.A.	N.A.	N.A.	N.A.	N.A.	N.A.	N.A.	N.A.
France	34,300	17,800	23,100	35,820	5,431	4,596	2,835	123,882

Country								
Gambia	N.A.	N.A.	N.A.	N.A.	391	343	263	997
Germany	200,000	66,000	70,100	92,606	9,886	8,961	5,101	476,958
Ghana	N.A.	N.A.	14,900	32,308	4,031	4,256	4,416	59,911
Greece	90,200	93,700	29,100	26,759	1,811	1,038	622	249,320
Grenada	N.A.	N.A.	10,600	6,372	645	636	481	18,734
Guatemala	15,400	25,600	87,900	77,578	13,567	16,229	14,415	250,289
Guyana	7,100	47,500	95,400	62,227	8,303	9,962	6,820	237,312
Guatemala	N.A.	N.A.	N.A.	N.A.	13,567	16,229	14,415	44,151
Guinea-Bissau	N.A.	N.A.	N.A.	N.A.	274	290	117	681
Haiti	37,500	58,700	140,200	179,644	27,120	20,268	12,314	475,746
Honduras	N.A.	N.A.	N.A.	N.A.	6,615	6,461	4,658	17,734
Hungary	17,300	11,600	9,800	8,839	1,273	1,284	1,024	51,120
Iceland	N.A.	N.A.	N.A.	N.A.	136	93	97	326
India	31,200	176,800	261,900	363,060	70,290	71,105	50,372	1,024,727
Iran	10,400	46,200	154,800	68,556	10,497	13,029	7,251	310,733
Iraq	N.A.	N.A.	N.A.	N.A.	4,985	5,196	2,460	12,641
Ireland	42,400	14,100	32,800	56,950	1,522	1,425	991	150,188
Israel	12,900	26,600	36,300	39,397	3,776	3,857	2,774	125,604
Italy	206,700	130,100	32,900	62,722	3,142	2,605	1,659	439,828
Jamaica	71,000	142,000	213,800	149,711	15,393	14,898	13,384	620,186
Japan	46,250	47,085	67,942	7,730	9,619	8,301	5,993	192,920
Jordan	14,000	29,600	32,600	35,470	4,593	3,980	2,935	123,178
Latvia	N.A.	N.A.	41,600	5,217	712	684	459	7,072
Lebanon	7,500	33,800	41,600	37,460	4,601	3,966	2,964	131,891
Lesotho	N.A.	N.A.	N.A.	73	6	13	5	97
Liberia	N.A.	N.A.	N.A.	N.A.	2,285	2,879	1,768	6,932
Liechtenstein	N.A.	N.A.	N.A.	11	4	0	0	15

(continues)

TABLE 1.2 Continued

Country	1961–70	1971–80	1981–90	1991–2000	2001	2002	2003	TOTAL
Lithuania	N.A.	N.A.	N.A.	7,898	1,735	1,787	2,266	13,686
Luxembourg	N.A.	N.A.	N.A.	N.A.	34	32	16	82
Macao (with Portugal)	N.A.	N.A.	N.A.	N.A.	N.A.	N.A.	N.A.	N.A.
Macedonia	N.A.	N.A.	N.A.	4,829	924	827	656	7,236
Madagascar	N.A.	N.A.	N.A.	N.A.	N.A.	N.A.	40	40
Malawi	N.A.	N.A.	N.A.	N.A.	70	56	62	188
Maldives	N.A.	N.A.	N.A.	N.A.	9	9	5	23
Mali	N.A.	N.A.	N.A.	N.A.	120	106	125	351
Malta	N.A.	N.A.	N.A.	547	57	45	37	686
Mauritania	N.A.	N.A.	N.A.	N.A.	117	124	131	372
Mauritius	N.A.	N.A.	N.A.	N.A.	84	83	57	224
Mexico	443,300	637,200	1,653,300	1,655,843	206,426	219,380	115,864	4,931,241
Moldova	N.A.	N.A.	N.A.	N.A.	9	17	N.A.	26
Mongolia	N.A.	N.A.	N.A.	204	103	136	153	596
Montenegro	N.A.	N.A.	N.A.	N.A.	N.A.	N.A.	N.A.	N.A.
Morocco	N.A.	N.A.	6,700	18,441	4,968	3,396	3,141	36,646
Mozambique	N.A.	N.A.	N.A.	N.A.	48	55	36	139
Myanmar	N.A.	N.A.	N.A.	N.A.	N.A.	N.A.	N.A.	N.A.
Namibia	N.A.	N.A.	N.A.	N.A.	54	47	40	141
Nepal	N.A.	N.A.	N.A.	N.A.	944	1,138	2,099	4,181
Netherlands	27,800	10,700	11,900	13,308	1,687	1,560	998	67,953
New Zealand	N.A.	N.A.	N.A.	7,246	1,214	1,129	884	10,473

Nicaragua	10,100	13,000	44,100	79,871	19,896	10,850	4,174	181,991
Niger	1,500	8,800	35,300	59,394	1,341	1,271	814	108,420
Nigeria	N.A.	N.A.	N.A.	N.A.	8,291	8,129	7,892	24,312
Northern Ireland	34,526	267,638	333,746	164,166	20,742	21,021	12,512	854,351
North Korea	N.A.	N.A.	N.A.	N.A.	55	61	76	192
Oman	N.A.	N.A.	N.A.	N.A.	3	10	8	21
Palau	N.A.	N.A.	N.A.	N.A.	N.A.	N.A.	N.A.	N.A.
Panama	18,400	22,700	29,000	19,825	1,881	1,695	1,178	94,679
Papua New Guinea	N.A.	N.A.	N.A.	N.A.	27	26	34	87
Paraguay	N.A.	N.A.	N.A.	4,337	408	359	209	5,313
Pakistan	4,900	31,200	61,300	104,224	16,448	13,743	9,444	241,259
Peru	18,600	29,100	64,400	89,487	11,131	11,999	9,444	234,161
Philippines	101,500	360,200	495,300	503,945	53,154	51,308	45,397	1,610,804
Pitcairn	N.A.	N.A.	N.A.	1	0	0	0	1
Poland	73,300	43,600	97,400	163,747	11,818	12,746	10,526	413,137
Portugal	179,300	104,500	40,000	22,916	1,651	1,331	822	250,520
Qatar	N.A.	N.A.	N.A.	N.A.	125	108	72	305
Romania	14,900	17,500	38,900	51,203	6,649	4,903	3,663	137,718
Soviet Union / Russian Federation[a]	15,700	43,200	84,000	462,874	20,413	20,833	13,951	660,971
Rwanda	N.A.	N.A.	N.A.	N.A.	148	217	109	474
Saint Kitts–Nevis	N.A.	N.A.	N.A.	4,006	466	343	312	5,127
Saint Lucia	N.A.	N.A.	N.A.	4,892	678	586	489	6,645
Saint Vincent	N.A.	N.A.	N.A.	4,762	563	481	324	6,130
Samoa	N.A.	N.A.	N.A.	N.A.	171	160	181	512
Yugoslavia/Serbia	46,200	42,100	19,200	20,996	6,240	10,401	3,008	148,145
Senegal	N.A.	N.A.	N.A.	N.A.	655	530	522	1,707

(continues)

TABLE 1.2 Continued

Country	1961–70	1971–80	1981–90	1991–2000	2001	2002	2003	TOTAL
Sierra Leone	N.A.	N.A.	N.A.	N.A.	1,884	2,250	1,496	5,630
Singapore	N.A.	N.A.	N.A.	N.A.	549	812	587	2,211
Slovak Republic	N.A.	N.A.	N.A.	N.A.	142	141	64	347
Slovenia	N.A.	N.A.	N.A.	N.A.	142	141	64	320
South Africa	4,500	11,500	15,700	20,838	4,100	3,880	2,200	62,718
South Korea	N.A.	N.A.	N.A.	N.A.	N.A.	N.A.	N.A.	N.A.
Spain	44,659	39,141	20,499	17,157	1,726	1,376	923	125,145
Sri Lanka	N.A.	N.A.	N.A.	9,655	1,507	1,534	1,246	13,942
Sudan	N.A.	N.A.	N.A.	N.A.	1,655	2,924	1,886	6,465
Swaziland	N.A.	N.A.	N.A.	N.A.	18	12	23	53
Sweden	16,700	6,300	10,200	10,095	1,692	1,387	966	47,340
Switzerland	16,300	6,600	7,000	11,841	1,304	1,010	636	44,691
Syria	N.A.	N.A.	N.A.	N.A.	3,368	2,567	1,944	7,879
Taiwan	N.A.	N.A.	N.A.	93,079	12,171	9,836	6,947	122,033
Tanzania	N.A.	N.A.	N.A.	N.A.	477	584	555	1,616
Thailand	5,000	44,100	64,400	41,041	4,291	4,175	3,158	166,165
Tibet	N.A.	N.A.	N.A.	N.A.	N.A.	N.A.	N.A.	N.A.
Togo	N.A.	N.A.	N.A.	N.A.	489	540	353	1,382
Tonga	N.A.	N.A.	N.A.	N.A.	328	335	239	902
Trinidad and Tobago	24,600	61,800	39,500	54,849	6,665	5,771	4,153	197,338
Tunisia	N.A.	N.A.	N.A.	N.A.	440	540	353	1,333
Turkey	6,800	18,600	20,900	38,212	3,229	3,400	N.A.	91,141
Tuvalu	N.A.	N.A.	N.A.	N.A.	N.A.	N.A.	N.A.	N.A.

Uganda	N.A.	N.A.	N.A.	N.A.	459	577	457	1,493
United Arab Emirates	N.A.	N.A.	N.A.	N.A.	461	472	380	1,313
United Kingdom	230,500	123,500	142,100	114,244	18,436	16,421	9,601	654,802
Ukraine	N.A.	N.A.	N.A.	141,279	20,975	21,217	11,666	195,137
Uruguay	N.A.	N.A.	8,300	4,252	545	539	473	14,109
United States	N.A.	N.A.	N.A.	N.A.	63	66	32	161
Uzbekistan	N.A.	N.A.	N.A.	N.A.	2,035	2,319	1,446	5,800
Vanuatu	N.A.	N.A.	N.A.	N.A.	5	8	3	16
Venezuela	N.A.	N.A.	N.A.	N.A.	5,205	5,259	4,038	14,502
Vietnam	4,600	179,700	401,400	286,145	35,531	33,627	22,133	963,136
Yemen	N.A.	N.A.	N.A.	N.A.	1,615	1,228	1,386	4,229
Zambia	N.A.	N.A.	N.A.	N.A.	269	312	282	863
Zimbabwe	N.A.	N.A.	N.A.	N.A.	476	492	358	1,326
Total	2,721,053	3,713,578	6,231,767	6,990,866	908,195	899,378	610,735	22,075,572
Dual-citizenship countries (%)	85	83	85	77	85	85	87	82

Note: N.A. = not available.

[a] Data here reflect the number of immigrants from the USSR through 1989 and from Russia from 1990 and beyond.

(continued from p. 12)

percent) are dual/multiple-citizenship-encouraging countries. From six of these countries, there has been a substantial, statistically significant increase in the numbers of citizens in the seven years between the two sets of figures. In 1990, the last enumerated census year, seven of the top ten countries of birth of the foreign-born population in the United States were from dual-citizenship-encouraging countries. These are the adults. Martin and Aleinikoff, "drawing on census data . . . estimate that over 500,000 children are born in the United States each year with more than one nationality."[35]

These numbers have attracted little notice. Further, as substantial or surprising as these figures may be, they do not tell the whole story of the number of potential dual citizens arriving and living in the United States. To further deepen our understanding of these numbers, we must turn to one other categorical source: illegal immigrants.[36]

Illegal Immigration

One source of dual citizenship in the United States that is rarely discussed is illegal immigration.[37] Illegal immigrants are relevant to the total number of potential dual citizens in the United States in two ways. First, the children of illegal immigrants born in the United States are American citizens by birth and therefore potential dual citizens by parental nationality. Second, illegal immigrants can, and have often, been legalized through various amnesty programs that the government has enacted over the years.

By its very nature, illegal immigration is hard to accurately quantify.[38] Nonetheless, various estimates have been made, some relying on quite sophisticated methodologies. In 1995, the INS attempted to estimate the number of illegal immigrants in the United States and arrived at a figure of about 5.0 million undocumented immigrants as of October 1996, with a range of about 4.6 to 5.4 million. The population was estimated to be growing by about 275,000 each year, which is about 25,000 lower than the annual level of growth estimated by the INS in 1994.

However, figures drawn from the 2000 census clearly indicated that these figures were much too low. As a result, the Census Bureau drastically revised its estimates. It now reports that the number of illegal immigrants in the country as of 2000 is over 8.4 million, with a range of between 7.6 and 8.8 million.[39] For the illegal population to have grown so much since the last estimates, it would have to have been increasing by between 400,000 and 500,000 people per year.

Although undocumented immigrants come to the United States from all countries of the world, relatively few countries add substantially to the illegal population. The annual growth of the illegal population can be grouped into four categories: (1) Mexico, with more than half the annual growth, adds just over 150,000 undocumented residents each year; (2) six countries—El Salvador, Guatemala, Canada, Haiti, Honduras, and the Bahamas—each add between 6,000 and 12,000 annually; (3) thirteen countries each add about 2,000 to 4,000 annually; and (4) the remaining countries add a total of about 30,000 undocumented residents each year. A large majority of the additions each year, totaling 65 percent, are from countries in the Western Hemisphere, all of which encourage dual citizenship.

How many illegal immigrants come from dual-citizenship countries? Complete figures for the revised 2000 census numbers are not yet available. However, the INS did provide estimates of the top twenty illegal-immigrant-sending countries in its 1996 estimates. Table 1.3 gives two sets of data on dual citizenship and illegal immigration. The data on the table's left-hand side assume an illegal population of 5 million (the old figures), and the data on the right-hand side assume the updated estimates of 8.5 million, keeping the percentages of national origin the same.

It is clear that nineteen of the top twenty (99 percent) illegal-immigrant-sending countries allow dual citizenship. Or, put another way, 99 percent of the total number of illegal immigrants entering this country from the top twenty illegal-immigrant-sending countries are from dual-citizenship-allowing countries. This of course underestimates the actual numbers, because the rest of the illegal immigration population in the United States is very likely to come from the remaining 131 dual-citizenship countries that send immigrants to the United States.

Consider Mexican illegal immigration. Mexico represents 54 percent of all illegal immigration, almost 3 million persons. However, these estimates are now recognized as too low. Assume that illegal Mexican immigration represents the same 54 percent of the new 8.5 million figures as it does for the 1996 figures. The new estimates would represent more than 4.5 million illegal immigrants from this single source. These numbers are substantial, as are their implications. The United States is adding millions of immigrants, who, because of the illegal nature of their presence, are even less likely to become integrated into the American national community than the 700,000 to 800,000 legal immigrants who arrive each year.

One response to the figures on illegal immigration is to say: So what? They are, after all, illegal immigrants and not citizens. Why worry about their national attachments if they are not citizens?

That argument would be more persuasive were it not for the interplay of empathy and pandering for partisan advantage that intersect in American immigration policy. Repeated calls for various "adjustments" and "regularization" are in fact de facto amnesties. The Bush administration proposal and the recently introduced McCain-Kennedy Bill are no exceptions.[40] Although

TABLE 1.3
Top Twenty Sending Countries of Illegal Immigrants (Estimated)

Country of Origin	Assuming 5 Million Illegal Immigrants (%)		Assuming 8.5 Million Illegal Immigrants (%)	
1. Mexico	2,700,000	(54)	4,590,000	(54)
2. El Salvador	335,000	(8)	680,000	(8)
3. Guatemala	165,000	(3)	255,000	(3)
4. Canada	120,000	(2)	170,000	(2)
5. Haiti	105,000	(2)	170,000	(2)
6. Philippines	95,000	(2)	170,000	(2)
7. Honduras	90,000	(2)	170,000	(2)
8. Dominican Republic	75,000	(.015)	127,500	(.015)
9. Nicaragua	70,000	(.014)	119,000	(.014)
10. Poland	70,000	(.014)	119,000	(.014)
11. Columbia	65,000	(.013)	110,500	(.013)
12. Ecuador	55,000	(.011)	93,500	(.011)
13. Trinidad and Tobago	50,000	(.011)	93,500	(.011)
14. Jamaica	50,000	(.011)	93,500	(.011)
15. Pakistan	41,000	(.008)	68,000	(.008)
16. India	33,000	(.006)	51,000	(.006)
17. Korea	30,000	(.006)	51,000	(.006)
18. Ireland	30,000	(.006)	51,000	(.006)
19. Peru	30,000	(.006)	51,000	(.006)
20. Portugal	27,000	(.005)	42,000	(.006)
OTHER	764,000	(15)	1,275,000	(15)
Total dual-citizenship immigrants in top twenty immigrant-sending countries (%)	4,236,000	(99.3)[a]	7,275,000	(99.4[a])

Note: Dual-citizenship countries are in bold.

[a]Percent given = total dual-citizenship illegal immigrants / all top twenty countries.

Source: U.S. Department of Justice, *2000 Statistical Yearbook of the Immigration and Naturalization Service*, table N; available at http://ins.gov/graphics/aboutins/statistics/bypage.htm.

the latter would require illegal immigrants already here to pay a fine in order to gain legal status, it would, in effect, allow them access to a queue well ahead of those who apply through standard procedures. It would also add hundreds of thousands of immigrants every year to the already substantial number of immigrants (over 700,000) who are allowed in every year. The bill would provide an incentive to become an illegal immigrant because it has become an officially sanctioned starting point for gaining legal status.

Dual Citizenship and the Geographical Concentration of Immigrants

Dual-citizenship numbers take some of their importance from the density and distribution of immigrants, their families, and fellow nationals. A national group of emigrants that made up 12 percent of the American population would have political significance even if they were not concentrated in particular localities simply by virtue of their total percentages. Yet numbers alone do not convey the power of these immigrant numbers. Measures of immigrant concentration do. That might be called the iron law of immigration: When immigrants first arrive, they cluster. They gravitate to regions where there are already large numbers of their fellow immigrants living. They gravitate to major metropolitan area cities where members of their groups have already established a presence. This is now becoming as true of smaller localities as it is of big cities.

Because the United States does not keep detailed records of the geographical location of members who have come from each of the 150 countries that allow some form of dual citizenship, it is not possible to know much about the concentration/dispersal of each specific group. Yet we can make some estimates. Recall that about 81 percent of all immigrants to the United States for the years 1961 to 2003 came from dual-citizenship-allowing countries.

In 2000, there were roughly 28.3 million foreign-born persons residing in the United States.[41] They were regionally distributed as follows: the Northeast, 6.4 million (10 percent); the Midwest, 3 million (4.8 percent); the South, 7.6 million (7.9 percent); and the West, 11.3 million (18.1 percent). Within these regions, there was further clustering. Six states had a foreign-born population of 1 million or more: California (8.8 million), New York (3.6 million), New Jersey (1.2 million), and Illinois (1.2 million). These six states accounted for 20 million (70.4 percent) of the total foreign-born population, yet they represent only 39.3 percent of America's total population. The concentration in these six states increased from 56.5 percent in 1960 to 70.4 percent in 2000. Four other states—Hawaii (16.1 percent), Nevada (15.2 percent), Arizona (12.9 percent), and Massachusetts (12.4 percent)—are well above the national average of 10.4 percent. By contrast, consider that thirty-three states, mostly in the South and Midwest, had an estimated foreign-born population of 5 percent or less in 2000.

Almost 50 percent of the growth in America's foreign-born population from 1960 to 2000 occurred in three states: California (1.3 to 8.8 million), Florida (0.03 to 2.8 million), and Texas (0.03 to 2.4 million). This has caused a regional shift in population concentration. For the West and the South combined, the foreign-born population grew from 2.9 to 18.9 million (26.6 to 66.7 percent). By 2000, Florida and Texas had replaced Pennsylvania and Massachusetts among the top six states for foreign-born population. According to a number of estimates, Hispanics will make up between 41 and 47 percent of California's population.[42] Remember that all the ethnic groups that make up the category of Spanish-speaking immigrants come from dual-citizenship-allowing countries.

Within particular states and statistical metropolitan areas, immigrants are particularly densely concentrated. Fifty-four and a half percent live in nine metropolitan areas of 5 million or more people. New York and Los Angeles, each with 4.7 million foreign-born persons, account for 33 percent of that population, although they are home to only 13.3 percent of the total U.S. population. Adding San Francisco (2 million), Miami (1.6 million), and Chicago (1.1 million) accounts for almost 50 percent of the foreign-born population, but only 20.5 percent of the total U.S. population.

Or viewed another way, the standard statistical metropolitan area consisting of New York, Northern New Jersey, and Long Island has a population that is 22.8 percent foreign-born. The area that includes San Francisco, Oakland, and San Jose has a population that is 28.3 percent foreign-born. Considering cities with 1 to 5 million residents, Miami had the highest foreign-born proportion—42.7 percent.

Some of the numbers can be understood by looking more directly at a particular city: New York. Cheng, using data from the New York City Department of City Planning for the years 1992 to 1996 (the last year for which these kinds of data were available), examined the top twenty countries of origin for New York immigrants.[43] The data show that eighteen of the top twenty countries of origin of New York City immigrants are dual citizenship countries. On average, almost 86 percent of immigrants in New York came from dual-citizenship-allowing countries. New York represents a diverse immigrant population, with Dominicans forming the most numerous group. In other cities and areas, the situation is different.

Consider California. Johnson divided the state of California into various regions and found that the percentage of persons of Hispanic descent had increased in every section of the state.[44] The 2000 census found that several sections of the state that had Spanish-speaking immigrants were approaching a majority of residents: the Central Coast, 33.8 percent; Inland Empire, 37.8

percent; San Diego, 28.9 percent; San Joaquin Valley, 39.8 percent; and South Coast, 40.9 percent. All these Spanish-speaking immigrants arrived from dual-citizenship-allowing countries.

This trend is no longer solely found in specific states or cities but is spreading to other administrative units on the local level. One observer noted, "There are more Hispanics in Cook County, Chicago, than in Arizona or Colorado or New Mexico."[45] Hispanics, almost all of whom come from dual-citizenship countries, accounted for about half the growth in the U.S. population since 2000. As a group in July 2004, they now number 41.2 million out of a national population of 293 million.

The immigrants from the roughly twenty Spanish-speaking, dual-citizenship-allowing countries of the world join immigrants from 130 other dual-citizenship-allowing countries that send immigrants to the United States. The results are an unprecedented number of immigrants and Americans who can claim dual citizenship status—including some groups of recent arrivals who are still very much emotionally connected with their "home" countries.

Of course, not every immigrant (or American for that matter) is rushing off to claim the benefits of dual citizenship. But the United States has been the destination for many millions of legal and illegal immigrants in the past few decades, and they have arrived in a country that has largely abandoned systematic efforts to integrate these new members into the American national community. We applaud their economic progress, when it happens, and believe, erroneously, that this is all it takes to develop an emotional connection to this country.

Dual Citizenship Considered

However you examine the figures on American immigration, one fact is clear: The United States is taking in many millions of immigrants every decade from countries that support and, in many cases, encourage dual citizenship. That fact makes this period of increased immigration important and substantially different from earlier periods of high immigration. This is one major difference, with enormous consequences for the American national community, but it is not the only one.

Then and Now—A Change in Perspective

Many Americans hold an idealized view of immigration. They understand immigration through the haze of a dimly known past and the erroneous assumption that immigration now is like immigration then. In many critical ways, it is not.

Older cohorts of immigrants came from countries they left behind to make a new life, not replicate an old one. In an early work on American national character, the English psychoanalyst Geoffrey Gorer wrote of immigration after the early English settlements in the United States: "With few exceptions, the immigrants did not cross the ocean as colonists to reproduce the civilization of their homes on distant shores; with the geographical separation they were prepared to give up, as far as lay in their power, all their past: their language, and the thoughts which that language could express; the laws and allegiances they had been brought up to observe, the values and assured ways of life of their ancestors and former compatriots; even to a large extent their customary ways of eating, of dressing, of living."[46] Why would they do this? The answer, Gorer thought, was to be found in the fact that most immigrants had, "escaped . . . from discriminatory laws, rigid hierarchical structures, compulsory military service and authoritarian limitation of the opportunities open to the enterprising and the goals to which they could aspire."

Today, immigrants also come to the United States in order to escape a lack of opportunity and its consequences—poverty, illness, lack of freedom, and harsh, difficult lives with little hope for a better future. However, they come with much less of an expectation that they will necessarily diminish their financial, national, and emotional ties to their home country—much less sever those ties altogether. There are many reasons for this. Some are technological, some political; but all result in the same fact: Today's immigrants to the United States not only *can* be more in touch with their home countries but *expect* to be and are. Moreover, their home countries encourage it. The generations of immigrants who came to this country in the early 1900s looking straight ahead are gradually being replaced by generations of new immigrants who increasingly are looking back.

Dual Citizenship and Immigrants' National Attachments

The chief concern about dual citizenship is that it encourages or results in shallower attachments to the American national community than would be the case if there were not stiff competition for immigrant loyalties. In fact, competition may be a misnomer because the United States, at present, does very little to meet the challenge of foreign attachments posed by dual citizenship. The "competition" for immigrant loyalties seems, most recently, one-sided. Some foreign governments aggressively court their foreign nationals for their own self-interest. The United States assumes, erroneously in my view, that economic success will necessarily lead to genuine attachment rather than just an instrumental relationship.

The well-being of the American national community depends on its citizens and leaders generally placing the well-being of the country first. Obviously, citizens can and do differ in understanding those interests. But it would be hard to argue that another country's interests should be given primacy or equivalence by large numbers of this country's dual-citizenship communities.

I want to make the point very clearly here. I am not arguing that dual-citizen immigrants represent a form of transnational fifth column. I do not envision many immigrants lining up to join al Qaeda. However, I can easily envision a more subtle kind of conflict, in which immigrants favor positions that are not necessarily in their new country's best interests but certainly are in the interests of their home country, or in which immigrants view their American attachments primarily through an instrumental lens.

Consider Mexico, for example. It has taken a number of steps to cement the allegiances of its nationals in the United States. The Mexican government favors voting rights in Mexico for American citizens and lenient welfare rules for new immigrants and their families. It also recruits Mexican American citizens to advise the Mexican government. Recently, the Mexican government hired an attorney to contest trespassing charges brought against one of its illegal nationals in the United States. The Mexican government feared "that a court may uphold the trespassing charges and so set a national precedent."[47] If that were to happen, many more jurisdictions might begin to pick up, detain, and deport illegal Mexican nationals, something the Mexican government was trying to stop from happening. All these initiatives are clearly in Mexico's self-interest—yet they are hardly in the interest of the United States, which is trying to maintain and develop its national community.

These are unprecedented circumstances. This country was, after all, founded on the idea that citizenship was based on a heartfelt attachment as well as a commitment to lofty ideals. However, as a result of foreign governments' dual-citizenship initiatives with the American national community, the United States could have thousands, perhaps hundreds of thousands, of its citizens voting in foreign elections. It could have a number of citizens running for and serving in elective office in a foreign country. It could have a number of its citizens serving as advisers to foreign governments. All these things are already happening to some degree, and they will likely increase in the future. The question as to what, if anything, the United States should be doing about these trends of foreign involvement and investment is an important issue.

The issue of multiple attachments also has implications for American national security. Consider U.S. national security agencies. They are scrambling to make use of America's diversity. The world in which they operate and in which they are particularly interested is neither Caucasian nor Christian or Western. Diversity is, in many ways, a treasured resource for national security.

A recent news article reported that the Central Intelligence Agency was turning away large numbers of Arabic-language linguists because they still had relatives abroad, leading to worries "that recruits could be blackmailed if their families were vulnerable."[48] This is a real concern but not the most central one. Security agencies must discern the allegiant from the conflicted. They must be able to separate those who are genuinely emotionally connected to the United States from those with more shallow attachments to this country. In the 1950s, these questions revolved around political loyalty, and partial answers could be found in support of or membership in groups and organizations in the service of the former Soviet Union. In the twenty-first century, questions of attachment take other forms and are not so easily answered by organization membership cards.

The CIA and similar organizations are not the only groups grappling with these issues. Americans more generally face them as well, only in different ways. As more and more citizens with emotional ties to other countries advance in their chosen careers, they will increasingly occupy positions of economic and political positions of power and responsibility. There is no reason why we cannot expect that they will aspire to be judges, representatives, governors, senators, and even presidents. There has already been a constitutional amendment introduced in Congress to allow persons not born and raised in the United States to assume the presidency.

There is one other aspect to the issue of attachments for the American national community in this period: national will and commitment in an age of terrorism. September 11 introduced Americans to the very difficult knowledge that there are smart, effective, and ruthless groups who want to inflict the most severe damage on this country and its institutions that it could manage. It can be safely assumed that Americans will be tested, perhaps severely, by these new circumstances. There will be times when our patience and staying power will be tested, and the strength of Americans' attachments will be a valuable national resource given that trying times almost certainly lie ahead. Conflicted or instrumental attachments will not be helpful in carrying us through. These are difficult issues but it is best that we give them some thought before they are fully upon us.

Notes

1. I use the term "dual citizenship" rather than the many other related terms for several reasons. The focus of this book is the United States and the implications of dual citizenship for its unique national and political culture. Americans have primarily defined these terms through the frame of citizenship rather than of nationality, and the term "dual citizenship" therefore speaks most clearly to the country's history and guiding frameworks.

2. The analysis advanced throughout does not deny the existence and importance of a national American culture and psychology. That set of relationships is discussed in chapters 2 and 3.

3. "The Functionality of Citizenship" (editorial), *Harvard Law Review* 110 (1997): 1814–31; the citation here is on 1817.

4. Along with "dual citizenship," the other terms are "multicultural citizenship," from William Kymlicka, *Multicultural Citizenship: A Liberal Theory of Minority Rights* (Oxford: Clarendon Press, 1995); "flexible citizenship," from Aihwa Ong, *Flexible Citizenship: The Cultural Logic of Transnationalism* (Durham, N.C.: Duke University Press, 1999); "transnational citizenship," from Rainer Baubock, *Transnational Citizenship* (Aldershot, U.K.: Edward Elgar, 1994); "postnational citizenship," from Yasemin Soysal, *Limits of Citizenship: Migrants and Postnational Citizenship in Europe* (Chicago: University of Chicago Press, 1994); "plural nationality," from Alexander Aleinikoff and Douglas Klusmeyer, eds., *Citizenship Today: Global Perspectives* (Washington, D.C.: Carnegie Endowment for International Peace, 2001); "global citizenship," from Richard Falk, "The Making of Global Citizenship," in *Global Visions*, ed. Jeremy Brecher, John Brown Childs, and Jill Cutler (Boston: Beacon Press, 1993); "international citizenship," from Kim Rubenstein and Daniel Adler, "International Citizenship: The Future of Nationality in a Globalized World," *Indiana Journal of Global Legal Studies* 7, no. 2 (2000): 519–47; "contextual citizenship," from Heinz Klug, "Contextual Citizenship," *Indiana Journal of Global Legal Studies* 7, no. 2 (2000): 567–74; and "denationalized citizenship," from both Linda Bosniak, "Citizenship Denationalized," *Indiana Journal of Global Legal Studies* 7, no. 2 (2000): 447–58, and Bosniak, "Denationalizing Citizenship," in *Citizenship Today*, ed. Aleinikoff and Klusmeyer. These terms are similar to, but not synonymous with, the more descriptive term "dual citizenship." Finally, the term "multiple citizenship" can refer to any of the above terms, because most countries that allow their nationals to have dual citizenship have no prohibition against their holding citizenship in more than one other country.

5. Dual nationality has long been recognized as an issue in the relationship among states, and they have found their way into various international treaties over time; Peter J. Spiro, "Dual Nationality and the Meaning of Citizenship," *Emory Law Journal* 46, no. 4 (1997): 1412–85. However, a review of these various treaties and related instruments like human rights protocols emerges with two key findings that are relevant to our concerns here: (1) "The limitations that international legal norms impose on a state's authority over nationality policy are unclear, but remain *decidedly modest*" (Aleinikoff and Klusmeyer, *Citizenship Today*, 65; emphasis added); and (2) "Despite the steady growth of adherence to these human rights instruments [treaties] commentators who have studied nationality law most closely in both its domestic and international aspects, have emphasized the *decisive role, and relative autonomy of states* in regulating national policy" (Aleinikoff and Klusmeyer, *Citizenship Today*, 69; emphasis added).

6. A number of cases are relevant to the circumstances through which American citizens may give up or lose their citizenship: *Perkins v. Elg* (1939), *Kawakita v. U.S.* (1952), *Mandoli v. Acheson* (1952), *Perez v. Brownell* (1958), *Trop v. Dulles* (1958), *Schneider v. Rusk* (1964), *Afroyim v. Rusk* (1967), *Rogers v. Bellei* (1971), *Vance v. Terrazas* (1980), and *Miller v. Albright* (1998). In 1986, following the Supreme Court's decision in *Afroyim v. Rusk* (387 U.S. 253), Congress repealed parts of the statutory provisions of American citizenship law by adding the key requirement that loss of citi-

zenship could occur only on the citizen's "voluntarily performing any of the following acts with the intention of relinquishing United States nationality"; Act of Nov. 14, 1986, § 18, 100 Stat. 3655, 3658, codified as amended in 8 U.S.C. § 1481 (1988). With that, the onus shifted to the government to demonstrate that a designated act had been performed both voluntarily and with the specific intent to renounce U.S. citizenship. See Thomas M. Franck, "Clan and Superclan: Law Identity and Community in Law and Practice," *American Journal of International Law* 90 (1996): 359–83.

7. T. Alexander Aleinikoff, *Between Principles and Politics: The Direction of U.S. Citizenship Policy* (Washington, D.C.: Carnegie Endowment for International Peace, 1998), 26–27; see also Jeffrey R. O'Brien, "U.S. Dual Citizenship Voting Rights: A Critical Examination of Aleinikoff's Proposal," *Georgetown Immigration Review* 13, no. 533 (1999): 573–95.

8. This is what happened to President Alberto K. Fujimori, whose parents were born in Japan, but who served as president of Peru until he fled that country to escape facing charges of murder and dereliction of duty. Prosecutors wanted to extradite him, but as the *New York Times* notes, "Japan says it will not return Mr. Fujimori because Japan rarely allows the extradition of Japanese citizens. Although it usually takes years to obtain Japanese citizenship, Mr. Fujimori won his in December, 2000, the month after he took refuge here (his parents, and some say Mr. Fujimori himself, were born there)." James Brooke, "Fujimori, the Exile, Repackages His Peruvian Past," *New York Times*, January 11, 2002.

9. The reasons for ignoring these circumstances vary. A country may simply not perceive the practice as sufficiently important or widespread to merit attention or action. Or it may serve its own purposes—political, economic, or cultural—by ignoring other ties from which they benefit. Or it may have legal prohibitions against the practice, which are weakened by another of that country's political institutions. E.g., as Franck points out, Australian law as legislated in 1948 appeared to withdraw citizenship from any Australian who "does any act or thing: (a) the sole or dominant purpose of which; and (b) the effect of which; is to acquire the nationality or citizenship of a foreign country." Franck, "Clan and Superclan," 359. Yet a recent court case there held that this provision did not apply to an Australian of partly Swiss origin who applied to the Swiss government for recognition of her *jus sanguinis* status as a Swiss citizen. The case thereby opened the door to recognition of dual nationality, because the court held that to lose Australian citizenship, the citizen's motive must have been to acquire Swiss citizenship rather than to obtain recognition of an already-existing status of foreign nationality.

10. Jones-Correa offers Bolivia, Honduras, and Venezuela as examples of Latin American countries that allow repatriation upon return. Michael Jones-Correa, *Under Two Flags: Dual Nationality in Latin America and Its Consequence for the United States*, Working Paper in Latin America 99/00–3 (Cambridge, Mass.: David Rockefeller Center for Latin American Studies, Harvard University, 2000), 32. Goldstein and Piazza add Haiti to this list. Eugene Goldstein and Victoria Piazza, "Naturalization and Retention for Foreign Citizenship: A Survey," *Interpreter Releases* 73, no. 16 (1996): 517–21; the citation here is on 1630. Israel's Law of Return establishes that any Jew may become an Israeli citizen upon taking up residence there (Israel already allows dual citizenship).

11. They are Bolivia, Chile, Ecuador, Costa Rica, Guatemala, Nicaragua, Paraguay, Peru, the Dominican Republic, Argentina, and Honduras. See Investigations Service, U.S. Office of Personnel Management, *Citizenship Laws of the World* (Washington, D.C.: U.S. Government Printing Office, 2001).

12. Jones-Correa, *Under Two Flags*, 2.

13. Recently, France and Germany, as part of their new political alliance, have worked on developing special citizenship reciprocity, whereby each country's citizens would automatically be citizens of the other—aside from the fact that both would share a common European Union citizenship. Presumably, in this case French Moroccans and other citizens of France's former colonies who elected to remain politically part of France would also become German citizens. Finally, along similar lines, Brooke has reported, "Under Portuguese law, all inhabitants of 'Portuguese India'—Goa and the northern coastal enclaves of Damão and Díu—were considered Portuguese citizens." Now, residents of these areas can gain Portuguese passports, making them at the same time European citizens. See James Brooke, "Indians Pursue Portuguese Passports as an Entry to Europe," *New York Times*, June 8, 2003.

14. Elaine Sciolino, "France Envisions a Citizenry of Model Muslims," *New York Times*, May 7, 2003; "Islam in Britain" (editorial), *Times* (London), May 2, 2003; Ian Johnson, "Lingering Muslim Extremism Perplexes Tolerant Germany," *Wall Street Journal*, September 20, 2002.

15. See Investigations Service, U.S. Office of Personnel Management, *Citizenship Laws*, 175.

16. These include Belgium, Brunei, Cambodia, the Congo, Croatia, Finland, Liberia, Luxembourg, Malawi, Mauritania, Moldova, Mongolia, Mozambique, Myanmar, Namibia, Nepal, Nicaragua, Oman, Pakistan, Palau, Qatar, Rwanda, Sierra Leone, Singapore, Samoa, Sudan, Swaziland, Sweden, Taiwan, Tanzania, Thailand, Tonga, Uganda, Ukraine, United Arab Emirates, Uzbekistan, Vanuatu, Venezuela, Vietnam, Yemen, Zambia, and Zimbabwe. See the specific country information in Investigations Service, U.S. Office of Personnel Management, *Citizenship Laws*.

17. Rodolfo O. de la Garza, Miguel David Baranoa, Tomas Pachon, Emily Edmunds, Fernando Acosta-Rodriguez, and Michelle Morales, *Dual Citizenship, Domestic Politics, and Naturalization Rates of Latino Immigrants in the U.S.* (Los Angeles: Tomas Rivera Center, 1996).

18. These include Capriotti & Associates, International Law, P.O. Box 2792, Portland, Oregon 97208–2792, http://www.capriotti.com; Aleinikoff, *Between Principles and Politics*, 28–29; Goldstein and Piazza, "Naturalization," 517–21; Eugene Goldstein and Victoria Piazza, "Naturalization, Dual Citizenship, and Retention of Foreign Citizenship: A Survey," *Interpreter Releases* 75, no. 54 (November 23, 1998): 1613–17; Ruta M. Kalvaitis, "Citizenship and National Identity in the Baltic States," *Boston University International Law Journal* 16 (1998): 238 (the citation here is to n. 184); K. Connie Kang, "Dual U.S.-Korean Nationality Nears," *Los Angles Times*, June 14, 1998; Norman Kempster, "Crises in Yugoslavia: 3,000 to 4,000 U.S. Civilians Believed Stuck, Many of Those Living in the Two Republics Hold Dual Citizenship," *Los Angeles Times*, April 3, 1999; Peter M. Schuck, *Citizens, Strangers, and In-Betweens: Essays on Immigration and Citizenship* (Boulder, Colo.: Westview Press, 1998), 223; Peter J.

Spiro, "Dual Nationality and the Meaning of Citizenship," *Emory Law Journal* 46, no. 4 (1997): 1412–85 (the citation here is on 1455, 1457–58); Jorge A. Vargas, "Dual Nationality for Mexicans?" *Chicano-Latino Law Review* 18, no. 1 (1996): 1–58 (the citation here is on 50, n. 198); Gianni Zappala and Stephan Castles, "Citizenship and Immigration in Australia," *Georgetown Immigration Law Journal* 13 (1999): 273; and Jones-Correa, *Under Two Flags*, 3, 5. In 2001, the Investigations Service of the U.S. Office of Personnel Management produced a comprehensive analysis titled *Citizenship Laws of the World* (Washington, D.C.: U.S. Government Printing Office, 2001), which was also consulted.

19. E.g., Goldstein and Piazza do not list Ireland, which does permit dual citizenship. More troublesome are inconsistencies that arise from conflicts between what two or more different authors assert as erroneous information. Thus, Goldstein and Piazza, "Naturalization," list the Philippines and India as non-dual-citizenship countries, whereas Peter M. Schuck—in "The Re-Evaluation of American Citizenship," *Georgetown Immigration Law Journal* 12, no. 1 (1997): 1–34 (the citation here is on 11); and in Schuck, *Citizens*, 222—says they are, for American-born children of Filipino and Indian nationals. The *Washington Post* has reported that India is considering a law to allow dual citizenship for its nationals abroad (Rama Lakshmi, "India Reaches Out to Emigrants: Millions Living Abroad Encouraged to Invest in Homeland," January 12, 2003)—which appears to suggest that Goldstein and Piazza were correct. That law has now been passed.

Along similar lines, Jones-Correa, *Under Two Flags*, lists Argentina as having limited dual citizenship (with other treaty countries), whereas Goldstein and Piazza, "Naturalization, Dual Citizenship, and Retention," make no such distinction. And finally, Goldstein and Piazza list the Netherlands as a country that does not allow dual citizenship, whereas an article by Schmitter-Heisler discusses the effects of the Dutch dual citizenship law passed in 1992. See Barbara Schmitter-Heisler, "Contents of Immigrant Incorporation," in *Immigration, Citizenship, and Welfare in Germany and the United States: Welfare Policies and Immigrants' Citizenship*, ed. Herman Kurthen, Jurgen Fijalkowski, and Gert. G. Wagner (Stamford, Conn.: JAI, 1998). In all cases of differences, inquiries were made of the appropriate embassies. In the few cases where this did not produce clarification, that country was not included. For the reasons noted above, and because the legal standing of dual citizenship is in flux in some countries, this list should not be considered final.

20. The strategy employed for this study was to accept as accurate countries listed as allowing dual citizenship by reputable academic authorities in the study of immigration. In some cases, when discrepancies arose, we e-mailed and called the embassies of those countries directly. After explaining our general interest in the subject and saying we would greatly appreciate their help we asked: (1) Whether your country now permits the children born of your nationals living abroad (for example, in the United States) to obtain or retain their citizenship in your country. (2) Whether your country now permits adult nationals living abroad to retain their citizenship in your country if they also become a citizen of another country (for example, the United States).

21. Tony Smith, *Foreign Entanglements: The Power of Ethnic Groups in the Making of American Foreign Policy* (Cambridge, Mass.: Harvard University Press, 2001).

22. E.g., recently, in India, Atal Behari Vajpayee, the prime minister, announced that "legislation would be introduced to grant dual citizenship to people of Indian origin living in 'certain countries,'" which officials later tentatively identified as the United States, the United Kingdom, Australia, New Zealand, Canada, and Singapore. According to a recent report by the consulting firm McKinsey & Company, the 20 million Indians living abroad generate an annual income equal to 35 percent of India's gross domestic product. Many of those reside in "certain countries" that have now been given dual citizenship.

23. G. Escobar, "Immigrants' Ranks Tripled in 29 Years," *Washington Post*, January 9, 1999; U.S. Bureau of the Census, *Current Population Reports: The Foreign-Born Population in the United States: March 1999* (Washington D.C.: U.S. Government Printing Office, 2000); Steven A. Camorata, *Immigrants in the United States—2000: A Snapshot of America's Foreign Born Population* (Washington, D.C.: Center for Immigration Studies, 2004); Eduardo Porter, "Estimate of Illegal Immigrants Reaches as Many as 8.5 Million for Some Experts," *Wall Street Journal*, August 14, 2001.

24. Camarota, *Immigrants*.

25. The figures that follow, unless otherwise noted, are drawn from U.S. Bureau of the Census, *Profile of the Foreign Born Population in the United States: 1997*, Current Population Reports Special Studies (Washington, D.C.: U.S. Government Printing Office, 1997), 8–49. Definitions of terms used are found in appendix A, 52–53.

26. Camarota, *Immigrants*.

27. Camarota, *Immigrants*; "Immigration Said to Keep Pace with 1990's," *New York Times*, November 26, 2002.

28. U.S. Bureau of the Census, *Current Population Reports*.

29. U.S. Bureau of the Census, *Coming to America: A Profile of the Nation's Foreign Born (2000 Update)* (Washington, D.C.: U.S. Government Printing Office, 2002), 1.

30. Camarota, *Immigrants*.

31. Samuel P. Huntington, *Who Are We? The Challenges to American National Identity* (New York: Simon & Schuster, 2004), 243. Spanish-speaking immigrants are not, of course, the sole source of our immigration numbers. Asian countries provided 7.2 million people in the foreign-born count, about 26 percent of that total figure. In 1970, those figures were 800,000 and 9 percent, respectively. China, the Philippines, India, and Vietnam provide a substantial portion of those immigrants. Three of these countries allow dual citizenship—India, Vietnam, and the Philippines.

32. Multilateral Investment Fund, Inter-American Development Bank, *Sending Money Home: Remittances to Latin America and the Caribbean* (Washington, D.C.: Inter-American Development Bank, 2004).

33. Immigration and Naturalization Service, U.S. Department of Justice, *Annual Report: Legal Immigration, Fiscal Year 1998, No. 2* (Washington, D.C.: U.S. Government Printing Office, 1999), 8. Immigration and Naturalization Service, U.S. Department of Justice, *Annual Report: Legal Immigration, Fiscal Year 1997, No. 1* (Washington, D.C.: U.S. Government Printing Office, 1999), 9. Both reports provide legal immigration figures for selected countries for the years they cover. As a result, some additional information is necessary to understand why the term "top twenty," though essentially accurate, is in quotation marks. One anomaly is that neither of the

two documents includes the countries making up the former Yugoslavia (Serbia and Montenegro, Croatia, Bosnia-Herzegovina, Macedonia, and Slovenia, all multiple-citizenship-allowing countries) in their list of top immigrant-sending countries. Yet with 10,750 immigrants in 1997 and 11,854 in 1996 coming from these countries in those two years, they certainly send more immigrants than several of the countries included in the document's list of high-sending countries. For these reasons, the numbers and percentages of multiple-citizenship-country immigrants as a function of the total number of listed top-twenty countries tend to underreport their magnitude.

One other anomaly of the table should be noted. The May 1999 report of 1995–98 immigration figures includes one country (Bangladesh) that is not included in the top-sending-country list in the January 1999 document reporting the immigration figures for 1994–97. The reports follow each of the countries listed back through several previous years. So the May 1999 report contains figures for Bangladesh for 1995 to 1998, even though it is not listed as a top sending country in the earlier January 1999 report, which covered 1994 to 1997. In that latter report, Ukraine is listed as a top immigrant-sending country and its immigrant-sending history is traced back from 1994 to 1997. However, Bangladesh is not listed in that report. Otherwise, the specific countries listed are the same. To more accurately reflect the realities of the data on high (top twenty) immigrant-sending countries, I have reported the Bangladesh data for 1998 but not for previous years, when the numbers are well below those of Ukraine, which is listed in that top-twenty group in the January 1999 report.

34. U.S. Bureau of the Census, *Profile of the Foreign Born Population in the United States: 2000*, Current Population Reports, Special Studies, Series P2–3-206 (Washington, D.C.: U.S. Government Printing Office, 2001), 19, 20.

35. David Martin and T. Alexander Aleinikoff, "Double Ties: Why Nations Should Learn to Love Dual Nationality," *Foreign Policy* (November–December 2002): 80.

36. One more element tends to increase dual-citizenship numbers among both legal and illegal immigrants: family size and fertility rates. Space precludes a detailed treatment, but some basic numbers may give a sense of the issue. In 1999, 25.4 percent of family households in which a foreign-born person was the householder consisted of five or more people. In contrast, only 13.2 percent of native family households were this large. Among foreign-born households, the proportion with five or more people varied from 40.1 percent when the householder was from Central America to 11.1 percent when the householder was from Europe. For Latin America generally, the figure was 33.0 percent (U.S. Bureau of the Census, *Current Population Reports*, 3). In June 2000, there were 7.9 million foreign-born women, in age categories fifteen to forty-four years, representing 13 percent of all women in the childbearing years. In the year preceding the census survey, 737,000 foreign-born women gave birth, resulting in a fertility rate of eighty-five births per thousand women; 42 percent of these were first births (9 percent and 58 percent, respectively, were second or later births). The fertility for native-born women was considerably lower at sixty-two births per 1,000 women (with 41 percent being first births). In the age categories twenty to twenty-four and thirty to thirty-four, fertility rates for foreign-born women exceeded those of native-born women by approximately thirty births per 1,000. Among foreign-born women, those of Hispanic origin had a "considerably higher fertility rate in 2000 (112 births

per thousand women) than those not of Hispanic origin, and a higher average number of births (1.8 per woman and 1.2 births per 1,000 women) respectively"; Amara Bachu and Martin O'Connell, *Fertility of American Women: June 2000*, Current Population Report P20–543RV, U.S. Bureau of the Census (Washington, D.C.: U.S. Government Printing Office, 2001), 3.

37. The two categories—illegal and undocumented immigrants—are separable, though often confounded by advocates of increased immigration. The difference may be succinctly stated. Illegal immigrants are those who enter this country with (as, e.g., with tourists who overstay their visas or those who sneak across borders) or without documentation—with the intention of, and by, evading the administrative reviews that would accompany legal applications or claims for residence. Undocumented immigrants are those who do not have relevant papers, not because they wish to evade the law, but rather because events in their countries of origin have resulted in a loss of their documentation. E.g., ethnic Muslims were stripped of their identification and other papers before being allowed to leave Serbia during the conflict in 1998. Many were offered an opportunity to resettle in the United States and other countries. They did so having lost their documentation, but they nonetheless went through an administrative review process before gaining admission. The same lack of documentation can be found in some cases of authentic requests for asylum. Immigrant advocacy groups prefer the term "undocumented" rather than "illegal" for obvious reasons. It helps to make it sound as if the estimated 8.5 million illegal immigrants living here all accidentally left their entry applications and identification material at home in their bureau drawers. And, of course, the legal and political standing of those who have gained entry by breaking U.S. laws differs from those whose genuine and dire (noneconomic) circumstances have left them without full documentation.

38. There have been attempts to do so; see Jeffrey S. Passel and Karen Woodrow, "1990 Decennial Census: Preliminary Research and Evaluation Memorandum No. 75, U.S. Bureau of the Census, Washington, D.C.," *International Migration Review* 18 (1994): 642–71; Robert Warren and Jeffrey Passel, "A Count of the Uncountable: Estimates of Undocumented Immigrants Counted in the 1980 Census," *Demography* 24 (1987): 375–93; Woodrow, "Preliminary Estimates of Undocumented Residents in 1990," Demographic Analysis Evaluation Project D2, Preliminary Research and Evaluation Memorandum No. 75, 1990 Decennial Census, U.S. Bureau of the Census, Washington, 1991; and Edward W. Fernandez and J. Gregory Robinson, "Geographic Distribution of Undocumented Immigrants: Estimates of Undocumented Aliens Counted in the 1980 Census by State," Population Division, U.S. Bureau of the Census, Washington, 1994. The technical mechanics of the preceding documents are beyond the scope of our interests here. A new, more sophisticated methodology for these estimates was developed at the INS and a report detailing some of the methods and findings was obtained, by Representative Lamar Smith, only by issuing a subpoena to the agency. The report, titled "Annual Estimates of the Unauthorized Immigration Population Residing in the United States and Components of Change: 1987 to 1999," was written by Robert Warren in the Office of Policy and Planning and is available from the author.

39. U.S. Bureau of the Census, "Executive Steering Committee for Ace Policy II, Report l, Appendix A, 13 October 2001," http://www.census.gov/dmd/www/pdflReportl

.PDF. Also see D'Vera Cohn, "Illegal Residents Exceed Estimate: Experts Analyzing New Census Figures Say 6 Million May Instead Be 9 Million," *Washington Post*, March 18, 2001; Porter, "Estimate of Illegal Immigrants."

40. Daryl Fears, "Immigration Measure Introduced," *Washington Post*, May 13, 2005.

41. The figures that follow, unless otherwise noted, are drawn from Dianne A. Schmidley, *Profile of the Foreign-Born Population in the United States*, Current Population Reports, Series P23–206, U.S. Bureau of the Census (Washington, D.C.: U.S. Government Printing Office, 2001).

42. Hans P. Johnson, "A State of Diversity: Demographic Trends in California Regions," *California Counts: Populations Trends and Profiles* (Public Policy Institute of California) 3, no. 5 (May 2002), available at http://www.ppic.org.

43. Mae M. Cheng, "Citizens of the World: New Americans are Increasingly Keeping Dual Allegiances," *Newsday*, August 7, 2000.

44. Johnson, "State of Diversity."

45. Quoted in D'Vera Cohn, "Hispanic Growth Surge Fueled by Births in U.S.," *Washington Post*, June 9, 2005.

46. Geoffrey Gorer, *The American People: A Study in National Character* (New York: W. W. Norton, 1948), 25.

47. Michael Powell, "New Tack against Illegal Immigrants," *Washington Post*, June 10, 2005.

48. Douglas Jehl, "C.I.A. Is Reviewing Its Security Policy for Translators," *New York Times*, June 8, 2005.

PART I

American National Identity: The Framework

CHAPTER 2

The Search for the Missing Link

WHAT UNITES AMERICANS? "E PLURIBUS UNUM"—OUT OF MANY, one—is our national motto. How that happens remains mysterious and shrouded in conventional, but incorrect, wisdom.

What is an American? Throughout the years of our history, there has been no shortage of answers to that question. Yet at this juncture in its history, the United States stands at a particularly difficult and dangerous crossroads. An accurate answer to that question is increasingly imperative.

Why is it so important now? One reason is that America's major institutions and traditions—including immigrant integration—have become matters of heated and divisive debate. It is also important because all these debates take place in the context of increased dangers from catastrophic terrorism, for which America is the chief enemy and target. In these circumstances, deep, strong national attachments are a necessity, not an option.

One critical question results: Does the United States have sufficient levels of cohesion and attachment among its diverse population to sustain the level of national integration necessary for democracy to survive and prosper? Many believe we already have the answer: Yes. President Bill Clinton asked, "Can we define what it means to be an American, not just in terms of the hyphen showing our ethnic origins?" His answer was in the affirmative. All we needed to do, he said was, define ourselves by "our primary allegiance to the values that America stands for and values we really live by."[1]

According to Tamar Jacoby, "Every schoolchild knows we are a unique nation not by blood or ancestry, *but by a set of shared ideas*."[2] Or again, what holds America together? "The ineluctable common core—is a set of ideas about how the American people ought to govern themselves."[3] Michael Walzer has argued that it is citizenship and the fact that it is easy to become an American that binds us together.[4] These values have traditionally been understood as "the American Creed." Cultural aphorisms like "democracy is the best form of government" or "everyone should have the right of free speech" garner almost uniform approval in public opinion surveys. And because everyone agrees, it is tempting to say that Americans have found the Holy Grail of political cohesion and attachment. But they have not.

That agreement is an illusion. One is reminded here of the classic study that found almost every American supported free speech, until asked about the first specific application of the principle that was controversial.[5] Of course, consensual agreement by itself is neither a necessary reflection of a desirable democratic process nor a reflection of deep emotional attachment. Alan Wolfe's study of American moral judgments, for example, found plenty of consensus in his in-depth interviews with Americans that were based on a disinclination to make judgments of any kind.[6]

The truth is that Americans may be united in the abstract but are increasingly disconnected. Americans live in a country where there is enormous and increasing technological interconnectedness but far less relatedness. Andrew Shapiro notes that "some forms of connectivity encourage separation; so paradoxically the Internet makes Americans more connected, but also more isolated."[7] Americans are more easily in touch with markets, news, and other aspects of their lives, but it does not necessarily follow that there has been an upsurge in interpersonal intimacy and knowledge.

The primary response to the issue of citizen disconnection has been institutional. The consensual response is that Americans need to revitalize their civic networks. Thus, in the 1990s, the United States had White House conferences on "Character Building for a Democratic Society," a "National Commission for Civic Renewal," and many other initiatives designed to revitalize the frayed fabric of our civic culture.

These important efforts proceeded on the idea that public psychology will follow the lead of civic institutions. That is, if you improve the civic infrastructure, you will increase the sense of connectedness and presumably the support for our democratic institutions. This may well be the case. But it is equally likely that public psychology *precedes* robust democratic civic connections. At any rate, it is difficult to imagine such efforts succeeding while America is engaged in what I term its "Second Civil War"—that is, the culture wars that have divided this country since the 1960s. The American Creed is small comfort when the basic institutions of American civic and cultural life have been bitterly contested for more than forty years. While the Creed has its place in American civic life, it does not provide the psychological glue that binds us together.

Psychologically, the chief question before us is: What is the basis for a person's attachment to his or her country? What does it mean to identify oneself as an American? What is so special about national identifications that are not true of other more narrowly focused identifications? And what are the implications of that understanding for the very large number of immigrants who have chosen to make the United States their home?

The Meaning of American National Identity

"American national identity" is a controversial term. Liberal theorists reject it as tainted by the excesses of nationalism, with which it is often, and erroneously, associated. Even conservatives have been wary of the term. At a forum on American identity, the moderator noted "significant resistance even to using the term, especially in its generic form, 'national identity,' among a largely conservative audience."[8] As Anthony Smith points out: "The process of self-definition . . . is in many ways the key to national identity, but also the element that has attracted the most doubt and skepticism."[9]

Some are convinced that the term has no possible empirical standing. Vincent, for example, notes, "The problem here is, how do we recognize the national identity and culture of Britain, Canada, Australia, Germany and America, or Israel? Is there a central public culture or distinctive set of *values* acknowledged by *all* citizens? Taking Britain alone, there are so many crosscutting differences of class, age, ethnicity, belief systems, and gender that making such a judgment seems simply frivolous."[10]

Yet making national identity dependent on whether *all* members of the community hold the exact same beliefs is a rather high and artificial standard. Moreover, Vincent appears to have confused the variation on any measure that one can get by looking at differences pertaining to the sociological categories that he mentions with the question of dispersal—that is, how much variance there is around the mean. It may well be that different sociological groups would have different levels of agreement on a value but still be in enough agreement to say that they hold compatible views. The more important mistake that Vincent makes, however, is a basic one. He equates national identity with values. This is a common mistake, especially in the United States, among politicians and theorists alike, where deference to "the Creed" as a unifying national factor has reached canonical status.

"National identity" is a term that currently has no common understanding. Meyers defines what he terms a "national identity approach" to immigration policy as focusing on how "the unique history of each country, its conceptions of citizenship and nationality, as well as debates over national identity and social conflicts within it, shape its immigration policies. . . . Much of this literature can be characterized as historical sociology or political sociology, and it builds upon social and psychological theories, and concepts such as national identity, nation building, prejudice, alienation and social closure."[11] If this sounds like a hodgepodge of different terms with little theoretical specification or connection, Meyers is perhaps to be excused. After all, he is not a psychologist. Even the father of the term "identity," Erik Erikson, was extremely vague as to its meaning.

In fact, there are a variety of approaches to understanding national identity. Some of these, like the national-trait psychology theories, are no longer in use—for good reason.[12] In examining the concept of national identity, therefore, it may be helpful to begin with some basic distinctions.

Does National Character Equal National Identity?

The idea that the character or psychology of a people is related to their capacity for particular kinds of politics has a long history in modern psychology and social science. But how, exactly, to understand that link has had its share of false starts.

National identity is not synonymous with national character. Early studies of national character were strongly influenced by cultural anthropologists like Ralph Linton and more specifically by the "culture and personality" work associated with Ruth Benedict, Margaret Mead, Clyde Kluckholm, and Henry Murray.[13] Those pioneers studied relatively small, homogeneous, and slowly evolving societies to chart the links among culture, socialization, and personality, on one hand; and the continuity of societal conventions (embedded in political, economic, religious, and social institutions), on the other. Perhaps not surprisingly, given the kinds of societies they studied, the links appeared solid. However, those who studied large, heterogeneous, and rapidly changing societies were certainly justified in asking what useful implications this genre held for them.

National character studies, a direct outgrowth of the "culture and personality studies" described above, were popular in the 1940s and 1950s. They tried to find antecedents of political institutions and cultural practices in very early childhood experiences.[14] The swaddling of Russian children, it was said, made them vulnerable to a lack of individual initiative. Along similar lines, national character studies argued that the authoritarian German family had made the country's citizens susceptible to a strong father figure.

Members of the early culture and personality school often wrote as if personality were culture writ large and viewed the former through the powerful, but scarcely refined, lens of early psychoanalytic theory. Those uncomfortable with a view of internal psychology as little more than a barely contained caldron of urges turned for life into instinctual stone had many legitimate questions to ask.

National Identity and the Nation

National identity obviously requires people to identify with something, and that something is often the nation. It is an easy, but conceptually erroneous, slip to then equate the nation with the identification itself and to discuss the latter as if it were synonymous with the former. Consider Smith's definition of the term "national identity," which is also the title of his book. He writes: "What we mean by 'national' identity involves some sense of political community, . . . [which] in turn requires at least some common institutions and a single code of rights and duties for all members of the community. It also suggests a definite social space, a fairly well demarcated and bounded territory with which the members identify and to which they feel they belong, . . . This is of course a particularly Western conception of the nation."[15]

There are some attractive elements in Smith's formulation. However, the state—as in the term "nation-state"—occupies a much different ontological status than the persons who make it up. It is probably a conceptual level-of-analysis error to equate them. Individuals, of course, are a part of the state and, neither alone nor in the aggregate, the state itself. Moreover, it is not the state but national identity that we wish to understand.

Smith is not the only scholar to run up against the overlapping psychological and structural meanings that occur in discussions of nation and national identity. Hugh Seton-Watson defines a nation as "a community of people bound together by a sense of solidarity, a common culture, a national consciousness"—all three obviously psychological.[16] Shortly, however, he adds that "a nation must share a common language, a common territory, a common economic life and a common mental make-up"—thus adding several structural elements to the mix.[17]

The same tendency—to mix structural and psychological elements—can be observed in Miller's discussion of national identity. He summarizes his view of national identity by saying it is a community constituted by (1) shared belief and mutual commitment, (2) a sense of shared history, (3) a particular territory (4) an active participation in the community, and (5) a distinct public culture. These, he believes, serve to distinguish nationality from other collective sources of personal identity.[18]

Miller, like others, has combined structural elements that help to define the nation with those individual psychological elements that are more clearly the province of national identity. In so doing, he may have distinguished national identifications from other forms of identification, but he has done so in a way that mixes two categories that need to be conceptually separated. What is needed to define national identity is a specifically psychological framing of that concept.

Does National Identity Equal Nationalism?

Another term with which national identity is often equated is "nationalism."[19] As early as 1937, the psychologist Floyd Allport suggested that the "nationalistic fallacy"—"the view that regards the nation as over-person, feeling, speaking and acting for itself"—often leads to war.[20] He then noted, "The writer [i.e., Allport] has perhaps not fairly distinguished between nationalism and patriotism. After all, it is not the nationalistic fallacy itself that leads to war, but the way in which it is used. . . . May we not keep our 'Nation,' but purge it of all sinister motives?"[21] In other words, patriotism and nationalism are drawn from the same conceptual reservoir—with nationalism being patriotism's evil twin.

Given the difficulty of disentangling patriotism and nationalism, and the slanting of nationalism as essentially aggressive, it is small wonder that the view that patriotism is essentially aggressive nationalism persists. Kosterman and Feshbach note that "'nationalism' and 'patriotism' were occasionally used interchangeably and conceptualized, for the most part, as negative internationalism."[22] The confusion was worsened by the classic study *The Authoritarian Personality*, which attempted to account for attitudes and psychology consistent with Nazi ideology. One of the study's subscales was conceptualized as "blind attachment to certain, uncritical conformity with the prevailing group ways, and a rejection of other nations as out-groups."[23] As Kosterman and Feshbach note, "Ironically, that subscale was named 'Patriotism'—ironic because Adorno and his associates had actually emphasized a distinction between *genuine* patriotism (as simply 'love of country') and pseudo-patriotism (which is what they were measuring) in the text describing the subscale." The distinctions between patriotism and nationalism were subsequently lost, and "'the badness' of nationalism became the overriding theme for many years to come."[24] Patriotism needs to be conceptually as well as politically rehabilitated.

Consider Conner's distinction between nationalism and patriotism. He writes: "Nationalism, as commonly encountered in the press, television news and even in most scholarly tracks, refers to the emotional attachment to one's state or country and its political institutions—an attachment more properly called PATRIOTISM. Nationalism refers to an emotional attachment to one's people—one's ethnonational group."[25] His view can be contrasted with that of Kosterman and Feshbach, who argue that agreement with statements like "I love my country" have very different places in an individual's psychology and attitudes than agreement with statements like "In view of America's moral and material superiority, it is only right that we should have the biggest say in deciding U.N. policy." They label the first cluster of questions patriotism, and the second nationalism.

Interestingly, both sets of questions are not strongly associated with each other and are associated differentially with other views and attitudes. So, for example, attitudes toward nuclear arms or readiness to go to war are not equally associated in the same ways or to the same degree with both sets of questions. The authors conclude that patriotism and nationalism, as they have measured them, are not ends of the same continuum but rather altogether different dimensions.[26] They appear not to realize that *how* they have measured nationalism has substantially compromised their findings.

The alert reader will notice the difference between Conner's definition of nationalism as simply an emotional attachment to one's people and Kosterman and Feshbach's definition of nationalism as being suffused with attitudes of competitive aggression and superiority. Statements such as "Generally, the more influence America has on other countries the better off they are," and "The important thing for the U.S. foreign aid program is to see that the United States gains a political advantage" stack the deck against a more neutral appraisal of nationalism. Others, like Sidanius and his colleagues, have followed Kosterman and Feshbach's lead in using these same questions to define nationalism.[27] The one-sided questions as a definition of nationalism are further reinforced by theories that define nationalism as the desire for national superiority that involves dominating or bettering other nations.[28]

So not only were the differences between patriotism and nationalism lost over the years, but also the very nature of nationalism itself has been confounded because it was equated with one form of it—a dominating and aggressive stance toward others. In view of this, it is therefore not surprising that Drukman's review of the social-psychological literature on nationalism, patriotism, and group loyalty concludes, "Patriotism seems to lead to strong attachments and loyalties to one's own group without the corresponding hostility towards other groups while nationalism encourages an orientation involving liking for one's own group and a disliking of certain other groups."[29]

Those errors and their consequences are still very much with us. Gomberg, to quote the title of his paper, believes that "patriotism is like racism."[30] His reasoning is that attempts to theorize about "moderate patriotism" founder on the shoals of real life. He gives as an example the war against Mexico in 1846 and the Vietnam War and asks what a moderate patriot would have done. In his view, support of either would make the moderate patriot the equivalent of a chauvinist patriot.

Yet Gomberg's strongest condemnation of moderate patriotism starts with the premise of universal morality: that all persons deserve equal respect and treatment. That being the case, he asks, "Doesn't this preclude favoring others of one's own nationality?"[31] Finally, he asserts, "I believe that it is racism. . . . The belief that favoring one's own nationality is wrong is based on the estimation that the practice contributes to the segregation and subordination of black people."[32] It would follow from this that most Americans do not consider blacks Americans—a position for which there is no empirical evidence.

Gomberg has a strong ideological stance toward the issues of patriotism. But he also fails to recognize that people develop feelings and attachments that are not always equal. People do not treat their parents or children in the same way as strangers. Moral absolutism—that any preference is discrimina-tory—is simply untenable from the standpoint of psychological life as it is actually lived.

Others have taken another route. They have constructed their theories of nationalism over many years by scrupulously avoiding any consideration of affect. Even when forced reluctantly to address the fact that feelings of emo-tional attachment to one's country are a profound source of cohesion, they have attempted to finesse that connection. One can gain some sense of their concerns by noting the title of Markell's recent paper: "Making Affect Safe for Democracy."[33]

Cosmopolitan Patriots in America?

In her book *For Love of Country: Debating the Limits of Patriotism*, Martha Nussbaum, a University of Chicago professor of law and ethics, asks, "Why should we think of people from China as our fellow citizens, the minute they dwell in . . . the United States, but not when they dwell in . . . China? What is it about the national boundary that magically converts people to whom we are both incurious and indifferent into people to whom we have duties of mutual respect?"[34]

Like many liberal theorists, Nussbaum is deeply suspicious of the psychol-ogy of national attachments. She agrees that "at bottom nationalism and eth-nocentric particularism are not alien to one another, but akin—that to give support to nationalist sentiments subverts, ultimately, even the values that hold a nation together because it substitutes a colorful ideal for the substan-tive universal values of justice and right."[35]

If Nussbaum is suspicious of national sentiment, she is downright skeptical of patriotism. Of that sentiment she writes: "This emphasis on patriotic pride is both morally dangerous and, ultimately, subversive of some of the worthy goals patriotism sets out to serve—for example, the goal of national unity in devotion to worthy moral principles of justice and equality."[36] She raises these issues in the abstract but is clearly criticizing the emotional and empathetic insularity of Americans. She does not attempt to answer them, but she does have a remedy.

She declares herself a cosmopolitan and professes allegiance to transcen-dent moral principles while affirming her identification as a citizen of the world. Being one, she wrote, "was often a lonely business," cut off "from the comfort of local truths, from the warm nestling feelings of patriotism, from the absorbing drama of pride in oneself and one's own."[37]

Nussbaum's condemnation of both nationalism and patriotism elicited varied responses. Among the many issues raised were the sole emphasis on the pathologies of patriotism (and, one might add, nationalism as well), the culture-bound nature of such terms as "justice" and "equality" (and, one might add, the narrow versions of some definitions of these terms), and the simple view of the political (and, one might add, the practical) issues involved in making the transition that she recommends.

The essential core of this debate is how one understands nationalism and patriotism. Both these concepts are related to rights and justice.

Liberal Rights and Communitarian Responsibilities

Many liberals support group rights because they result in what the liberals view as more democracy, equality, and justice. However, this support is tempered by a belief in maximizing individual freedom. Some liberals reconcile the two by viewing group rights as ultimately empowering the individual. Yet the problem of the exit and selection of group membership poses unresolved issues for the strong support of group rights.

Moreover, these liberal theorists have had little to say, at least until recently, about the impact of ever-expanding rights on the claims a community might reasonably make. That omission has been responsible for the rise of communitarians, who emphasize that shared values are the only source of social cohesion.[38] They locate these shared values—loyalty, shared responsibility, and doing what is right—primarily in civil society, which includes the institutions of family, work, and a range of voluntary associations.[39]

Neither liberal nor communitarian theorists have addressed their relationship with nationalism—in particular with American nationalism. Clearly, they are highly ambivalent. Liberal theorists champion individualism but laud the development of the state, so long as it pursues values they favor.[40] Like communitarians, they see the development of these values as the province of civil society. Yet as a result of some suspicion of the state, liberal theorists have retained a degree of antipathy toward nationalism and its expression. Vincent, in fact, claims that "liberalism is utterly incompatible with nationalism."[41]

Nationalism is, of course, a form of emotional attachment that helps connect individuals to the state—and not necessarily to civil society. But paradoxically, the very same assumptions that underlie the commitment to group-based rights that many liberal theorists support should also lead to support for the virtues of nationalism. Advocates of group rights correctly point to the important psychological functions that groups perform for individuals. Feelings of attachment, acceptance, and belonging are all powerful motives in human life. Their existence leads to individual psychological benefits. The absence of such feelings is a roadblock to the values that liberals affirm—fulfillment, freedom, rationality, subjective satisfaction, and so on—the ends of a liberal society.[42]

The national community is another form of community. It, too, is quite capable, as I will argue, of fostering those very same feelings of attachment, acceptance, and belonging. And, as I have argued above, it is instrumental in helping to develop and maintain the very structures and institutions that support liberal initiatives.

Some liberals have been suspicious of nationalism's association with aggression, xenophobia, and uncritical loyalty. But this raises a dilemma: How will liberal theorists reconcile their support for individual freedom with the knowledge that individuals find meaning by being embedded in communities—the national community chief among them? One response is constitutional patriotism,[43] or so-called liberal nationalism.[44]

Constitutional Patriotism

The great spoiler of democracies in the minds of liberal theorists is affect. And historically, there is much evidence that unimpeded nationalist fervor can destroy older democracies, smother the development of new ones, and make life for their neighbors—none of whom are far away in today's world—dangerous. The list—Nazi Germany, Romania, ex-Yugoslavia, Rwanda, Nigeria, Afghanistan, to name a few—is long. That danger is real. Yet as Markell puts it, "Liberals have tried to exchange the dangerous romance of *polis* and *partia* for the calm certitudes of reason."[45]

The most famous thinker associated with the "constitutional patriotism" effort is Jürgen Habermas.[46] The basic thrust of this effort is to redirect affect away from its usual object—the state—and toward more abstract universal principles. Habermas distinguishes between attachment to prepolitical objects—family, ethnos, and nation—and more "mature" object attachments—an abstract set of principles that can serve as a common denominator among diverse members and views of a society.[47] The point of affective connection then will be universal principles, not specific historical communities. Even when Habermas slightly revises his formulation to include some acknowledgment of the importance of specific, historically located communities, he still emphasizes "attachment to the political order and the principles of Basic Law."[48]

Habermas seems to be offering here a version of the American Creed, buttressed by a small, tamed measure of psychological attachment. Yet his work leaves several psychological questions unanswered. Do not community attachments precede abstract attachments? Or to put it another way, Does not Freud precede Piaget? The answer in both cases is yes.

Are people more likely to identify affectively with abstract principles rather than their specific historically constituted communities? No evidence of that appears in historical practice so far, except for a handful of contemporary political theorists who urge this view and presumably share it. Indeed, it is quite likely that some theorists, including Habermas, have confused cause and effect. Support for abstract principles, like the Creed, depends on a prior condition: community attachment.

Psychologically and developmentally, it is clear that affective attachments to the community come first. Yet that argument can be taken a step further. It seems plausible to say that the binding of affect to national community begins the process of binding the individual to those very abstract principles that help to define the community. After all, the Creed is presented and taught as an important part of the national community to which the individual has already emotionally bonded. In this sense, identification with the Creed is not accomplished in spite of affective bonding with the national community but, on the contrary, because of it.

Liberal Nationalism

Tamir argues that "the liberal tradition, with its respect for personality autonomy, reflection, and choice, and the national tradition, with its emphasis on belonging, loyalty, and solidarity . . . can indeed accommodate each other."[49] One reason for this is that there is more community in liberalism than commonly acknowledged, and more liberalism in nationalism than is commonly acknowledged.

Liberal nationalism, according to Tamir, rejects the extremes of both liberalism and nationalism. She presents nationalism as offering "a set of moral values worthy of respect and serious consideration."[50] What are these? The national community can foster care and cooperation; it can provide an understanding of why we feel closer to those who share our community, it allows the community to agree on principles of justice, and it can help to facilitate better relationships with those outside the community.

Tamir's defense of the liberal nationalism she envisions stands in stark contrast to those who are still hostile or skeptical about the blend.[51] Yet, as Levinson notes, "Tamir is considerably more liberal than she is nationalistic."[52]

Being liberal means, of course, that individual rights would be respected, even if that included not necessarily giving primacy to the political community. Another reason to embrace liberal nationalism is that while individuals are necessarily embedded in communities, these communities would need to be liberal ones. Moreover, adherence to a national community would be "voluntary," echoing Sandel's view of citizenship responsibilities.[53]

Tamir's reconciliation of liberalism and nationalism is accomplished by being pitched at a highly abstract level and by ignoring real-world psychology. The first is not necessarily a drawback for an "ideal theory" or one that begins with the theorist's own views of human nature. It is, however, a decided drawback to neglect real-world psychology when the theory put forward is used to advocate policies that will affect people in practice, not just theory. The questions that Tamir asks of liberal nationalists—Should I prefer my liberal beliefs to my national commitments? Are liberal values truly rational, and nationalist values emotional and inexplicable? Is the difference between the two, then, a difference between reason and emotion?—are good ones. Yet they are not easily answered in any evidentiary way by political theory. Political theory conceptualizes conjectures in response to these questions, but that is not the same as answering them.

Notes

1. William J. Clinton, "Remarks at the University of California San Diego Commencement Ceremony in La Jolla, California" (June 23), *Weekly Compilation of Presidential Documents* 33, no. 25 (1977): 871–915. Theorists on both the left—Michael Walzer, *What It Means to Be an American: Essays on the American Experience* (New York: Marisilio, 1996)—and the right—Samuel P. Huntington, *American Politics: The Promise of Disharmony* (Cambridge, Mass.: Belknap Press, 1961)—have been united in the belief that the Creed is all that Americans need to unite their country. Huntington has since modified his position, arguing that Americans need more than the creed to unite them; Huntington, *Who Are We? The Challenges to American National Identity* (New York: Simon & Schuster, 2004).

2. Tamar Jacoby, "What It Means to Be American in the Twenty-First Century," in *Reinventing the Melting Pot*, ed. Tamar Jacoby (New York: Basic Books, 2004), 294.

3. Ibid., 310.

4. Michael Walzer, "What Does It Mean to Be an 'American'"? *Social Research* 57, no. 4 (1990): 591–614. His use of quotation marks around the word "American" and a close reading of his article leave one unsure whether he believes there is anything distinctive about those who live in the United States other than that fact.

5. James W. Prothro and C. M. Grigg, "Fundamental Principles of Democracy: Basis of Agreement and Disagreement," *Journal of Politics* 22 (1960): 276–94.

6. Alan Wolfe, *One Nation After All: What Middle-Class Americans Really Think about: God, Country, Family, Racism, Welfare, Immigration, Homosexuality, Work, the Right, the Left, and Each Other* (New York: Penguin Books, 1998).

7. Andrew L. Shapiro, The Control Revolution: How the Internet Is Putting Individuals in Charge and Changing the World We Know (New York: PublicAffairs, 1999), 118–20.

8. The conference was held under the auspices of the Center for the American Founding and was held in May 1998. The quote is from David March of the Heritage Foundation in an e-mail message to the author dated May 22, 1998.

9. Anthony D. Smith, *National Identity* (Reno: University of Nevada Press, 1993), 17.

10. Andrew Vincent, "Liberal Nationalism: An Irresponsible Compound?" *Political Studies* 65 (1997): 275–95; the citation here is on 291, and the emphasis is mine.

11. Eytan Meyers, "Theories of Immigration Policy: A Comparative Analysis," *International Migration Review* 34, no. 4 (2000): 1245–82; the citation here is on 1251.

12. An analysis of trait theories of American national identity can be found in Stanley A. Renshon, "American Identity and the Dilemmas of Cultural Diversity," in *Political Psychology: Cultural and Cross Cultural Foundations*, ed. Stanley A. Renshon and John Duckitt (London: Macmillan, 2000).

13. E.g., see R. Linton, *The Study of Man* (New York: Appleton-Century-Crofts, 1930); and Linton, *The Cultural Background of Personality* (New York: Appleton-Century-Crofts, 1945); A. Kardiner, with R. Linton, *The Individual and His Society* (New York: Columbia University Press, 1939); Ruth Benedict, *Patterns of Culture* (New York: Mentor, 1934); Benedict, *The Chrysanthemum and the Sword* (Boston: Houghton Mifflin, 1946); Margaret Mead, *And Keep Your Powder Dry* (New York: Morrow, 1942); and C. Kluckholm and H. A. Murray, eds., *Personality in Nature, Society, and Culture, Second Edition* (New York: Alfred A. Knopf, 1953).

14. Alex Inkeles and Daniel J. Levinson, "National Character: The Study of Modal Personality and Socio-Cultural Systems," in *The Handbook of Social Psychology*, 2nd edition, vol. 4, ed. G. Lindzey and E. Arronson (Reading, Mass.: Addison-Wesley, 1978–79).

15. Smith, *National Identity*, 9. Notice the easy slide from the structures and psychology of national identification to their equation with a nation. In fact, a nation could be defined by the existence of a national identity.

16. Hugh Seton-Watson, *Nations and States: An Inquiry into the Origins of Nations and the Politics of Nationalism* (Boulder, Colo.: Westview Press, 1977), 2.

17. Seton-Watson, *Nations and States*, 5.

18. David Miller, *On Nationality* (Oxford: Clarendon Press, 1995), 21–47.

19. The literature review that follows draws on Rick Kosterman and Seymour Feshbach, "Toward a Measure of Patriotic and Nationalistic Attitudes," *Political Psychology* 10, no. 2 (1989): 257–74.

20. Floyd Allport, "The Psychology of Nationalism: The Nationalistic Fallacy as a Cause of War," *Harper's Monthly*, August 1927, 291–301; the citation here is on 293.

21. Ibid., 300.

22. Kosterman and Feshbach, "Toward a Measure," 259.

23. T. W. Adorno, Else Frenkel-Brunswick, and Daniel J. Levinson, *The Authoritarian Personality* (New York: Basic Books, 1950), 1070.

24. Kosterman and Feshbach, "Toward a Measure," 259.

25. Walker Conner, "Beyond Reason: The Nature of the Ethnonational Bond," *Ethnic and Racial Studies* 16, no. 3 (1993): 373–89; the citation here is on 374, and the emphasis is in the original.

26. Kosterman and Feshbach, "Toward a Measure," 271.

27. Jim Sidanius, Seymour Feshbach, Shana Levin, and Felicia Pratto, "The Interface between Ethnic and National Attachment: Ethnic Pluralism or Ethnic Dominance?" *Public Opinion Quarterly* 16 (1997): 102–33, table 2; see also Jim Sidanius and Roland R. Petrocik, "Communal and National Identity in a Multiethnic State: A Comparison of Three Perspectives," in *Social Identity, Intergroup Conflict, and Conflict Reduction*, Rutgers Series on Self and Social Identity, vol. 3, ed. Richard D. Ashmore

and Lee Jussim (London: Oxford University Press, 2001). Schatz and Staub write: "In our research, we assessed militaristic nationalism with a modified version of a nationalism measure developed by Kosterman and Feshbach." Robert T. Schatz and Ervin Staub, "Manifestations of Blind and Constructive Patriotism: Personality Correlates and Individual–Group Relations," in *Patriotism in the Lives of Individuals and Nations*, ed. Daniel Bar-Tal and Ervin Staub (Chicago: Nelson-Hall, 1997), 240.

28. Daniel Bar-Tal, "Patriotism as a Fundamental Belief of Group Members," *Politics and the Individual* 3 (1993): 45–62; Stephen Worchel, with Dawna Coutant, "The Tangled Web of Loyalty: Nationalism, Patriotism, and Ethnocentrism," in *Patriotism*, ed. Bar-Tal and Staub, 193; and Leonard W. Doob, *Patriotism and Nationalism: Their Psychological Foundations* (New Haven, Conn.: Yale University Press, 1964), 6.

29. Daniel Drukman, "Nationalism, Patriotism, and Group Loyalty: A Social Psychological Perspective," *Mershon International Studies Review* 38 (1994): 43–68; the citation here is on 63; see also Worchel and Coutant, "Tangled Web," 192.

30. Paul Gomberg, "Patriotism Is Like Racism," *Ethics* 101 (1990): 144–50.

31. Gomberg, "Patriotism," 147.

32. Gomberg, "Patriotism," 148.

33. Patchen Markell, "Making Affect Safe for Democracy," *Political Theory* 28, no. 1 (2000): 38–63.

34. Martha Nussbaum, "Patriotism and Cosmopolitanism," in *For Love of Country: Debating the Limits of Patriotism*, by Martha Nussbaum (Boston: Beacon Press, 1996), 14. An excellent review of Nussbaum's book may be found in Veit Bader, "For Love of Country," *Political Theory* 27, no. 3 (1999): 379–97.

35. Nussbaum, "Patriotism," 5.

36. Nussbaum, "Patriotism," 4.

37. Nussbaum, "Patriotism," 15.

38. Christopher Lasch, "The Communitarian Critique of Liberalism," *Soundings: An Interdisciplinary Journal*, Spring–Summer 1986, 60–76.

39. E. J. Dionne, "The Quest for Community (Again)," *American Prospect*, Summer 1992, 49–54.

40. William Galston, *Liberal Purposes: Goods, Virtues and Diversity in the Liberal State* (New York: Cambridge University Press, 1991).

41. Vincent, "Liberal Nationalism," 279.

42. Galston, *Liberal Purposes*.

43. Jürgen Habermas, "Political Culture in Germany since 1998," in *The New Conservatism Cultural Criticism and the Historian's Debate*, ed. and trans. Shierry Weber (Cambridge, Mass.: MIT Press, 1989); and Markell, "Making Affect Safe."

44. Yael Tamir, *Liberal Nationalism* (Princeton, N.J.: Princeton University Press, 1993).

45. Markell, "Making Affect Safe," 38.

46. Jürgen Habermas, "Citizenship and National Identity: Appendix II," in *Between Facts and Norms: Contributions to a Discourse Theory of Law and Democracy*, trans. William Rehg (Cambridge, Mass.: MIT Press, 1996), 496.

47. Relevant here as well is Ignatieff's distinction between civic nationalism and ethnic nationalism. The first redirects the strong feelings of group identity towards

patriotic ideals of equal rights and democracy, while the second reaffirms ties based on blood and ethnic lines—a much narrower basis of inclusion. Michael Ignatieff, *Blood and Belonging: Journeys into the New Nationalism* (New York: Farrar, Straus & Giroux, 1993), 1–7.

48. Quoted in Markell, "Making Affect Safe," 51.

49. Tamir, *Liberal Nationalism*, 6.

50. Ibid., 95–96.

51. Vincent, "Liberal Nationalism."

52. Sanford Levinson, "Is Liberal Nationalism an Oxymoron? An Essay for Judith Sklar," *Ethics* 105 (1995): 626–45; the citation here is on 629.

53. Tamir, *Liberal Nationalism*, 87.

CHAPTER 3

A Theory of American National Identity

In this chapter, I put forward a theory of American national identity and attachment. I also provide an account of how and why it works. The elements of the theory are one part belief and two parts psychology. The belief portion of American national identity is the American Creed, that series of beliefs about the nature and virtues of our democratic traditions. The Creed by itself, however, does not provide an adequate understanding of American national identity. That understanding can only be reached by also focusing on America's national psychology, which grows out of the country's historical experiences and the missing link that binds these two together: patriotism. Patriotism, that widely feared and disparaged concept, is the bonding mechanism through which pluribus becomes unum. It is these psychological mechanisms that connect Americans to each other and to an American national identity.

Huntington's book on American national identity neglects patriotism and substitutes in its place the foundation of Judeo-Christian belief. Of course, America certainly was and to some degree still is a Christian country. But there are many views of the Christian God, even among the many churches counted among his believers. And many Christians find they have more in common with those who may have different theological beliefs than with other Christians. Judeo-Christian principles are certainly central to the Anglo-Western conceptions of justice and the institutions that are derived from them. But emotional attachments to these institutions or the concepts that underlie them are a matter of patriotism, and the American Creed is more than religious belief.

National identity is a term with many meanings and a long history. In the past, one meaning of national identity was simply a reflection of national psychology. This at first was associated with sets of specific psychological traits that were presumed to characterize whole countries (e.g., Bulgarians were noted for their plodding endurance and taciturn energy). When that approach lost favor, it became associated with the national character school of psycho-analytically framed cultural anthropology. Here, scholars looked for evidence of German authoritarianism in the family, of Russian passivity in the swaddling practices with babies, and so on.

When this approach fell out of favor, researchers began to look for modal characteristics in the culture at large. As Leonard Doob noted of these efforts, "Glib summaries of the modal personality tendencies of a nation must be viewed with deep suspicion."[1] Still, Doob thought there were discernible psychological differences among national groups. The question was how best to get at and understand them.[2]

Researchers armed with survey methodology thought they had an answer. They took a large sample of individual attitudes within countries and used it to characterize a country's civic culture and the psychology that underlies it,[3] Later, Ron Inglehart, using cross-national data, examined the ways in which different historical and psychological experiences influenced the distribution of values and associated motivations within societies.[4]

These efforts, flawed as they were, built on an essentially correct understanding—namely, that every intact culture was characterized by practices and institutions that both helped to create but also reflected individual psychology. The concept of national identity provides some advantages in that regard.

The term "national identity" is psychological without being reductionist. It signifies a process, an identification, and a qualifier—national—that lead directly to three questions. What is American national identity? Of what does it consist? And what are its implications for national attachment and integration?

American National Identity: Meaning and Operation

An identity is a person's understanding of who he or she is. What is required of most well-functioning persons is that they assemble and arrange the parts of their identity in a way that gives integrity to their own interior psychologies—their hopes, ambitions, and values—and yet are in sufficient accord with the world in which they live that they can find a comfortable and productive fit.

This is both easy and difficult in America. It is easy because there are so many choices and little pressure to make difficult ones. It is difficult for exactly those same reasons.

In the United States, the choice of identities or its elements need not be permanent, and it is quite possible to have numerous identity elements in play at any one time. One can be a parent to one's child and a child to one's parents. At the same time, one can be a husband, professor, Jew, American, and so on.

Two things seem clear about modern identity. First, there are a very large number of possible identity elements from which to choose; and second, choose you must. The desire to embrace every identity is to fail in developing a coherent one.

This follows from the fact that not every identity element can be embraced, that some will be more important than others. Choices between or among identity elements are most necessary when two or more vie for consideration or primacy—say, one's identity as a parent and as a professor. Faced with two such elements in conflict, some choose their professional identities, others do the reverse, and many attempt to balance them. In most American life circumstances, the conflicts are modest and the opportunities to find balance available.

Yet it is only when one has to make choices that the arrangement of one's identity truly comes into focus. It is easy, for example, to be a liberal, a cosmopolitan, an American—and many other things. It is less easy to be both a Muslim and a Jew.

Ordinarily, in the United States, we can engage aspects of our identities when we wish, and there is often, as with our identities as citizens, no penalty for failure to enact them at all. As a result, many Americans can avoid the pressure or even the internal motivation to sharpen the shape of their identities.

Where does national identity fit into this cacophony of possibility identity elements? The answer lies in Smith's observation that, "of all the collective identities in which human beings share today, national identity is perhaps the fundamental and inclusive. . . . Other types of collective identity—class, gender, race, religion—may overlap or combine with national identity, but they rarely succeed in undermining its hold."[5]

In the United States, one's national identity as an American is essential to national cohesion and integration. Why? When Vincent skeptically asks, "What is so special or what is the special virtue of national loyalty above other group loyalties?"[6] the answer seems quite straightforward. It is the one and most inclusive category with which all the diverse elements of this society may identify. It allows for Catholics to identify with Protestants and each to identify with Jews and Muslims. It allows Hispanics to identify with South Asians. It even allows the possibility for Democrats to identify with Republicans. In psychology, as in algebra, two elements equal to a third are equal to each other.

America's Hidden Identity

American national identity is, in many ways, a hidden identity. I mean this in two ways. First, in spite of criticisms leveled at the George W. Bush administration regarding the use of the word "patriotism" after September 11, 2001, the U.S. government has actually done very little to develop and solidify feelings of national attachment and identity. Between 1836 and 1920, over 120 million copies of the patriotically oriented McGuffey readers were sold. Schools had civics classes that stressed American principles, history, and ideals.[7] No longer. As Diane Ravitch has documented at great length, "Educational materials are now governed by an intricate set of rules to screen out language and topics that might be considered controversial or offensive."[8] This applies to advocacy groups from both the right and the left sides of the political spectrum. Yet, certainly for the latter groups, materials that foster ethnic or racial identity are preferred to those that foster national identity. Today's civics preparation is a far distance from the "education for civic consciousness" that the famous Chicago sociologist Morris Janowitz called for almost twenty-five years ago.[9]

Not only has the government shied away from too close an association with fostering a national identity; it has, in important respects, systematically gone in the opposite direction, especially regarding ethno-racial categories. How many citizens in the United States identify as Americans? There is no answer. Why? Apparently, the government is uninterested in the question, or perhaps afraid of the answer. Since the 1980 census, it has not asked an ancestry question that might allow people to answer "American." Nor did it include a question on American identification in the 1990 or 2000 censuses, or another of the Current Population Surveys. It should.[10]

A second and perhaps primary reason that American national identity is hidden is that it is normally latent. Ordinarily, Americans do not spend much time thinking of themselves as Americans or of the role that their American identity plays in their overall set of identity elements. Before September 11, American national identity was lost in a cacophony of debate over the importance and primacy of race, ethnicity, and gender, what David Hollinger aptly labeled the ethno-racial pentagon.[11] At the same time, schools, museums, history, and almost every other major element of American national culture and institutions were, to use the dainty but nondescriptive word, "contested." That word hardly conveys the ferocity of the attacks. No wonder American identity got lost in the process.

September 11 changed that. The fact that the United States was being targeted for destruction, as were Americans more generally, was a direct and stark reminder that as much as we might differ among ourselves on racial and ethnic issues, all of us were Americans to the rest of the world. In short, what had been taken for granted quickly became something to think about, and one result was the dramatic upsurge in patriotic sentiment.

In the words of the *Washington Post*, the terrorist attacks of September 11 "triggered a broad surge in national feelings of pride, confidence and faith in America and many of the country's key institutions, according to a national survey."[12] To cite just one finding, nearly everyone—97 percent—now said they would rather be citizens of the United States "than of any other country, also up from 2000." A January 14, 2001, Gallup Poll found that 55 percent of those sampled were "extremely proud to be Americans." A March 10, 2002, *Washington Post* poll asking that same question found that 74 percent now felt that way.[13]

Doob noted that "patriotism can give rise to nationalism; if the beloved society is threatened."[14] Yet, interestingly, the surge of national connection after September 11 led to feelings of more national intercitizen solidarity. When a poll asked in 1988 whether Americans were united and in agreement about the most important values, or are greatly divided when it comes to them, 62 percent said Americans were divided. Yet, in a November 26, 2001, Gallup Poll asking the same question, 74 percent said Americans were united. Catastrophic terrorism succeeded in underscoring the fact that we are all in the same boat.

The fact that patriotism surged after September 11 and resulted in greater feelings of attachment to the country still does not tell us much about its relationship to American national identity. Patriotism is certainly a key to national attachments; but just as clearly, it is not synonymous with national identity. So what is national identity, and what role specifically does patriotism play in it?

In his otherwise excellent review of *American Identity and Americanization*, Paul Gleason employs the term "American identity" interchangeably with "American nationality" and "American character" and argues that "they are more or less synonymous."[15] They are not. He later argues that American identity primarily consists of "the formal principle, namely commitment to the universalist ideals of Americanism"—in other words, the American Creed.[16] This is conventional wisdom—and a common error.

In the sections that follow, I propose that American national identity is actually an amalgam of three interconnected elements: an attachment to what America stands for; a set of essential psychological characteristics that help both to define American national psychology and facilitate individuals' negotiating America's social, political, cultural, and institutional currents; and patriotism. Patriotism, I will argue, is much more complicated than a mere "love of country."

The first element—what America stands for—is the set of ideals and aspirations that have traditionally been characterized as the American Creed. The second set of elements is matters of individual psychology that are instrumental and necessary for a well-realized and productive life within the confines of this particular culture. The third, patriotism, is the emotional bonding element that attaches people to the ideals that the country aspires to, and the psychology that allows them to share with their fellow citizens a sense of shared experience.

Let us begin then with a provisional understanding of American national identity given these elements. *American national identity is primarily a psychological attachment to one's national community, its institutions and practices, the people who constitute it, the psychology of its way of life, and the ideals for which it stands.*

The American Creed

The United States is now more racially, ethnically, religiously, and culturally diverse than at any time in its history. There are advantages to such diversity. A country can be enriched by different points of view, traditions, and contributions. In a diverse world, ethnic and racial pluralism can provide a bridge of understanding and contact. However, there is a tension between diversity and tradition, especially when cultural and institutional practices have been under siege, as they have been in the United States for over forty years.

Liberal theorists and their allies are at the forefront of arguments for substantial and fundamental change. Cultural conservatives argue that many of the changes suggested by liberals would have the paradoxical effect of weakening the very culture they are charged with improving. Worse, they would also result in the "Disuniting of America."[17]

Yet America's "Second Civil War" has also led to the search for solutions—in Higham's words, "rediscovering what values can bind us together." Many believe that can be accomplished by a common commitment to national values.[18] The commitment to national values is of course the province of the American Creed—that set of beliefs that presumably unite all Americans. It has also functioned as a rationale for admitting, without much follow-through, immigrants of widely varying skills, religious beliefs, ethnic identities, and nationality. So long as they accept the Creed, it is said, they can become Americans.

The American Creed, according to Huntington, is the belief in liberal democracy and its associated practices. It involves the rule of law, the virtues of democracy, and the importance of freedom, justice, and equality. Some are not convinced that the Creed has lived up to its billing. Rogers Smith argues that Huntington's formulation (and presumably the political leaders and theorists who support it) is "at best a half truth."[19] Why? Because, according to Smith, the United States has never been as liberal as supporters of the Creed have suggested, and one can see this discrepancy most clearly in the various limitations placed on citizenship and participation in the nineteenth century.

Smith's point is a fair one. Yet one must ask: Do those limits represent the rule or its reception? Further, one might ask: Have the limits increased or decreased over time? And one might further ask: Is Huntington's faith in the Creed still no better than a half-truth *today*?

In fact, there are more substantial reasons to doubt the power of the Creed to unite a divided country. However, they have little to do with history of illiberal limits and much more to do with the limits of idealized political aphorisms as a unifying force in national communities. Discussions of the Creed often fail to appreciate that true emotional attachment entails much more than high-level aphorisms.

In one respect, the Creed has been a part of American cultural development from its inception. Yet in another, it dates back to World War I, when Americans were divided about the wisdom of involvement. When Baltimore mayor James H. Preston offered a prize of $1,000 for the winning essay on Americanism,[20] the winner was William Tyler Page, who characterized his creed as a "summary of the fundamental principles of American political faith, as set forth in its greatest documents, its worthiest traditions, and by its greatest leaders."[21] The document was widely disseminated, and it is still included in American information almanacs.

The full text of the American Creed reads: "I believe in the United States of America as a Government of the people, by the people, for the people; whose just powers are derived from the consent of the governed; a democracy in a republic; a sovereign Nation of many sovereign states; a perfect union, one and inseparable; established upon those principles of freedom, equality, justice, and humanity for which American patriots sacrificed their lives and fortunes. I therefore believe it is my duty to my country to love it; to support its Constitution; to obey its laws; to respect its flag; and to defend it against all enemies."

It is easy to see that this Creed actually contains two elements. The first is what is normally considered its core—constitutionalism, democracy, and so on. Yet there is another aspect, which has to do with commitment (American patriots sacrificed their lives and fortunes) and emotional attachment (it is my duty to my country to love it). In works of liberal theorists, we hear much of the first and very little of the second.

Ignoring people's emotional connections to their country is an obvious problem with relying on the Creed. A major difficulty with a focus on values is that they are too abstract. Who does not believe in democracy? Who is against opportunity? Once again, one is reminded of the classic study that found that almost every American supports free speech, until asked about the first specific application of the principle that was controversial.[22]

The consequences of conducting the analysis of these issues at the rarefied level of highly abstract categories easily leads to conflicts over who really is a rightful heir to the values being discussed. This often leads to a focus on artificial similarities, or an ambivalent and ultimately confused effort to stake out an Olympian middle ground. So, on many contentious issues, like a permissive stance toward dual citizenship, many theorists will argue that their views represent the best realization of "democratic values." It is difficult to make informed judgments about such matters when the analysis is presented at such a highly abstract theoretical level.

At a stratospheric level, Americans may agree that democracy is best. However, that has not exempted any of the country's major social, cultural, or political institutions or patterns of traditional practice from acute conflicts over the specific ways in which they are constituted and operate. That is, after all, the meaning of the phrase "culture wars."

The Creed will not rescue the United States from its substantial cultural, psychological, and political divisions—for three reasons. First, it is too abstract. People can agree with many things in the abstract, but American politics takes place in the contentious—sometimes savage—here and now of real problems and policy debates.

Second, the Creed is almost entirely cognitive. It resides in the realm of the mind, not the emotions. Looking back one year later after September 11, the *New York Times* editorialized in part, "Although America was bound together by emotion on Sept. 11, 2001, America isn't bound together by emotions. It's bound together by things that transcend emotion, by principles and laws, by ideals of freedom and justice that need constant articulation."[23]

That view is common but wrong. Yes, one can have positive attachments to abstract aphorisms, but those are not the binding glue of national attachment. One does not die for an aphorism, such as "Democracy is the best form of government." People are willing to die in the service of their country because of their emotional attachments to it.

Third, an emphasis on the Creed almost completely neglects the importance of the psychological characteristics that can and do unite us as a people. The Creed suggests that Americans are bound together because they share support at the stratospheric level for what amounts to cultural clichés. Yet there is another level at which Americans share something fundamental that helps bind them together—their psychologies.

American National Psychology

America does have a national psychology, but it is not to be found solely, or even primarily, in early child-rearing practices. Nor does it consist of a limited set of traits that everyone shares. And it is not to be found in any so-called national character—essential characteristics to which every American must adhere.

American national psychology is built on the motivational foundation of those who first came here.[24] They were looking for a new and better life, one in which their skills could be put into the service of their ambitions. Others came looking for the freedom to express their religious views and the opportunity to build a society consistent with them.

Freedom and opportunity came together in a particular way in the religious colonies, but in quite another way in those searching for economic advancement. In neither was freedom or opportunity an isolated, absolute value. In the case of religious freedom, it was embedded in a strong community context, and in the case of economic opportunity, it coexisted with a strong belief in public social and political equality.

The common denominators of those early settlers were ambition, the courage to pursue it, and the freedom that it took to realize it. Those who came here gave up familiarity—no small matter—and took large risks. No book or rumor could adequately prepare these settlers for what they faced. Those who stayed and realized their ambitions for a better life had to be able to persevere through hard times and circumstances—of which there were many.

The physical realities of frontier conditions required a psychology of courage, independence, and self-reliance. Opportunity required talent and hard work to take advantage of it. America was rich in promise, but only for those able to survive, persist, and even thrive in difficult circumstances.

Settlers who prospered had to adapt. The past could no longer operate as a ready crutch. Each new challenge, and there were many, demanded its own solution. Thus, those early Americans were forced by necessity to honor the present more than the past and to solve problems rather than apply timeless principles. In short, a forward-looking pragmatism became a necessity as well as an outlook.

Often having nothing more than their own ingenuity in dealing with novel circumstances, Americans became pragmatists. They focused on what worked. America was not at first a country of revolutionary innovations, but in many ways pragmatism did prove ultimately to be revolutionary. At any rate, a pragmatic approach proved successful, and its repeated success led to a culture-wide sense of can-do optimism.

Those settlers who undertook this new life hoped, of course, that they would succeed. However, beneath this hope was a conviction that their efforts would count, and that their success, if it came, would be a matter of hard work and luck or providence, but not of luck alone. In short, these pioneers had an expectation of personal effectiveness when combined with faith in their destiny, allowing them to have some confidence, hope, and therefore optimism.

We can see at once that these traits encompass, but are quite different from, the Protestant ethic. The latter focused on hard work and delay of gratification. Yes, many Americans subscribed to that ethic, and Huntington is correct, to a point, in making it an element in the answer to his question "Who are we?" But the emphasis on work and gratification delay alone does not adequately convey the range of American national psychology, nor why it is an intrinsic part of economic capitalism.

Early Americans were ambitious risk takers, with the courage of their aspirations. They were willing to endure enormous hardships, not once or twice, but repeatedly. The new Americans needed resilience. America is often called the land of second chances, and for good reason. The opportunity for reinvention accompanied the risks of failure in a free capitalist society. You could try, try again, but you first needed to be able to pick yourself up off the floor to do so. Success in the United States was substantially oriented toward the future and the present, rather than the past. Big ambitions were, of necessity, coupled with a pragmatic bent. What counted was what worked.

Above all, people were the authors of their own salvation—in both religious and secular terms. Individual effort, not fate, became the key to successful effort. "God helps those who help themselves" became another American aphorism for the ages.

My point here is not that every American had then or has now high levels of each of these psychological elements. Miller quotes David Hume as remarking that the vulgar think that everyone who belongs to a nation displays its distinctive traits, whereas "men of sense" allow for exceptions.[25] Miller suggests thinking of this issue in terms of Wittgenstein's metaphor of a thread whose strength does not reside in a single strand running though the length of a garment but rather in the overlapping of many fibers. The United States was built on this particular combination of psychological elements, and they have been primary ingredients of its national culture for the past 230 years and counting.

These elements of American national psychology constitute the psychological center of gravity for American national culture. They historically provided individuals, and still do, with the psychological keys with which to unlock the riches of opportunity and to fulfill their responsibilities as free citizens. By providing opportunity, America fostered ambition. By encouraging freedom, America placed a premium on being prepared to make use of it.

Americans did not acquire these psychological capacities in a vacuum. Institutions helped to develop and support them. The United States was not a feudal society, so anyone's station in life could advance or decline. As a result, families had to prepare their children for success, however that might be defined. Because hard work and perseverance were a central part of success, families had an incentive to instill the virtues and necessities that underlay it—diligence, seriousness of purpose, resilience, the expectation of accomplishment through effort, setting and meeting goals, balancing responsibilities and pleasure, and so forth.

The work of the family as a psychologically preparatory institution was supplemented and reinforced by other American institutions—most notably the school and the workplace. Schools taught subjects, but in doing so required further development of the habits of success. Material had to be mastered, tests passed, and focus developed. The national habit of acquiring more skills and knowledge for the eventual rewards they were assumed to bring developed rapidly over time. At first some primary education was the norm, then high school. For most, college became a reachable expectation.

All these were considered preparatory for "making it." Here, too, the psychological lessons began in childhood and continued. Ambition, prudent risk, hard work, and the ability to sustain oneself through vicissitudes all helped to foster and reaffirm the psychological lesson of American experience woven into the basic fabric of American institutional life.

I am painting here in broad strokes. Obviously, not every American acquired and developed these characteristics to the same degree. However, what does seem clear is that the basic cultural foundations of American society—freedom and capitalist opportunity—provided the basic psychological setting within which Americans had to live and prosper. There is a necessary relationship, I think, between America's national culture and the psychological characteristics that foster success within it.

American National Psychology and Immigration

Every country rewards the psychology that it favors, and America is no different. Does this mean that national integration of immigrants ought to take place primarily at this basic psychological level? Not wholly, but psychology does play a role.

American nationality has distinctive psychological elements. America is a nation that prefers and works to develop a specific set of psychologies in its citizens. Americans prefer self-reliance to dependence, moderation to excess, optimism to futility, pragmatism to rhetoric, and reflection to impulsiveness—to name just a few.

Americans applaud immigrants who show ambition, try to achieve work-related excellence, are anxious to move toward self-sufficiency, and who remain pragmatic and optimistic about themselves and their new circumstances. Americans can appreciate immigrants' struggles to maintain community as they pursue their ambitions. Americans can appreciate immigrants' desire for political, economic, and social equality. Yet Americans also appreciate immigrants' striving toward achievement, self-reliance, and emotional attachment to their new country.

Several of the psychological elements of success in this culture are, of course, associated with the core characteristics of the Protestant ethic. Yet some, like Aleinikoff, assert that concerns with assimilation mask a demand to conform to what he terms "Anglo/White culture."[26] The same criticism is made by those who argue that Americanization implies "the notion that there is a single white, middle-class mainstream culture that accounts for the economic and cultural success of the United States."[27]

The genius of American national culture, psychology, and identity is that over time they have become decoupled from ethnicity, religion, and even race. Successive waves of immigrants—the Irish, Jews, blacks from Trinidad or the Bahamas, educated Hispanics of all nationalities, South Asians, Chinese, and Japanese—were certainly not Protestant, Anglo, or "white." Yet all these groups have found a successful place in American society. Not a place realized without difficulty, not a place where everyone is a success, but a place nonetheless.

Becoming an American, then, is not simply a matter of agreeing that democracy is the best form of government. It is a commitment to a psychology and the way of life that flows from it. And it ultimately entails an appreciation of, a commitment to, and even a love and reverence for all that being an American stands for and provides.

The United States has its Creed and a national psychology. Are these sufficient to develop the sense of attachment and integration that is so necessary to democratic functioning in an increasingly diverse country? No. There is one more absolutely essential element that helps to unite and bond both the Creed and American psychology: patriotism.

Patriotism: The Missing Link

Patriotism is the missing link of American national identity. It is the glue that binds American psychology with American support of the Creed. It is the emotional amalgam that makes real diversity possible.

This is not a conventional view of patriotism. Most discussions of patriotism, as noted, see it as a simple, or a simplistic, aggressive love of country. Given that it is a linchpin of American national culture, it is surprising that there is little in the way of sustained theory about patriotism. As Nathanson notes, "There has been surprisingly little serious discussion about patriotism. People who are avidly patriotic see no need to discuss something of such evident value, while people who see patriotism as dangerous and undesirable may think that rational discussion will have no effect against so powerful an emotion."[28]

That discussion is complicated by the political nature of that term. Calls to be patriotic, or alternatively questions about someone's lack of patriotic attachment, carry substantial weight in political life. According to Morray, "Patriotism, loyalty to the state is very much a part of good American character." Yet it is also "the last resort of scoundrels," and "the last infirmity of noble minds." In addition, it is also clear that "it is a virtue upon which the free societies must depend."[29] Clearly, Curti is correct—"patriotism has served several and varied national and group interests simultaneously."[30]

Critics of patriotism point to the fact that it can be used as a basis for accusations of disloyalty, or as a method of demanding political conformity. It has been used for both these purposes. Yet even after September 11, the strong surge in patriotic feelings did not unleash a torrent of hypernationalism. In June 1994 and again in June 1999, 21 percent of Americans described themselves in a Gallup Poll as "extremely patriotic." In January 2002, that figure had risen to only 24 percent.

Even more telling are American views on the United Nations. Asked in an ABC / *Washington Post* Poll on March 17, 2003, whether they approved or disapproved of the way in which that organization had handled the situation with Iraq and Saddam Hussein, only 25 percent approved and 75 percent disapproved. Yet in that same poll, when asked, "In the future, do you think the United States should continue its usual relationship with the United Nations, or do you think the United States should show less cooperation and support for the United Nations?" a total of 70 percent said the United States should continue as usual. When asked whether in the future the United States should feel freer to use force without U.N. authorization, 66 percent said no.[31] So, clearly, the rise in patriotism did not result in the rise of hyperpatriotism, or strong public sentiment, that this country should be free to do whatever it wanted internationally. In short, the fact that patriotism has been misused on occasion should not blind us to either its virtues or its functions.

Understanding Patriotism

What exactly is patriotism? Most theoretical discussions have concentrated on setting out distinctions between "good" and "bad" patriotism, much like liberal theorists have recently sought to parse the distinction between nationalism and patriotism. Thus Staub distinguishes between "blind' and "constructive" patriotism,[32] Johnson distinguishes between "pseudo-patriotism" and its real kind,[33] and Fletcher equates patriotism with loyalty and urges that the latter be "enlightened."[34] Most social psychology theorists see patriotism as a set of feelings and identifications,[35] but they fail to tell us what these feelings are, or how and why they develop.

Thanks to an excellent collection of essays edited by John Bodar, we know that expressions and understandings of patriotism in the United States have varied over time.[36] And we also know that it is fostered, "because the nation directly satisfies personal needs by government programs that increasingly touch more and more people."[37] But the question remains: What is it?

What Is Patriotism? Varieties of National Attachment

The definitions of the words "loyalty" and "patriotism" have changed over time. That is why I prefer the term "national attachments." Yet there is a theoretical reason to believe that whatever name is used for the phenomenon to which they refer, patriotism is far more than a simple love of country or a thoughtlessly aggressive defense of it. Patriotism is much more complicated than either its supporters or critics allow.

I see patriotism, or national attachment, as including (1) a warmth and affection for, (2) an appreciation of, (3) a pride in, (4) a commitment and responsibility toward, and (5) support of the United States—its institutions, its way of life and aspirations, and its fellow members. "Love" is a summary term that covers all these things. Yet each of these elements deserves to be looked at more closely. Each is important to understanding the critical mediating role of national attachment between American national psychology and national identity. And these elements are also critical in understanding how national attachment is related to the integration of immigrants, and citizens, in the American national community.

National attachment begins with feelings of warmth and affection. Love encompasses such feelings but does not exhaust them. One feels warmth toward a person, or in this case an "object,"[38] as a result of generally favorable experiences with it. These experiences begin early.

Primary nationality, the one that we are born into, begins to take root very early, indeed before the child is born. The history and practices that brought a particular couple together are themselves influenced by the cultural expectations and understandings that they acquired while growing up in their country and culture. How they prepare for their child and how they relate to her is also conditioned by the same factors. And of course, the parents speak to the child in their own language, soon to be his, and as he grows are the guides and interpreters of the culture that he must learn and transverse. Being embedded in, and attachment to, one's country of origin begins early.

Children begin to incorporate the symbols of their nationality and country very early. An early study found that 25 percent of a sample of first graders in Tennessee chose the American flag as the "best," and that by the seventh grade the number doing so was 100 percent.[39] That study was later replicated in an urban-suburban New York school district and it found that kindergarten children put the Stars and Stripes first.[40] Weinstein found that the first notions of another country, ours as "good," and other countries as "bad" in children as young as five years old.[41] Piaget's colleague and disciple, Marie Jahoda, found that a child's emotional attachments to his country clearly begin much earlier than the cognitive development level necessary to sustain an intellectual understanding of the concepts.[42] Indeed, that is precisely the fulcrum of their life-long power. Summing up a variety of such early studies, A. F. Davis concludes, "The main lesson . . . is how early and closely they conform to a relatively stable and complex order of preferences appropriate to their American nationality. . . . It runs through all grades, it is common to boys and girls, impervious to the syllabus and remarkably resistant to background factors like family social status or region."[43]

What is the point of these studies? Just this: Loyalty and feelings of attachment to a nation begin at a primal age and become increasingly consolidated as the child develops. That is why people are willing to die for their country, why great national accomplishments bring pride, and why the symbols of a country—its flag, its constitution—carry such great emotional weight and political power.

The feelings of warmth and affection for the country stem in part from its embodiment of the familiar and our need for and comfort with it. Our lives are intertwined with an uncountable number of common experiences that start with our language, our ways of knowing and understanding the world, and growing up in the United States.

These experiences are mixed with feelings of warmth toward that to which we are emotionally attached. It is natural for children to identify with their country when both parents are lifelong community members. In the world of nations, they know only what they experience.

Just because national attachment begins before people can think about it does not mean they do not do so once they are older. In the course of one's life, it is a rare country indeed that does not sometimes anger or disappoint its citizens. The United States is no exception to this obvious fact. National attachments are a complex amalgam of many different experiences.[44]

And, in fact, that is exactly how Americans view it. Americans rank among the most patriotic people in the world, but they are very far from having a "my country right or wrong" mentality. For example, Americans are justly proud of their democracy, and they highly rank their country's influence in the world, its economy, and its history and scientific achievements. Yet, they are less proud of their "fair and equal treatment of all groups in society."[45] Or, to use another example drawn from the same cross-national survey, Americans are prone to take a strongly pro-American stance. For example, close to 90 percent say that they would rather be a citizen of this country than any other, and almost 80 percent say this country is better than "most other countries."

Does this sound chauvinistic? Consider that 62 percent of Americans *disagree* with the sentiment that "the world would be better off if people from other countries were more like us." Americans may love their country, but they do not see it as a required model for others. Consider, too, that almost 70 percent of Americans in that same survey would not support their country if they thought it was wrong.[46] A cynic might argue that the statistic is meaningless because Americans never think their country is wrong, but the evidence even from this survey refutes that view. Americans are proud of their recognized achievements, but not of the gaps between ideals and practice in group relations.

The patriotism of Americans appears more accurately viewed as a commitment that is based on a fair assessment of what is true for any country, that it both succeeds and stumbles in pursuit of the virtues to which it aspires and may even lay claim.

The best remedy for either idealization or angry disappointment is realism. This, in turn, requires knowledge of both the real successes and disappointments in living up to this country's ideals, which is the common legacy of most nations. Yet this is precisely what Americans and immigrants alike lack—a realistic knowledge of America's many virtues along with its sometimes glaring deficiencies. A watered-down curriculum that runs afoul of group sensitivities or inaccurate glorifications of one or another ethnic groups' contributions do nothing to foster a mature, realistic sense of national attachment.

Developing a realistic understanding of the country is important for another reason. It is the basic ingredient of appreciation. Americans are often unappreciative of their circumstances because they take so much for granted. State-of-the-art medical knowledge, telephones, paved roads, comprehensive sanitation systems, pure water, free primary and secondary education—the list is enormous. September 11 demonstrated something profound. Americans depend on the federal government and its constituent institutional elements for the most basic necessities of national life—physical and emotional security among them. Security is, of course, among the most basic functions of a national government, and Americans have every reason to expect their government to provide it. Yet expectation does not rule out feelings of appreciation. And therein lies one of the dilemmas of contemporary American life. Many Americans are quicker to express their expectations and demands than they are their appreciation. Either through ignorance or psychology, they take what they have for granted, without appreciating the accomplishments it represents.

Freedom, for example, is precious—just how much so is difficult to appreciate when it is so often taken for granted. The same is true for opportunity, or even free public education, or the safety net, or any of the myriad programs and infrastructure advantages that have become so much a part of American life that they are rarely considered.

They should be. Perhaps a free post–high school trip to any number of countries that lack these foundations would provide some comparative perspective. Appreciating what we have can only help citizens to resolve to keep it, and to understand how each American is part of a larger community purpose.

Appreciation—that is, realistic appreciation—is related to yet a third element of patriotic psychology: pride in the accomplishments of the national community. Americans can and do take pride in their democratic institutions and national accomplishments. And this pride, of course, requires identification. When a person expresses pride in "our" accomplishments, he or she is identifying as part of the group that can rightly claim to be responsible for the achievement.

Along with feelings of warmth, affection, and appreciation, patriotism requires a sense of commitment and responsibility, a stance of care toward the country's institutions, ways of life, and fellow citizens. "Ask not what your country can do for you, but what you can do for your country," John F. Kennedy famously urged in his inaugural address.[47] Like other forms of deep emotional attachment—a child's love for parents, a parent's love for a child, a couple's love—the feelings associated with patriotism lead to an ethic of care. Patriots not only wish their country well or take pride in it; they also try to help nurture it and are willing to sacrifice for it.

Finally, patriotism leads to feelings and expressions of support for the country. This does not necessarily result, as we have seen, in a view that supports a country regardless of what it does. So what, then, does support mean? This element of patriotism has become particularly muddled in recent political debates. Critics of one policy or another remind us that criticism of government policies is an important American tradition and that it is patriotic to be critical.

The first of these statements is most certainly true. However, the second neglects the fact that criticism alone is not an adequate understanding of all that is encompassed by the term "patriotism." Patriotism requires that criticism be contextualized by feelings of warmth and appreciation of what the country is or is trying to do in undertaking the initiatives that bring "patriotic criticism." A parent who constantly berates his or her child for the child's "own good" would lead us to wonder about the nature of their attachment. So, too, a critic who constantly berates his or her country as a result of "patriotic duty" would lead us to wonder about the nature of the attachment. Criticism alone as a primary expression of patriotism is like a racing car stuck in low gear; if it does not make use of the other gears, the engine will be torn apart.

One mistake that is often made in discussing national attachments is to speak of "the country" as if it were a single object. It is not. Actually, what we too easily refer to as "our country" embodies a number of elements, and each has its place in the development of national attachments.

A country has national institutions. It has a way of life. And it contains a community of members who share these national attachments. Its institutions are the major embodiment of its ideals and an irreplaceable method of translating them into common practice. A country has a way of life, a way of doing things—culturally, politically, and psychologically. These, too, are a part of what "our country" means. Last, but certainly not least, a country is a community, and a community is a group of people who see themselves belonging to, and being tied together by, their common ties of national attachment.

National attachments thus reflect consideration of all these elements. There is nothing static about them. Consider institutions. The office of the presidency can be esteemed or demeaned by the person occupying it. Religious institutions can be damaged by unscrupulous behavior, as can any institution over time. A country's ways of doing things can change as well. To take one important contemporary example, the massive influx of immigration has forced many institutions to adjust. Hospitals must hire translators, for example, or important government documents must be made accessible to people who do not yet speak English. The national community is like an extended family, and the sense that we are all more alike—as Americans—than not is a critically important set of identifications to encourage. At present, America does not.

So attachment begins with feelings of warmth and affection for various aspects of the national community, but it certainly does not end there. How does one develop feelings of warmth and affection for a country? Given that attachment to one's country begins early in life, the puzzle of patriotism is how best to build on that foundation.

Being appreciative of the various aspects of our national community allows one to feel pride in it. Now it is true that excessive pride precedes a fall, but pride need not necessarily result in hubris or arrogance. Pride must be leavened by a realistic appraisal of the successes and stumbles of a country in pursuit of its aspirations.

Pride also serves a community purpose, however. As has been noted, to take pride in something is to feel that it is partially yours—another form of attachment. To feel that it is partially yours is one path toward feeling responsibility for it. Pride begets caring, caring begets a sense of responsibility, and this results in a widening of the emotional circle of commitment and attachment.

American National Identity and Immigrant Integration

It would take some time to spell out the bonding implications for immigrants that come with these various elements of attachment. Only a start can be made here. A warmth and affection for one's country is a primary form of attachment and can obviously help individuals weather the vicissitudes of life in the United States. Some of these elements may be present in incipient form even before an immigrant arrives. Others may take time to develop. But all of them are affected in some ways by the pulls of dual citizenship and its implications for national attachment.

At the level of national psychology, it seems clear that many immigrants endure substantial hardships to come here. Like their counterparts in earlier American history, they take the risks associated with their decision to build a better life for themselves and their families. In doing so, most commit themselves to dislocation and in so doing deny themselves the comfort of the familiar.

There is, of course, more of a safety net in America now than there was in previous periods of high immigration. But given the immigrant's status, especially those with little education or technical skills, it is no Shangri-La.

Immigrants must also embrace the ethic of hard work, be able and willing to build for a better future in lieu of an easier time in the present, endure disappointments, maintain resilience, retain optimism, be willing to take risks but hedge them with prudence, and so on. In all these ways, they should find a hospitable cultural environment for their psychologies in relation to the national psychology clusters that have helped define and build this country. To the extent that there is, and continues to be, a match at these two levels—the micro and the macro, if you will—American national psychology is a helpful starting point for integrating new arrivals.

Many immigrants also arrive here with at least one other basis for one strong element of national attachment: appreciation. They arrive from countries where opportunity is limited and the hope for a better life thwarted. They have, as so many Americans have not, experienced the true deprivations that can accompany the lack of opportunity. Yet this country is not yet theirs. Their life narratives here have just begun, and they have yet to be linked with the many millions who preceded them and whose large experience mirrors theirs.

It is possible, over time, that their initial feelings will deepen and expand. That appreciation will lead to warmth, and to a sense of both belonging and membership. Over time, if they are so attuned, they can become more realistic about America—and be able to see it as it is—with all its virtues and its faults. They will also more fully begin to understand our culture, ways of life, and the institutions that support them. It will then be possible for "ours" and "theirs" to blend and an American identity to emerge. In time, they will share the pride of our successes and the disappointments of our setbacks. They and their children will not forget or dishonor their heritage. Every American has at least one. But increasingly, they will find themselves and their children oriented toward this country—its unfolding history and debates, and those of their fellow Americans. Gradually, their story and their family's stories will join that great stream of American stories. And as generations turn one into another, what starts as a small beginning in national attachment will have developed into one indistinguishable from millions of their fellow countrymen and countrywomen.

That is one possible generational progression, but it is by no means guaranteed. Several dangers loom. America has always believed that it can leverage the self-interest of new immigrants and gradually transform it into genuine attachment. In an age of entitlement and narcissism, this transition is ever more difficult. When segments of the American population look out for "number one" and ask, if only to themselves, "What's in it for me?" psychological attachments are harder to develop.

Many immigrants who come here do so in the hope of returning to their "home country" at some point. They are immigrants, but they are also sojourners—here, but not permanently. They are here for what the country has to offer, with no real incentive to develop and cement their ties here. Psychologically, they are mostly unavailable for the kinds of attachments that lead to permanent identifications. The United States has had such immigrants in the past, but they have not represented the majority of the immigrants who came to settle. Today, one can be a sojourner-immigrant much more easily, and therein lies a serious problem for this country's national community and civic culture.

The rise of globalism exacerbates these dilemmas. Substantial mobility among international cosmopolitans leads to a lessening of commitments to any particular place—its institutions, ways of life, and people. The central frame of reference for such people is their own realization of the good life, and it is tied to the psychology of consumption and gratification more than to a particular community. This, of course, is not the case for the many millions more who travel to the United States in search of a better life.

The problem of multiple loyalties for new immigrants begins with the fact that early attachments are very strong. Americans most likely cannot and, in my view, ought not attempt to sever or destroy these attachments—they are part of an individual's personal identity. This does not mean, however, that the United States has no stake or right to attempt to develop real attachments to this country, attachments that go beyond immigrant self-interest.

Consider remittances. Immigrants send hundreds of millions of dollars back to their "home" countries. It is clear that in doing so they want to help their families, their towns, and their country. Yet what responsibilities do they feel toward America? If national attachment consists, in part, of a commitment and responsibility toward one's country, where is the evidence of an immigrant's commitment and responsibility to this country? Would it not be furthered by devoting some portion of these resources to local immigrant communities in the United States rather than to hometown communities in the home country?

Or consider the idea that national attachment reflects support for this country and community. Should immigrants support illegal immigrants because they are of similar nationality? Should immigrants support national policies that encourage native languages when English has been a key element of American national integration for past, present, and future immigrant groups? Foreign governments have been pushing both policies, and many immigrant advocacy groups within the United States have followed suit. Is this an illustration of building attachments to the American national community?

If an American national identity consists of a *primary* psychological attachment to one's national community, how is that to be accommodated within the confines of dual citizenship? "Primary" does not mean exclusive, but it does mean predominant. It does not mean a partial identification. Nor does it envision even an equal one.

The 50 percent American, for whom both sides of the hyphen are equal, means in reality that both sides have equal weight in a person's psychology and that in any particular instance the scale could tip to one side or the other. The person might or might not identify with his or her American community. The person might or might not identify with its institutions and practices. The person might or might not identify and feel a sense of kinship with the others who make up that community or the ideals toward which they strive. And he or she might or might not feel a commitment to this national community.

Shallow attachments prevent integration into the American national community. When attachments are directed elsewhere, attachments are unavailable for the commitments that flow from an identification with the United States. It is impossible to view this as a positive development for the future of this country.

Notes

1. Leonard W. Doob, *Patriotism and Nationalism: Their Psychological Foundations* (New Haven, Conn.: Yale University Press, 1964), 83.

2. Ibid., 80–85.

3. See Almond and Verba's landmark five-nation study of political culture. It is arguably one of the most influential political science books of that decade. They relied

on national surveys and focused on culture as embedded in the beliefs and attitudes that support different political practices. Building on the culture and personality school, they viewed political culture as the result of a set of interrelated personal, institutional, and historical experiences. "Subject" and "participant" political cultures differed because each family, school, social, and later political experience shaped, then reinforced a particular view of one's self in the world. In short, congruence and coherence were still the foundations of the culture's impact on psychology and the political practices they shaped. Gabriel Almond and S. Verba. *The Civic Culture* (Princeton, N.J.: Princeton University Press, 1963).

4. Inglehart's influential studies approached political culture and its implications from another perspective. He views culture as embedded in values, which are, in turn, a reflection of the level of need satisfaction that a society has achieved. See R. Inglehart, *Cultural Shift in Advanced Industrial Society* (Princeton, N.J.: Princeton University Press, 1990); and Inglehart, *Modernization and Postmodernization: Cultural, Economic and Political Change in 43 Countries.* (Princeton: Princeton University Press, 1996). Building on Maslow's need theory of personality and psychological development, Inglehart argues that the satisfaction of more basic human needs (physiological, safety, esteem, and belonging needs) frees up individuals and societies to be concerned with other, postmaterial, concerns. Abraham Maslow, *Motivation and Personality* (New York: Harper Brothers, 1954).

Inglehart finds that different historical generations, within the same culture, can have vastly different psychological experiences. In his work, culture's impact on the psychology of political views and practices is no longer a function solely of family, institutional, or political experience but also of historical circumstances, during which it unfolds. Thus, does the modern sometimes reaffirm the traditional, albeit in new ways, as Ingelhart's use of generational analysis recaptures and updates Benedict's insistence on the importance of history to cultural psychology analysis. Ruth Benedict, *Patterns of Culture* (New York: Mentor, 1934), 232.

5. Smith's observation; Anthony D. Smith, *National Identity* (Reno: University of Nevada Press, 1991), 143.

6. Andrew Vincent, "Liberal Nationalism: An Irresponsible Compound?" *Political Studies* 65 (1997): 275–95; the citation here is on 291.

7. Walter Berns, *Making Patriots* (Chicago: University of Chicago Press, 2001).

8. Diane Ravitch, *The Language Police: How Pressure Groups Restrict What Students Learn* (New York: Alfred A. Knopf, 2003), 16.

9. Morris Janowitz, *The Reconstruction of Patriotism: Education for Civic Consciousness* (Chicago: University of Chicago Press, 1983).

10. Canada does much better on this score. Having developed a Ministry of Multiculturalism, it has become very interested in the self-identifications of Canadians. In their 2001 census they asked: "When asked about the ethnic origins of ancestors, fully 39% said 'just Canadian.'" Matthew Mendelson, "Birth of a New Ethnicity," *Globe and Mail*, June 9, 2003. One wonders what result would come from a well-phrased question that allowed respondents to choose from among: a plain American response, a hyphenated response with emphasis on either side of the hyphen, or both equally weighted, a pan-ethnic or panracial response.

11. David Hollinger, *A Postethnic America: Beyond Multiculturalism* (New York: Basic Books, 1995).

12. Richard Morin, "Poll: National Pride, Confidence Soar," *Washington Post*, October 25, 2001.

13. A comprehensive compilation of opinion polls on the subject of patriotism, both before and after September 11, can be found in Karlyn Bowman, ed., "Polls on Patriotism," AEI Studies in Public Opinion, April 2003, available at http://www.aei.org/publications/pubID.14889/pub_detail.asp. The figures in these paragraphs are drawn from that report.

14. Doob, *Patriotism*, 6.

15. Paul Gleason, "American Identity and Americanization," in *Harvard Encyclopedia of American Ethnic Groups*, ed. Stephan Thernstrom (Cambridge, Mass.: Harvard University Press, 1980), 31.

16. Ibid., 56.

17. Arthur A. Schlesinger Jr., *The Disuniting of America: Reflections on a Multicultural Society* (New York: W. W. Norton, 1992).

18. Jeffery C. Alexander and Neil J. Smelser, "The Ideological Discourse of Cultural Discontent: Paradoxes, Realities, and Alternative Ways of Thinking," in *Diversity and Its Discontents: Cultural Conflict and Common Ground in Contemporary American Society*, ed. Neil J. Smelser and Jeffrey C. Alexander (Princeton, N.J.: Princeton University Press, 1999), 3; see also Samuel P. Huntington, *American Politics: The Promise of Disharmony* (Cambridge, Mass.: Belknap Press, 1961), 23; see also John Higham, *Strangers in the Land* (New Brunswick, NJ: Rutgers University Press, 1955).

19. Rogers M. Smith, "The 'American Creed' and American Identity: The Limits of Liberal Citizenship in the United States," *Western Political Quarterly* 41 (1987): 225–51; the citation here is on 226.

20. This overview is drawn from Thomas V. DiBacco, "Simple Creed Sums Up Basics for Americans," *Washington Times*, October 1, 2001.

21. Quoted in ibid.

22. James W. Prothro and C. M. Grigg, "Fundamental Principles of Democracy: Basis of Agreement and Disagreement," *Journal of Politics* 22 (1960): 276–94.

23. "America Enduring" (editorial), *New York Times*, September 11, 2002; emphasis mine.

24. This discussion draws on Stanley A. Renshon, "American Identity and the Dilemmas of Cultural Diversity," in *Political Psychology: Cultural and Cross Cultural Foundations*, ed. Stanley A. Renshon and John Duckitt (London: Macmillan, 2000).

25. David Miller, *On Nationality* (Oxford: Clarendon Press, 1995), 26–27.

26. T. Alexander Aleinikoff, "Between National and Post-National: Membership in the United States," *Michigan Journal of Race and Law* 241 (1999): 9453.

27. Eugene Garcia and Aida Hurtado, "Becoming an American: A Review of Current Research on the Development of Racial and Ethnic Identity in Children," in *Toward a Common Destiny: Improving Race and Ethnic Relations in America*, ed. Willis D. Haeley and Anthony W. Jackson (San Francisco: Jossey-Bass, 1995), 162.

28. Stephen Nathanson, "Should Patriotism Have a Future?" in *Patriotism in the Lives of Individuals and Nations*, ed. Daniel Bar-Tal and Ervin Staub, editors (Chicago, Nelson-Hall, 1997), 311.

29. The three preceding quotations are found in Morray and refer, respectively, to comments made by Samuel Johnson, Arnold Toynbee, and John Foster Dulles; Joseph Morray, *Pride of State: A Study in Patriotism and American National Morality* (Boston, Beacon Press, 1959), xii. The often-quoted Johnson phrase is only attributed to him by James Bosworth and has never been authenticated. One reason to question this quotation is that Johnson apparently thought better of patriotism than the quote allows. In his 1774 address to the electors of Great Britain, he said, "It ought to be deeply impressed on the minds of all who have voices in this national deliberation, that no man can deserve a seat in parliament, who is not a patriot. No other man will protect our rights: no other man can merit our confidence. A patriot is he whose publick conduct is regulated by one single motive, the love of his country; who, as an agent in parliament, has, for himself, neither hope nor fear, neither kindness nor resentment, but refers every thing to the common interest." Samuel Johnson, *The Works of Samuel Johnson*, vol. 14 (Troy, N.Y.: Pafraets & Company, 1913), 81.

30. Merle Curti, *The Roots of American Loyalty* (New York: Athenaeum, 1968).

31. These data are drawn from Karlyn H. Bowman, ed., "America after 9/11: Public Opinion on the War on Terrorism and the War with Iraq," AEI Studies in Public Opinion, June 2003, which has a comprehensive listing of polls on the subjects referenced in the title of the report; available at http://www.aei.org/publications/pubID .16974,filter./pub_detail.asp.

32. Ervin Staub, "Blind versus Constructive Patriotism: Moving from Embeddedness in the Group to Critical Loyalty and Action," in *Patriotism*, ed. Bar-Tal and Staub.

33. Gary R. Johnson, "The Evolutionary Roots of Patriotism," in *Patriotism*, ed. Bar-Tal and Staub, 81–82.

34. George Fletcher, *Loyalty: An Essay on the Morality of Relationships* (New York: Oxford University Press, 1993), 151.

35. Herbert C. Kelman, "Nationalism, Patriotism, and National Identity: Social-Psychological Dimensions," in *Patriotism*, ed. Bar-Tal and Staub, 166, sees it as "an ideology—or a set of attitudes and beliefs—that refers to an individual's attachment and loyalty to their nation and country." Stephen Worchel, with Dawna Coutant, "The Tangled Web of Loyalty: Nationalism, Patriotism, and Ethnocentrism," in *Patriotism*, ed. Bar-Tal and Staub, 192–93, say it "consists of acts and beliefs based on securing the identity and welfare of the group without regard to either self-identity or self-benefit. This definition equates nation with nationality and fails to appreciate that identifications and attachment with one's country can be a very important part of self-identity."

36. John Bodnar, ed., *Bonds of Affection: Americans Define Their Patriotism* (Princeton, N.J.: Princeton University Press, 1996).

37. Morton Grodzins, *The Loyal and the Disloyal: Social Boundaries of Patriotism and Treason* (Chicago: University of Chicago Press, 1956), 21.

38. That term is used here in the psychoanalytic sense of any person, place, or thing that has ontological or psychological standing.

39. E. L. Horowitz, "Some Aspects of the Development of Patriotism in Children," *Sociometry* 3 (1940): 329–41.

40. E. D. Lawson, "The Development of Patriotism in Children: A Second Look," *Journal of Psychology* 55 (1963): 279–86.

41. Eugene A. Weinstein, "The Development of the Concept of Flag and the Sense of National Identity," *Child Development* 28 (1957): 167–74.

42. Gustav Jahoda, "The Development of Children's Ideas about Community and Nationality," in *Growth and Change: A Reader in Political Socialization*, ed. Charles G. Bell (Belmont, Calif.: Dickenson, 1973).

43. A. F. Davis, "The Child's Discovery of Nationality," *Australian and New Zealand Journal of Sociology* 4 (1968): 107–25; the citation here is on 114.

44. One mistake often made in discussions of national attachment is to assume that love is the only feeling that is possible toward one's country. In fact, like other affections, national attachments can encompass more than one feeling. If you can be attached to an object, you can be disappointed by it. If you love an object, you can idealize it—failing to see it for what it really is. And, if you are attached to a disappointing object, you can become angry at it—sometimes in an intense way.

45. These figures are drawn from Davis, "Child's Discovery," table 5.

46. Davis, "Child's Discovery," appendix 2, table 4.

47. John F. Kennedy, "Inaugural Address," January 20, 1961; available at http://www.jfklibrary.org.

PART II **Domestic Challenges to American National Identity**

CHAPTER 4

Multiculturalism and National Identity

AMERICAN NATIONAL IDENTITY IS BESET BY CENTRIFUGAL FORCES from both above and below. Domestically, the rise of political and cultural demands for group identity represents one influence. Internationally, the rise of transnationalism and its attendant loosening of national ties represent the other. That both are operative at the same time is an unprecedented challenge, and not simply to the nation-state itself. Rather, it is a particular challenge to the integration and cohesion of the diverse groups that constitute the American national community.

The United States has now had forty-plus years of intense cultural conflict, which has affected virtually all its major social and political institutions. As a result, the tens of millions of new immigrants arriving in this country in the decades since the early 1960s have landed in the middle of a cultural battle zone. Not surprisingly, given these circumstances, immigration itself has become one more area of cultural and political conflict.

In the immediate wake of the September 11, 2001, terrorist attacks, some of these conflicts seemed to subside.[1] However, the respite proved temporary. Almost immediately, intense partisanship, driven by cultural and political divides, displaced civic solidarity.[2] Today, these conflicts smolder and flare up like the aftermath of a raging fire.[3]

The Civil War really tested the cultural and civic bonds that united this country's disparate interests. That crisis confronted America's leadership, and especially its president, with a very profound, but basic question—one that had first surfaced and had been last faced by the Founding Fathers: Could America share a common future without a common culture?[4] The answer, over which the war was fought, was that it could not.

There are many ways to be divided—along class, racial, ethnic, religious, and political lines. Since the Civil War, the United States has, for the most part, avoided the intense violence but not the conflict that has been associated with these fissures elsewhere. America's unique contemporary contribution to the theory of divided societies is as a stable, long-standing constitutional republic in which partisan political conflict has both reflected and helped to stimulate even more intense cultural conflict.

These conflicts frame the true meaning of our "culture wars." In reality, of course, there are many such wars. There are the abortion wars, school wars, military culture wars, gender wars, family wars, language wars, history wars, and museum wars —not to mention the wars over flags, statues, and pledges of allegiance at school or as part of our naturalization ceremonies. Not surprisingly, our politics, like our culture, have become mired in bipartisan trench warfare.

My shorthand term for this is America's "Second Civil War."[5] Now, for the second time in its history, this country faces a real question of how to maintain a stable and effective relationship between America's "unum" and "pluribus." Unlike the first Civil War, this one does not pit commerce against agriculture, urban centers against rural traditions, or North against South. Rather, it is being waged in *every* section of the country. Unlike the first Civil War, the antagonists cannot take refuge in the primary institutions in their part of the country—their family or their religious, social, cultural, or political organizations. Today, these are precisely the places where the conflicts are occurring.

The consequences of these conflicts are found not in body counts but in the retreat from common ideals, abandoned cultural values, and floundering institutions. Expanding claims for group rights, and acerbic debates regarding their legitimacy and limits, have furthered a deep cultural divide. Every conceivable group—some deserving, others less so—have demanded legitimacy, parity, and, in some cases, preference.

American National Culture: Worth Keeping?

Some applaud the centrifugal developments associated with multiculturalism. They view the decline of key American cultural traditions, and especially its "dominant elites," as a necessary step in developing a less "hegemonic," more democratic society.[6] And it would be hard not to acknowledge the shadows of our national history—the racism, the exclusive practices, the prejudices against those who were not white, male, and Protestant.

It is true that the United States has had a mixed—and in some cases poor—historical record in its treatment of American Indians, Americans of African descent, Americans of Asian descent, women, and others.[7] This is not the entire story, of course. Smith amply documents the fact that the United States has had multiple traditions—some exclusionary, others inclusive.[8] Strains of both traditions continue today.

American Traditions: Which Ones?

How much genuine white supremacist thinking actually exists, much less pervades American society, is an open question. The evidence suggests that such views exist but that they are by no means representative. Most Americans, according to available data, show no particular difficulty with the fact that whites will be in a minority sometime after 2050 if recent demographic trends continue. Most Americans of all races and ethnicities support better race relations—although there remain honest and legitimate differences as to how they can best be accomplished.

Those who believe that whiteness is the only acceptable color in America must explain why Eastern European ethnics were originally discriminated against when they began to arrive in this country in large numbers.[9] They must further explain how these ethnics came to be integrated into American society. If white is the only acceptable color and Protestantism the only acceptable religion, critics must explain why Asian Americans account for a higher percentage of college graduates than non-Asians—being neither white nor Protestant. And they need to explain how it is possible that the median salary for Asian college graduates working full time one year after graduation is $27,637, while the comparable salary for whites is $23,637.

Those who believe that American society is simply continuing its long history of oppressing and marginalizing minority groups must explain the circumstances that led those major groups to cede power to the marginal. Jennifer Hochschild has assembled a partial list of those historical circumstances.[10] They include the prohibition of any law of primogeniture in the Constitution; separation of church and state in the First Amendment, which gave people with all religious convictions, or none, equal political standing; decisions in state constitutional conventions of the 1820s and 1830s to open the franchise to property-less white men; the Civil War, and the institutionalization of its outcome in the Thirteenth, Fourteenth, and Fifteenth Amendments to the Constitution; policies in the nineteenth century that established the principle and sometimes the practice of free (tax-supported) public schools for all (nonenslaved) children; the Sixteenth Amendment, which permitted an individual income tax; the Nineteenth Amendment, which granted the franchise to women; the laws and policies of the New Deal, especially with regard to social security, which provided the foundation for a social welfare state; the laws and policies of the New Deal, especially with regard to the right to unionize, which gave workers some countervailing leverage against employers; the McCarran-Walter Act of 1952, which finally permitted all legal immigrants to become naturalized citizens; the Twenty-Fourth Amendment, which abolished the poll tax; the Twenty-Sixth Amendment, which lowered the age of enfranchisement to eighteen years; and the judicial decisions and civil rights laws of the 1950s through the 1970s that granted political equality, at least formally, to all adult citizens regardless of race, gender, or disability status. "One could add others," she writes, "but that is a rather compelling list."[11]

Assimilation? To What?

America's traditional answer to the question of how to encourage the integration of new immigrants has been assimilation. Assimilation carries with it the implication that there *is* a national American identity and culture.[12] It also carries the implication that immigrants choosing to come here should, in good faith, try to embrace it. There are many good reasons for them to do so. And as noted, many immigrants do share some of the basic elements of American national culture—ambition and risk taking, to name two—or they would not undertake the difficult physical and psychological costs of immigration.

Yet the concept of assimilation is "contested," to use a somewhat dainty postmodern term that hardly does justice to the fierce assault on it as a normative and descriptive model. Some sociologists see the term "assimilation" as harboring "deep layers of ethnocentric pretensions" and the experience associated with it as a physically and emotionally harmful experience.[13] Many multiculturalists see it as an attempt to strip immigrants of their identity.

Yet assimilation has provided the framework for the many benefits immigrants have enjoyed. Most immigrants come to the United States not to express their ethnicity but to seek political and economic freedom. Those benefits are built on and supported by the very same primary cultural traditions that are now being increasingly questioned—merit and hard work as a vehicle for mobility, independent thinking within a strong framework of values and ideals, moderation in character, tempered self-interest, and so on.

Consider the psychology of ambition. People come here to improve their circumstances. They want to do better and are willing to endure great hardships in order to have the opportunity. Does ambition and the hard work that accompany it provide a psychological foundation for the culture and society that developed in the United States? Of course. Capitalism without ambition is unthinkable.

Assimilation to those primary American psychological and cultural traditions would seem, on its face, to be instrumental in helping immigrants achieve the goals for which they came. They are important to the country itself, as well.

However, if there are good reasons for immigrants to assimilate into American culture, there are hazards in doing so uncritically. Even immigrants who arrive in this country with the psychology, values, and beliefs that parallel those of traditional American culture might wonder whether assimilation to a debased national culture is beneficial.[14] Studies show, for example, that television and adversarial youth culture undermine the values of hard work and family values with which many immigrants arrive.

Immigration researchers have found that length of residence for immigrant children in San Diego was associated with spending less time on homework and more time watching television.[15] Also, a 1988 study by the National Research Council found that adolescents born in the United States to immigrant parents suffer poorer health and engage in riskier behaviors than children born in other countries who then move here with their parents.[16] That, not surprisingly, led to lower grade point averages. Paradoxically, then, immigrant groups that might be helpful in revitalizing traditional American cultural values like hard work, the importance of merit, and feelings of pride and attachment to the nation are faced with becoming integrated into a culture in which these very basic ideals are themselves under attack or in decline.

Nor can Americans count on immigrant groups to answer problems here that Americans have not already addressed themselves. A 1998 study by the National Center for Health Statistics showed soaring birthrates among teenagers of Mexican origin that were more than twice the rate of the nation's teenagers as a whole, and more than three times the rate of white teenagers.[17] Equally disturbing is the fact that the figures revealed that Hispanics born in this country were more likely than Hispanics who moved here from their homeland (primarily Mexico) to give birth as teenagers, and to have children outside marriage.[18] Indeed, these findings suggest that continuing high levels of this immigration stream may contribute to the development of a Hispanic/Mexican "underclass" in a country that has had little success in addressing or resolving similar problems among Americans of African descent.

Arriving in a culture that contains powerful and corrosive elements raises the question: How much should immigrants and citizens alike accommodate themselves to such forces? Immigrants may well look elsewhere, most notably to their home countries and cultures, if they begin to worry about the fate of their families in this country. Given the ease of international communication and transportation, erasing boundaries of time and geography may mean that immigrants will seek sources of identity elsewhere—anywhere but in the United States.

As this is happening, most public debate has centered on whether and to what extent new immigrants are an economic asset or liability. Economic analysis, however, while important, misses a much more central issue, namely, how to integrate enormous numbers of new immigrants into a national culture and identity that are, themselves, increasingly questioned.

Needed: A Primary Culture

Must cultural, psychological, and political diversity leads to a fragmented and dysfunctional national identity? It is not a baseless question. Is the opposite of fragmentation Anglo-Western domination? Some apparently think so. James Davidson Hunter, in his book *Cultural Wars*, argues that "*cultural conflict is ultimately about domination.*"[19] The word "domination" implies subjugation. And if Hunter is correct, it is not surprising that our culture wars are fought with no quarter given to a state of exhaustion and stalemate.

Is it true that all cultural conflict is ultimately about domination? Not necessarily. A more central and useful question, given our current circumstances, is not whether the United States has a dominant culture but whether in a democratic, pluralist republic like ours it is still important to have a *primary* one. Is America's tradition of inclusion compatible both with the wide range of personal and political choices associated with our liberal traditions and with the cultural *primacy* of certain core American traditions like individualism, opportunity, merit, and responsibility? The wager that this country has made for 230 years is that both are not only possible but also necessary.

The question "What does it mean to be an American?" has never been easy to answer. Yet in the past four decades, new and more basic and unsettling questions have emerged. Is there an American national identity? Should there be one? Some worry about how we can maintain and further develop common understandings and purpose in a diverse country. Others ask what useful purpose such worries serve when we live in a postmodern era and when our allegiances ought to be global.

Paradoxically, arguments over assimilation assume a stable, coherent culture into which immigrants are assimilated. As the many battles that constitute our culture wars make clear, this is increasingly not the case. The major psychological and cultural traditions that underlie American national culture have themselves become sharply disputed.

As noted, high levels of immigration over an extended period of time have dramatically altered the ethnic and racial composition of the country. By 2050, as noted above, America will contain no real majority racial or ethnic group.[20] Some advocates, counting on a coalition of what they see as the oppressed, are hoping to turn James Madison's warnings about the tyranny of the majority on its head. In place of the tyranny of the majority, they look to the day when a coalition of the minority will acquire hegemony. Others are wondering how America will manage to integrate so many culturally diverse newcomers while retaining its core identity as a country built primarily, but not exclusively, on Western European intellectual, legal, ethical, and cultural traditions.

Does America need a *dominant* culture? Our history suggests that the answer is no. Does America have a primary culture? The answer is and ought to be yes. The two are not the same. A dominant culture requires compliance. It maintains a "do it or else" stance toward newly arriving immigrants, other cultural traditions, and its own citizens. In that sense, America does not have a dominant culture.

The basic stance of American primary culture is more or less, not either/ or. It does not demand that an immigrant's original language never be spoken or that an immigrant sever all previous emotional ties. Rather, it asks immigrants to make a degree of commitment to America's basic cultural traditions and identity and to make a good-faith effort to become involved and emotionally connected to this country where they now live, which has opened itself to them. These do not seem to be unreasonable requests.

Few argue that new immigrants should never speak the language of their home country. What they do say, for very practical reasons, is that immigrants should learn English as quickly as they can.

English became the preeminent language of the United States because it was the language of most of those explorers who settled the country, and of the major institutions they built. A rapidly growing country required a common language.

Few here argue that immigrants should cut off all ties to their countries of origin. What does seem reasonable to urge is that these ties generally recede in favor of more robust connections to the country to which they have chosen to migrate.

From its inception, the United States has comprised various cultural strands. These strands have developed and become integrated into the fabric of our national community. That tradition continues today.

"Welcoming"

Many believe that the United States should be, but is not, welcoming to new immigrants. In its most general form, this "welcoming" can be understood as a general respect and appreciation for the immigrant's beliefs and sensibilities. That is hardly controversial.

Yet some advocates of immigrant group identity seek more than general respect and appreciation. They often ask for acceptance *regardless* of the nature of immigrants' beliefs or practices. These issues range from the central to the peripheral. For example, some immigrants to the United States have strong views on the limits that should be imposed on women and on members of their respective groups. Some do not accept the distinction drawn between public and religious life in this country. Others believe that killings to avenge honor are permissible.

In Iraq, after the overthrow of Saddam Hussein, the *New York Times* reported, "Long forbidden, long hidden, the whips of mortification were flagellating today as Iraq's Shi'ite Muslim majority celebrated its newfound political freedom and potential political power. 'For 25 years they were hidden in our houses,' said a man from the Shi'ite south as a group of young men lashed their backs in rhythm with whips made from chains. 'The father taught his son.'"[21] Do such practices fall under the heading of freedom of religion in the United States? What does "welcoming" mean in these circumstances— tolerance, acceptance?

Other difficulties of a more practical matter emerge when different cultural traditions meet. In France, a debate has broken out over Muslim women who refuse to remove their veil before a photograph is taken for their French identity card.[22] In the Netherlands, a bastion of multicultural tolerance, a brutal murder by young, supposedly culturally well-integrated Muslim youths has created an uproar of calls for stronger measures against radical elements, in spite of the fact that all new immigrants must attend "integration classes."[23] The balance between tolerance of new immigrant cultures and traditional practices in the immigrant's new country is not just a European problem. In Orlando, a Muslim woman sued to be allowed to shield her face for her state driver's license photograph. Her attorney argued that such a requirement violated her rights to privacy, freedom of religion, due process, and free speech.[24] She lost.

The issue is not limited to one new ethnic group. Sikhs in Britain have insisted that they be allowed to wear their traditional headdress rather than hard hats when working on a construction site. Should they be allowed to forgo wearing motorcycle helmets, as others must? Barry has examined these and similar dilemmas in the context of British culture. Briefly, he shows that most of the cultural traditions that become issues are themselves the product of continuous development within the home culture, and in a number of cases can be further adapted to a new culture, when necessary.[25] The very same dynamics are at work in the demand for special religious exceptions from the requirements for humane animal slaughter for Jews and Muslims.[26] If the cultural traditions of immigrants are not immutable within their own home cultures, why must they become so when transplanted to a new one?

The "immutable culture" argument can sometimes take tricky turns. In 2003, CNN Television reported that the practice of veiling oneself for driver's license photographs is *not* the practice in Muslim countries. In Bahrain, Egypt, Jordan, Kuwait, Oman, Qatar, and the United Arab Emirates, veils may not be used for such identification photographs. In Iran, women wear a traditional chador that does not cover their face, and in Saudi Arabia women are not allowed to drive.

The issues that confront the United States with its new ethnic mix go much deeper than whether a group should be allowed exemption from an occupational safety law. "Welcoming," Americans are told, requires the adjustment of our cultural and political practices to help make immigrants feel more at home. "Welcoming" should mean that learning English must be balanced against every effort to ensure that immigrants and their children retain their native language. If the result is that immigrant children do not learn enough English to have true functional proficiency (reading, writing, and speaking), adjustments must be made. Voting machines and ballots must be available in foreign languages, with no time limits of any kind placed on that aid. Driving and other state licensing examinations must also be available in foreign languages, with no time limits set for being able to take them in English. None of this, it is emphasized, is really a problem so long as we all believe in the American Creed.

In truth, American culture has responded positively in many ways to its new arrivals. Consider the maternity wards of American hospitals. In 2002, the *Washington Post* reported:

> Faced with an influx of immigrant mothers over the past decade, delivery rooms across the Washington area are increasingly adapting not just to unfamiliar languages, but also to a new set of traditions and taboos. Holy Cross has become adept at assembling all-female teams of obstetricians, nurses, anesthesiologists, and neonatologists to attend Muslim women whose religion forbids examination by male health workers. The maternity ward has also learned to keep special biohazard containers on hand for patients, usually from African countries, where the tradition is to take the placenta home and bury it. Prince George's Hospital Center in Cheverly allows women to give birth in a variety of positions according to their native custom. Inova Fairfax Hospital in Falls Church often bends its five-person limit on visitors in the delivery and postpartum rooms to accommodate Latin American women who want extended family members close by.[27]

I quote this report at length because it suggests the range of accommodation that is being made, and in my view legitimately so. The story of assimilation is so often presented as if a rigid, demanding American culture requires every change of immigrants but does little or nothing to accommodate their needs and views. This is far from the truth.

Group Rights

Group identity and individual identification with ethnic and other groups has a long history in the United States. Historically, groups have provided networks for mobility. They have also provided psychological comfort for the difficult processes of transition in a new country.

Multiculturalism has not changed these functions of group identity. What it has changed, and dramatically, are expectations regarding its duration and consequences. What was once understood as a transitional stage is now considered, by some, a permanent and necessary part of how Americans think of themselves. As a result, multicultural advocates demand that every basic American institution respond to the need of ethnic and other disadvantaged groups to be seen as members of that group and be treated accordingly.

That treatment often takes the form of special programs, rules, and resource allocations designed to benefit the specific groups. This may take the form of preferences in university admissions or in private industry. It can take the form of proposals with regard to political representation—as districts with boundaries set to ensure that members of these groups will be able to win elective office. Or it can take the form of expecting dispensation from the ordinary rules of standard behavior because of cultural dispositions.

Group Rights and "Oppression"

Political theorists like Iris Young provide what they believe are the theoretical underpinnings of such policies.[28] Young starts with the assumption that certain groups experience pervasive "discrimination and oppression."[29] Who is in these groups? They include "women, blacks, Hispanics, other Spanish speaking Americans, Asian Americans, gay men, lesbians, working-class people, poor people, and mentally and physically disabled people."[30]

There is much to puzzle over in the five criteria Young uses to ascertain "oppression" and "discrimination." Consider "the poor," one of her oppressed groups. Are they excluded from the workplace? They are most likely poor as a result of not working, or working in a job that is low paying. Why do they not try to find a better job, or any job? Young believes the reason is oppression; in fact, she states that "we live in a society with deep group oppressions."[31] Young appears to equate intergroup disparity with oppression, but surely there are important distinctions.

Blacks in South Africa and in the American South were subject to a racial caste system that was clearly oppressive. Jews in Germany, peasants in Stalin's Russia, and bourgeoisie elements in Mao's China all clearly qualify as oppressed. But do the poor in modern America qualify as oppressed in these terms? Surely not.

Special Rights

Differentiated citizenship involves granting special rights to those oppressed groups.[32] They are required, Young argues, because "the privileged are usually not included to protect and further the interests of the oppressed."[33] Yet, as noted above, Hochschild has documented a number of historical occasions in the United States when those with power have voluntarily given up a substantial portion of their privileges.

A special right is different from the general rights that all share, in that it is specifically bestowed on the "marginal group," presumably and paradoxically by the very "oppressive groups" that hold power. These rights include having special representatives in the decision-making bodies of the country, having their special advocacy groups funded by the government, requiring decision makers to be "obligated to show that they have taken these perspectives into account," and "having veto power over specific policies that affect a group directly."[34]

Elsewhere, Young argues for special cultural rights, for example, the right to have the state facilitate the development of ethnic languages and continued publication of government documents in minority languages.[35] Some others have supported these ideas on the grounds that they promote inclusion.[36] Yet it is difficult to see how they accomplish that purpose.

Many questions arise: How many groups would there be, and who would decide that question? Who would or would not be counted as a member of the group, and who would decide those questions? As Young notes, "Groups are fluid, they come into existence and fade away."[37] The same could be asked of individual identifications with various groups. The increasing prevalence of intermarriage and thus multiethnic and multiracial couples and individuals presents an enormous problem for this scheme.

Black Enough?

A large problem, then, is who exactly would represent these oppressed groups. Advocates of group representation insist that it must be members of the oppressed groups themselves. This is called "mirror representation," which presumes that "minority groups can only be fully 'represented' by someone who shares their gender, class, occupation, ethnicity, language, and so on."[38]

Yet this is a tricky matter. Advocates of mirror representation argue that no amount of empathy can jump the barriers of experience.[39] That is why whites cannot represent blacks, men cannot represent women, and so on.

Still, there are a number of problems with this approach to representation.[40] If oppressed groups get special representations, why should nonoppressed groups exert any effort to be empathetic toward them? Indeed, their time would best be spent concentrating their efforts on wholly representing their own. American politics would, instead of trying to build bridges, build moats.

Of course, the lack of empathy is a two-way street, so to speak. Oppressed groups concentrating on sharpening the range and understanding of their oppression and making demands based on it would have little incentive to reach out to other groups, except as a coalition of the oppressed against their oppressors. This is formula for conflict, not national community.

The issue of mirror representation is even more divisive than resolving the question of whether privileged groups can represent oppressed groups. Consider this question: Can a Midwestern woman who has chosen to stay home and raise her children full time represent an ardent feminist who has not? Both are women and therefore members of that oppressed class, but Midwestern stay-at-home moms are hardly the kind of representation that fits this model.

This is not a matter of theoretical musings, but of real-life politics. In Washington, Mayor Anthony Williams, who is an African American, has been criticized for not being "black enough." He has quite an impressive list of accomplishments in a city that has had many famously corrupt and criminal politicians before him (e.g., Marion Barry).[41] Yet with his Ivy League degrees, suits and bow ties, and preference for making tough economic decisions, he has been characterized as insufficiently attentive to black concerns. In a *Washington Post* opinion piece, an African American *Washington Post* reporter wondered whether the city was "losing its flavor" because of the larger number of whites who were returning to the city because of the changes wrought by Mayor Williams. Her article had been stimulated by a question on a flyer she had been handed: "Is the Chocolate City Turning Vanilla?"[42]

These and similar controversies raise good questions: Who are the authentic representatives of a group, and how that will be decided? Random selection within a given universe is clearly the best guarantee of representation. Yet this is not what advocates mean when they press for more democracy and more justice. What they want represented is a very narrow slice of the ideological diversity that exists in most groups.

Young and her advocates present their ideas for a radical remaking of American democracy as a response to its history. In fact, theirs is a narrow, highly ideological view of American history.[43] Advocates of group rights—or "deep diversity"[44]—insist that it is the only formula that will allow a multinational state to remain united.

The Consequences of Special Rights: Inclusion or Conflict?

Advocates of group rights barely mention the idea that with rights come responsibilities. Without a discussion of both, it is hard to see how special rights do not become just another form of oppressive privilege, but in reverse.

The vehement opposition to any dilution of racial and ethnic preferences on the part of those who support them suggests that once in place they will be extremely hard to remove. There is always some disadvantage to be overcome.[45] As Offe notes, "Expiration (or even review) clauses are typically missing in such arrangements." "As a result," he argues, "group rights are granted as permanent rights."[46]

How do we know which issues groups should have veto power over? Young mentions "reproductive rights for women," as a major example.[47] Yet she then acknowledges that "a right to pregnancy and maternity leave and the right to special treatment for nursing mothers" is highly controversial among feminists today.[48]

Drawing lines for group rights is a difficult process, which reflects the challenges of understanding groups as undifferentiated—women, blacks, Hispanics, and so forth. For instance, once you begin to assign veto power to groups, you must ask *which* area and *what* groups. What would be the area of veto power of blacks? Is it education, housing, welfare, or race relations? All these areas hold special importance for blacks. Yet they hold special importance for many other groups as well—in fact, for most Americans. Should Hispanic veto power be limited to language? Would Koreans have the same veto power? What areas of public policy should gays and lesbians be given veto power over? With every group claiming veto power over the areas that can legitimately be said to affect them (almost every national policy affects many groups), what happens to the core idea of citizenship interests for the common good?

The goal of building a coalition of the oppressed, leading to more political and social harmony, seems farfetched. It is far more likely that this arrangement would sharpen the distinction among groups and thus heighten conflict. Will blacks get along better with Koreans or Hispanics with Arabs because each group is more sharply defined and socialized to view their loss as another's gain? The genius of requiring groups to build large coalitions, in the best American tradition, is to blur the lines of conflict and work for common purposes.

Toward One America—How?

Advocates of group rights claim to speak for the betterment of those they champion but do not necessarily listen to what those group members say. No better evidence of this can be found than in reading through the transcripts of town hall meetings during President Bill Clinton's race initiative, One America.[49]

Here is Vanessa Cordero asking the group to remember that "this is not black and white in America. . . . It's hurt me all these years that I've been in the United States, since 1957, that all I hear is black issues and white issues."[50] Another young woman has a similar concern. Referring to the segregation she witnesses on her campus, she asks, "White people hang out here, and black people hang out there. And as a Hispanic and coming from a Mexican background, where does that put me? I'm neither one."

Here is McHoughton Chambers, the biracial child of a mixed marriage, struggling to find his identity. He expresses his concern that people only see half of who he is and that they often neglect to see the other side of his biracial makeup. Another student, Erika Sanders, eloquently evokes her experiences as a black student in an all-white school: "I feel like I live in two different worlds. When I go to school, sometimes I feel the burden to speak for all of black America. And slowly, I'm helping my classmates to realize that I'm not all of black America; I'm Erika."[51]

What do these narratives have in common? They share something extremely basic yet profound. These individuals are all asking, each in their own way, to be taken as the unique persons that they are. They do not ask to be representatives of groups or to be represented by them. Erika Sanders does not want to speak for all African Americans. She would prefer that her friends get to know her as who she is: Erika. McHoughton Chambers does not wish to be known for half his biracial identity, whichever half is emphasized. He wants to be known as who he is: both. However paradoxical, it seems that the road to One America lies through the path of individualism.

What of Ethnicity?

The path to One America may well lie in the direction of individualism. But what about ethnicity? Ethnic identification remains a strong element of the identity of many Americans, especially those in the primary immigration cohorts that I would define as the first, second, and perhaps third. As it turns out, there is some suggestive evidence on this matter.

In the 1980 census and the 1979 Current Population Survey, the government asked a straightforward ancestry question.[52] Multiple answers were accepted and then coded, including "American" as an ethnic ancestry response. In spite of a format and instructions that discouraged the selection of an "American" identification, out of a total population of 226.5 million, 13.3 million (almost 6 percent) selected "American." Another 6 percent declined to choose any specific ancestries—a group that Lieberson believes contains at least some of "a new group of White Americans who are unable to specify any ethic ancestry."[53]

The sociologist Richard Alba's ethnic identity survey carried out between May 1984 and June 1985 found declining attachment to traditional ethnic identifications.[54] This indicates that "a reshaping is under way, in my estimation—a new ethnic group is emerging among whites."[55] It is, however, not the same as Lieberson's "unhyphenated white" group. The new members of this group, he writes,

> do not define themselves solely in terms of being an American identity (although some do much of the time). . . . Rather they continue to define themselves as European in terms of origin. But, in contrast to the past, . . . the different European ancestries are not seen as the basis for important social divisions; instead *they create the potential for social bonds having an ethnic character, founded on the perception of similar experiences of immigration and social mobility.* This new group can be called . . . European American.[56]

These data, along with the desire for individualism, give some sense of how ethnic identities might be supplemented by a more American one. Ethnicity will not disappear, if Alba and Lieberson are correct, but rather over generations it will fade. In terms of the discussion of American national identity in chapter 3, traditional ethnicity will move from the center to the periphery and lower in the hierarchy of necessary identity elements.[57]

The italicized portion of the Alba quotation above suggests another important mechanism: the sharing of a common experience. One of the hallmarks of a national identity is a shared set of experiences. Immigrants who come here already share a major psychological element of American national identity with Americans: ambition. And as they work their way through and into the American system, they will also acquire a set of common generational and historical experiences. These common experiences can lead to common bonds, and these in turn can become one basis of emotional attachment. It is another important path to One America.

Notes

1. See Somini Sengupta, "Sept. 11 Attack Narrows the Racial Divide Effects," *New York Times*, October 10, 2001; Rick Lyman, "At Least for the Moment, a Cooling Off in the Culture Wars," *New York Times*, November 13, 2001; David Rogers, "House Leaders Bury Hatchet," *Wall Street Journal*, September 20, 2001; and David Rosenbaum, "Congress Joins in Support of President," *New York Times*, September 21, 2001.

2. "The Return of Partisanship" (editorial), *New York Times*, October 13, 2001; Charles Babington, "Era of Bipartisanship Ends Before It Begins," *Washington Post*, March 9, 2001.

3. For a contrary view, see Andrew Sullivan, "Life after Wartime: Lighten Up—The Culture Wars Are Over," *New York Times*, March 18, 2001.

4. Charles Kessler, "The Promise of American Citizenship," in *Immigration & Citizenship in the 21st Century*, ed. Noah M. J. Pickus (Lanham, Md.: Rowman & Littlefield, 1998), 18.

5. Stanley A. Renshon, *America's Second Civil War: Dispatches from the Political Center* (New Brunswick, N.J.: Transaction Press, 2002).

6. Cf. Dale Maharidge, *The Coming White Minority: California's Eruptions and America's Future* (New York: Times Books, 1996). Also see John Isbister, *The Immigration Debate: Remaking America* (New York: Kumarian Press, 1996); and Isbister, "Is America Too White?" in *What, Then Is the American, This New Man?* ed. E. Sandman (Washington, D.C.: Center for Immigration Studies, 1998).

7. These views are summed up by Juan F. Perea, "Am I an American or Not? Reflections on Citizenship, Americanization and Race," in *Immigration & Citizenship in the 21st Century*, ed. Pinkus, 50. But for a different perspective, see Kessler, "Promise of American Citizenship."

8. Rogers M. Smith, *Civic Ideals: Conflicting Visions of Citizenship in U.S. History* (New Haven, Conn.: Yale University Press, 1997).

9. John. J. Miller, *The Unmaking of Americans: How Multiculturalism Has Undermined America's Assimilation Ethic* (New York: Free Press, 1998).

10. Jennifer L. Hochschild, "Black and White Americans' Ambivalence about Equality, or Did Tocqueville Get It Wrong?", paper prepared for conference on America's Ambivalent Egalitarianism: Facts and Perceptions, Gerst Program in Political, Economic, and Humanistic Studies, Duke University, Durham, N.C., April 3–4, 2003.

11. I am indebted to Jennifer Hochschild for permission to draw on this list from her as yet unpublished paper. She asked that the list be viewed in the context of how easy it is for Americans, especially—though not only—whites, to resist claims of equality. Personal communication, April 6, 2003.

12. On assimilation generally, see R. A. Kazal, "Revisiting Assimilation: The Rise, Fall, and Reappraisal of a Concept in American History," *American Historical Review* 100, no. 2 (1995): 437–71. On the question of the demise of assimilation, see Nathan Glazer, "Is Assimilation Dead?" in *Multiculturalism and American Democracy*, ed. Arthur M. Melzer, Jerry Weinberger, and M. Richard Zinman (Lawrence: University of Kansas Press, 1998).

13. Rubén G. Rumbaut, "Assimilation and Its Discontents: Between Rhetoric and Reality," *International Migration Review* 31, no. 4 (1997): 923–60.

14. Alexander Portes and Min Zhou, "Should Immigrants Assimilate?" *Public Interest*, Summer 1994, 18–36.

15. Rumbaut, "Assimilation," 17; see also Peter D. Salins, *Assimilation American Style* (New York: Basic Books, 1996), 56–57.

16. National Research Council, *From Generation to Generation: The Health and Well-Being of Children in Immigrant Families* (Washington, D.C.: National Research Council, 1998). According to Kathleen Mullan Harris (quoted in the press release accompanying the study), who headed the study of 20,000 randomly selected students, "Foreign-born youth experience fewer physical health problems, have less experience with sex, are less likely to engage in delinquent and violent behavior and are less likely to use controlled substances than native-born youth." E.g., foreign-born Mexican

youth are less likely than native-born youth of Mexican parents to miss school for a health or emotional problem, to have learning difficulties, to be obese, or to suffer asthma. They also are less likely to have had sex, to engage in delinquent or violent acts, or to use three or more controlled substances.

17. M. Healy, "Latina Teens Defy Decline in Birth Rates," *Los Angeles Times*, February 13, 1988; Steven A. Holmes, "Hispanic Births in U.S. Reach Record High," *New York Times*, February 13, 1998.

18. Barbara Vobeja and P. Constable, "Hispanic Teens' Birth Rate Ranks First of Ethnic Groups," *Washington Post*, February 13, 1998.

19. James Davidson Hunter, *Cultural Wars: The Struggle to Define America* (New York: Basic Books, 1997), 52; emphasis in original.

20. The relevant statistics are available from U.S. Bureau of the Census, "Projections of the Population of the United States by Age, Sex and Race: 1992–2050," *Current Population Reports*, P-125–1092 (Washington, D.C.: U.S. Government Printing Office, 1992); and U.S. Bureau of the Census, *Statistical Abstract of the United States*, 115th ed. (Washington, D.C.: U.S. Government Printing Office, 1995), table 12.

21. Daniel Wakin, "Scenes of Ritual Flagellation Resonate at Mosque," *New York Times*, April 25, 2003.

22. Elaine Sciolino, "France Envisions a Citizenry of Model Muslims," *New York Times*, May 7, 2003.

23. Andrew Higgins, "Rude Awaking: A Brutal Killing Opens Dutch Eyes to Threat of Terror," *Wall Street Journal*, November 22, 2004,

24. "Orange County Judge Ruling Limits Muslim Women's License Case," *Saint Petersburg Times*, May 17, 2003.

25. Brian Barry, *Culture and Equality* (Cambridge, Mass.: Harvard University Press, 2001), 44–45, 49–50, 319–21.

26. Ibid., 35, 40–44, 295–96, 319–21.

27. Nurith C. Aizenman, "A Rebirth of Traditions: Maternity Wards Adapt to Immigrants' Needs," *Washington Post*, May 12, 2002.

28. Iris Young, "Political and Group Difference: A Critique of the Ideal of Universal Citizenship," *Ethics* 99 (1989): 250–74; and Young, *Justice and the Politics of Difference* (Princeton, N.J.: Princeton University Press, 1990). To a lesser extent, also see William Kymlicka, *Multicultural Citizenship: A Liberal Theory of Minority Rights* (Oxford: Clarendon Press, 1995).

29. Young, "Political and Group Difference," 261. She lists five conditions: (1) exploitation [little benefit from the work they do]; (2) excluded from participation—primarily from the workplace; (3) they live and work under the authority of others with little autonomy; (4) they are stereotyped but also invisible in society; and (5) they suffer random violence. Young denies that her list of the oppressed represents "an unworkable proliferation" of aggrieved groups (*Justice*, 197). But according to one estimate, it covers about 80 percent of the U.S. population; Kymlicka, *Multicultural Citizenship*, 145. Also see Will Kymlicka and Wayne Norman, "Return of the Citizen: A Survey of Recent Work on Citizenship Theory," *Ethics* 104 (1994): 325–81, and especially here 373, n. 26. Having arrived at the radical conclusion that all those persons in the many groups she lists are oppressed and discriminated against, it is a small step

to the equally radical solution she proposes: "differentiated citizenship"; Young, "Political and Group Difference," 258.

30. Young, "Political and Group Difference," 187–89.

31. Ibid., 262.

32. Ibid., 269, n. 20.

33. Ibid., 262.

34. Ibid., 261–62.

35. Ibid., 272.

36. Kymlicka and Norman, "Return of the Citizen," 273; see also Kymlicka, *Multicultural Citizenship*, 83, 108–11. Kymlicka's support is somewhat surprising, given that in his often-cited book on multicultural citizenship, which is often portrayed as advocating unqualified acceptance for Young's position, he is actually quite skeptical that his ideas could or would work (pp. 131–51).

37. Young, "Political and Group Difference," 260. Also see Claus Offe, "Homogeneity and Constitutional Democracy: Coping with Identity Conflicts through Group Rights," *Journal of Political Philosophy* 6, no. 2 (1998): 113–41; the citation here is on 125–30.

38. Kymlicka, *Multicultural Citizenship*, 138.

39. Anne Phillips, "Dealing with Difference: A Politics of Ideas or a Politics of Presence?" *Constellations* 1, no. 1 (1994): 74–91; the citation here is on 76. Also see Boyle, "Home Rule for Women: Power Sharing between Men and Women," *Dalhousie Law Journal* 7 (1983): 790–809; and Martha Minnow, "From Class Action to Ms. Saigon: The Concept of Representation in the Law," *Cleveland State Law Review* 39 (1991): 269–300.

40. Kymlicka, *Multicultural Citizenship*, 139–40.

41. Twomey reports the following: "Capitol Hill applauds the mayor. The downtown suits do, too. The city has come-visit ads on national television, and he's the pitchman, a role Marion Barry probably could not have played. Notorious services— pothole patching, trash gathering, phone answering—are U-turning. James H. Jones, a Ward 4 advisory neighborhood commissioner, found that leaf collection these days is simple (no more mandatory bagging), dependable and frequent, three things it wasn't. The control board is gone, bond ratings are up, and city agencies are emerging from receivership. Anthrax struck; the mayor's team coped." Steve Twomey, "Mayor's Pluses Don't Please Everyone Despite Progress in City, Many Question Williams's Focus and Attitude," *Washington Post*, February 28, 2002.

42. Natalie Hopkinson, "Outlook," *Washington Post*, June 17, 2001; see also William Raspberry, "Racism's New Flavor," *Washington Post*, July 13, 2001.

43. Smith, *Civic Ideals*; Hochschild, "Black and White Americans' Ambivalence"; Kessler, "Promise of American Citizenship"; and Thomas G. West, *Vindicating the Founders: Race, Sex, Class and Justice in the Origins of America* (Lanham, Md.: Rowman & Littlefield, 1997).

44. Charles Taylor, "Shared and Divergent Values," in *Options for a New Canada*, ed. R. L. Watts and D. G. Brown (Toronto: University of Toronto Press, 1991).

45. Thomas Heller reports a discussion at Stanford among Asian students and faculty as to exactly which special accommodations should be granted to each group.

After Chinese, Japanese, and Korean representatives spoke, he writes: "Finally, it was suggested that although the least represented groups [like Southeast Asians] were the most recent historical populations, and therefore had suffered the least historical discrimination in America, their exclusion from populations made them the subjects of virtual discrimination [*they would have been discriminated against if they had been allowed to enter*] as manifested by their absence from American history." Thomas C. Heller, "Modernity, Membership, and Multiculturalism," *Stanford Humanities Review* 5, no. 2 (1997): 5 (emphasis mine). In other words, they were not here to be discriminated against, but would have been had they been here, so that they too count as an oppressed group.

46. Offe, "Homogeneity," 132.

47. Young, "Political and Group Difference," 262.

48. Ibid. Along similar lines, Representative Judith Biggert (R-Ill.) introduced what she thought was a family-friendly bill to allow workers a voluntary choice between paid overtime at time and a half and unpaid leave time calculated on the same basis. According to the *Times* reporter who broke the story, "Lobbyists for dozens of unions as well as some women's groups have flocked to Capitol Hill to fight the bill." Steven Greenhouse, "Bill Offers Option of Compensatory Time," *New York Times*, May 10, 2003. Other women's groups have welcomed the bill as a vehicle for greater personal and family flexibility.

49. Stanley A. Renshon, "Leadership Capital and the Politics of Courage: The President's Initiative on Race," in *One America? Political Leadership, National Identity, and the Dilemmas of Diversity*, ed. Stanley A. Renshon (Washington, D.C.: Georgetown University Press, 2001), 347–93.

50. William J. Clinton, "Remarks in a Roundtable Discussion on Race in Akron" (December 3), *Weekly Compilation of Presidential Documents* 8, no. 33 (1997): 1959–69.

51. Clinton, "Remarks."

52. Stanley Lieberson, "Unhyphenated Whites in the United States," *Ethnic and Racial Studies* 8, no. 1 (1985): 159–80; the citation here is on 171. Also see Stanley Lieberson and Mary C. Waters, "The Ethnic Responses of Whites: What Causes Their Instability, Simplification, and Inconsistency," *Social Forces* 72, no. 2 (1993): 421–50.

53. Lieberson, "Unhyphenated Whites," 172. Lieberson and Waters ("Ethnic Responses," 443, 444) later reported that "the number of children reported as 'American' is 25% more than the number expected if parents had exactly reported children's ancestry." Moreover, when both parents' self-identify as American, 94.4% of their children do as well. Interestingly, when parents report a mixed ethnic (not American) background, 3 to 5 percent of their children end up classified as "American." They see this process as a by-product of increasing intermarriage affecting both marriage partners and their children. Since interethnic marriage is increasing, as are the numbers of persons entering the fourth plus generation after arriving here, the authors believe this is a significant development in identification trends in the United States.

54. Richard D. Alba, *Ethnic Identity: The Transformation of White America* (New Haven, Conn.: Yale University Press, 1990), 321.

55. Ibid., 312.

56. Ibid., 312; emphasis mine.

57. Some movement along these lines already appears to be happening. An Associated Press report on the 2000 census noted "a decline in the number of people identifying themselves as being of Irish, German and other European ancestries. A relatively small, but growing, number of people who live in the United States are simply calling themselves American. . . . The number of people who wrote in 'American' as their ancestry increased to 20 million in 2000 from 13 million in 1990." Associated Press, "Immigration Said to Keep Pace with 1990s," *New York Times*, November 26, 2002.

CHAPTER 5

Hyphenation and National Identity

MULTICULTURAL ADVOCATES BEGIN WITH THE PREMISE THAT A PERson's attachment to an ethnic or racial group is, and ought to be, the primary anchor of his or her identity. They often see national and group attachments as antagonistic rather than compatible, and they urge individuals to resolve this conflict by placing ethnic and racial attachments ahead of American national community attachments. Among those concerned with the nature and quality of the connections that Americans have to each other and their country, this is understandably controversial. In this respect, Nathan Glazer is mistaken; we are not all multiculturalists now.[1]

In placing group identity over national identity, multiculturalists enter "the politics of difference." Michael Walzer argues correctly that "engaged men and women tend to be multiply engaged," by which he presumably means that multiple attachments are a fact and a by-product of an active civic life.[2] Yet, he says, American citizenship is indeed anonymous because it does not require a full commitment to American (or any other) nationality.[3] Maybe. But what level of commitment does it require?

Theorists like Walzer appear to answer: Not much.[4] In the case of hyphenated Americans, he writes, "It doesn't matter whether the first or the second name is dominant."[5] And further, "An ethnic American is someone who can live his life as he chooses, *on either side of the hyphen*."[6] Walzer agrees with Horace Kallen's 1920s brand of liberal pluralism—that individuals really do find their most basic satisfactions in groups, and that ethnic and religious groups provide the most intimate personal relationships and the most intense aspects of emotional life.[7]

Liberals on the Primacy of Group Life

Walzer's position appears to be buttressed by psychological research that finds groups do provide powerful support for individual identity. Of course, the obvious questions are: Which groups and what satisfactions?

101

Walzer writes: "For support and comfort and a sense of belonging, men and women look to their groups; for freedom and mobility, they look to the state."[8] Leaving aside the striking omission of married and family life as one obvious source of comfort and belonging, one wonders why so many Americans then turned to Washington and the president for comfort, reassurance, and protection in the wake of the September 11, 2001, terrorist attacks. Indeed, at times of national tragedy, like the Oklahoma bombing or the assassination of John F. Kennedy, we are much more likely to turn to leaders and other national symbols than we are to visit the websites of the NAACP or the Mexican American Legal Defense and Education Fund (MALDEF).

In fact, national attachment might just provide at least some of the basic emotional satisfaction that Walzer reserves for ethnic and religious groups. Richard Rorty writes that multiculturalism, "in the name of the 'politics of difference,' refuses to rejoice in the country it inhabits. It repudiates the idea of a national identity and the emotion of national pride."[9]

Identifying as an American

Perhaps one reason that Michael Walzer can be disinterested to the point of opposing an American national identity is his inventive, but dated and now inaccurate, solution to the problem of identity and hyphenation. In his view, there is no reason to worry about the relative emotional weight of the terms on each side of the hyphen because *both* are American. He writes:

> It is not the case that Irish Americans, say, are culturally Irish and politically American, as the pluralists [theorists] claim. . . . Rather they are culturally Irish American and politically Irish American. Their culture has been significantly influenced by American culture. . . . With them and with every ethnic and religious group except the American Americans, hyphenation is doubled.[10]

This is an attractive idea and may even have been correct at one time for some groups. Yet notice what this view assumes. It assumes first and foremost that the Irish and "every group" have not only become acculturated—which is to say successful at adapting the surface manifestations of the culture—but also assimilated, that is, identifying with and integrating the core elements of American culture, its patterns of values, understandings, and psychology.[11] Wearing blue jeans is acculturation; believing that individualism trumps group identity is one core element of American psychology and belief. One must question whether all new immigrants are both acculturated *and* assimilated.

Further, using the Irish to represent all groups is questionable on several grounds. The Irish are unlike many other ethnic groups in several ways. They

come from an English-speaking culture, and a culture that has Western traditions as part of its heritage—both of which help facilitate a relatively easy
transition to American culture. Of course, this does not mean that those who
do not come from an English-speaking or Western culture cannot make the
transition. Many have and continue to do so. My point is that the degree of
difficulty associated with doing so is lessened when English is the primary language and Western culture is not foreign.

Moreover, generations of the Irish have now grown up in the United States
and have had several centuries to become Americanized ethnics.[12] The Irish
have been here long enough to both embrace their ethnic group heritage as a
method of mobility and to also allow it to recede once newer generations have
achieved mobility.

The Irish are, of course, European ethnics. The sociologist Richard Alba,
who studied European ethnics, found that "it is hard to avoid the conclusion
that ethnic experience is shallow for the great majority of whites [European
ethnics]."[13] Even by a generous standard of counting, he could find "no more
than one-fifth of native-born whites, who hold intensely to an ethnic identity."[14] Yet this is hardly the pattern of the non-European ethnics for which
we have data.

Are Hispanics Irish?

Consider the Pew Hispanic Center's 2002 survey of 3,000 persons of Hispanic
or Latino background. Among the many useful questions this survey asked
were those that concerned national and ethnic identity. The findings provide
a dramatic caveat to Walzer's double-hyphen theory—we are all Americans
now—and Alba's data on the decline of ethnicity among white Europeans.

The survey asked respondents about the terms they used to describe themselves and found "a large majority of Latinos (88%) indicate that they often
identify themselves by the country where they or their parents or ancestors
were born, for example as a " 'Mexican' or a 'Cuban.' They are almost as likely
to . . . use the term 'Latino' or 'Hispanic.' By contrast they are much less likely
to use the term 'American' (53%)."[15]

Yet percentages tend to obscure the fact that we are discussing large numbers of actual people, numbers in the millions. In July 2004, Hispanics num-
bered 41.3 million out of a national population of nearly 293 million.[16]
Because the Pew Hispanic survey is a stratified sample meant to reproduce,
within a small margin of statistical error, the general Hispanic population of
the United States, we can use its figures to gain some idea of the actual numbers involved with some confidence. So to say that 88 percent of the sample
has referred to themselves primarily in terms of their nationality of origin is
to say that almost 36 million immigrants of Hispanic descent have likely done

so. To say that 81 percent have used a pan-ethnic term to identify themselves means that more than 33 million persons of Hispanic descent are likely to have done so.

One other set of questions, asked only of those *not* born in this country, concerned which country respondents considered their homeland: their country of origin or the United States. Sixty-two percent choose their country of origin.[17] When reminded that "some countries allow people to be legal citizens of their country, even if they are also U.S. citizens," and asked if they were citizens of their home country, 86 percent said yes.[18] If extrapolated to 2004 figures, that would translate into more than 35 million Hispanics who consider themselves citizens of their home country. Approximately 15 percent (more than 6 million) said they had voted in elections in their "home" country since arriving here.[19] It is findings like these that fuel concerns, voiced most recently and forcefully by Samuel Huntington, that "the persistent inflow of Hispanic immigrants threatens to divide the United States into two peoples, two cultures, and two languages."[20] And, he might have added, two identities.

Hyphenation and Identity: Parity versus Primacy

There are several ways to look at the Pew data. One can say that self-identification as an American does reflect some level of integration as attachment increases over generations. Yet one can also point with equal authority to the fact that the country-of-origin and pan-ethnic identifications strongly persist into even the third generation and beyond.

A critical question then becomes, which of these self-identifications is primary? The Pew survey asked respondents which if any of the three identifications they tended to use as their only identification, or which they tended to use first, second, or third.[21] The choices were a country-of-origin identification, a pan-ethnic identification, or an American identification. Our interest here is in those who picked one of the three either as the only one or the first of the three possibilities. The answers are intriguing.

Those who use their country-of-origin identification "only" or "first" constitute 54 percent of the total sample. Those who use a pan-ethnic identification first or only constitute 24 percent of the sample. Finally, those who use an American identification only or first constitute 21 percent of the sample. Translating these percentages into actual numbers of people, it means that after two or more generations here, almost 22 million people still self-identify primarily as members of their ancestral country. And it means that after two generations or more, 24 percent or more than 9 million still make primary use of pan-ethnic identification.

These figures change with length of residence in the United States. Among the foreign born, 68 and 24 percent prefer a country-of-origin or a pan-ethnic identification, respectively, to an American one. Among the native born, those numbers are 29 and 23 percent—lower, but still a majority choosing a non-American identity. These numbers are also related to citizenship status. The Pew survey found: "As might be expected, citizens are much more likely than non-citizens to identify as 'American,' (33% vs. 3%). Nonetheless, Hispanics who are American citizens are still more likely to identify themselves by country of origin (44%) than to identify themselves as primarily 'American,' (33%) or as a 'Latino' or "Hispanic' (22%)."[22]

Allow me to state the point again: Latinos who are American citizens prefer a country-of-origin or pan-ethnic identification (66 percent) to an American one (33 percent). Again, speaking in terms of numbers of real people, that means about 27 million Latinos living here and holding American citizenship prefer not to identify primarily as Americans.

The Pew survey deals with adults, but it is interesting to compare its data with a study that deals with children and young adults. Portes and McLeod found that 25 percent of second-generation children in Southern Florida and Southern California in 1992 identified themselves with a "non-hyphenated Latin nationality" (e.g., Mexican), despite the fact that they had been born and raised in the United States.[23] The sociologist Rubén Rumbaut surveyed over 5,000 immigrant family children. Half were U.S.-born children of immigrants, and half were foreign-born children who immigrated here before they were twelve (the "1.5 generation").[24]

Rumbaut offered each child the opportunity to self-identify by (1) national origin (e.g., Jamaican, Hmong), (2) hyphenated identity (e.g., Mexican American, Filipino American, (3) a plain American identity, or (4) a pan-racial/ethnic identity (e.g., Hispanic, Latino, black).[25] He found a definite trend of adapting a hyphenated American identity from the foreign-born children to those born here (from 32 to 49 percent), and he sees this as indicating a significant assimilative trend. Yet this trend does not apply to all groups.

The most assimilative groups appear to be the Latin Americans, "with the very notable exception of Mexicans. Among the U.S. born less than four percent of Mexican American-descended youth identified as American (the lowest proportion of any group)."[26]

Moreover, among second-generation Mexicans, "a very substantial number identified as Chicano, virtually all of them U.S. born and all of them growing up in California."[27] In fact, a quarter of all Mexican-descended second-generation students self-identified as Chicano. In other words, compared with other second-generation immigrant children (e.g., Asians), Mexicans were far more likely to select a pan-racial/ethnic identity that *did not* include some American component.

The Meaning of Hyphenation

The problem with Rumbaut's study and others like it is that they assume a great deal about the emotional commitments involved in adopting an ethnic American identity and make no effort to further clarify the important differences such terms contain.[28] Consider the hyphenated Irish American identity. Does that person consider himself or herself to be an *Irish* American, an *Irish American,* an Irish *American,* or an *American* of Irish descent? Each of these possible permutations reflects a different level of psychological identification with, and arrangement of, some of the basic building blocks that form our identity. One could almost array these terms from left to right in terms of the degree of an American identification—given an ethnic element.

This somewhat commonsensical view receives some empirical support from a study by Aguirre and his colleagues.[29] Using data from 11,000 Hispanic households, they asked an open-ended question about identity self-definitions and then asked respondents to rank their importance to them. The most prevalent categories were Mexican, Chicano, American of Mexican descent, and American. Using a statistical technique (discriminate function), they write that the choice "validates the arrangement of these ethnic identities into an assimilation continuum." In other words, the choice of identifications *does* reflect something important about attachments and, more specifically, that non-American identifications are associated with a failure to assimilate.

It seems very unlikely that for most Irish their "home country" identifications were either equal to, or more important than, their American identity. Indeed, Alba, whose study included many of Irish descent, noted that "many respondents were at pains to assure the interviewers that they are American far more than Irish Americans or German-Irish Americans."[30] Do these sound like members of a group who do not care which side of the hyphen they live on, if any?

Moreover, the Irish did not demand that Gaelic be taught in their schools, that American history textbooks extol unique Irish contributions, or that the Irish be granted special political or cultural rights, like veto powers over legislation that might affect their group or reserved representation in political institutions. All these are elements of contemporary multiculturalism, and they underscore the differences between assimilation then and ethnic separatism now.

Can anyone seriously argue that such an identity would be chosen as Rumbaut found was the case in second-generation immigrants from Mexico?[31] He found that almost half his respondents selected a pan-racial/ethnic identity, or that another 8 percent of these adolescents would select an identity exclusively allied with national origin. Would a random sample of Irish or Jewish American second-generation children find over 50 percent whose *selected* self-identification did not include an American element? I think not. They wanted to be *Americans*.

The focus on Hispanic identity does not mean this is only a Hispanic issue. They are representative of a new climate in the United States regarding cultural and identity integration. Immigrants from many countries are arriving in vast numbers during the period when the domestic climate has shifted. In fact, they are not the only group struggling to reconcile their attachments to the country they have chosen as their new home.

Consider in this respect Muslim immigrants. In one of the few systematic, in-depth studies of identifications of Muslim immigrants with their country of origin and the United States, Kambiz GhaneaBassiri, an Iranian doctoral student at Harvard University, found that they are extremely ambivalent about this country. More specifically, he found "a significant number of Muslims, particularly immigrant Muslims, do not have close ties or loyalty to the United States."[32] Indeed, his questionnaire showed that 45 percent of his sample of Muslims in Los Angeles and a third of those who had converted to Islam felt more allegiance to a foreign country than to the United States. Thirteen percent were not certain to whom they felt more loyal.

Or consider a survey undertaken by the Council on American-Islamic Relations of mosque leadership in the United States.[33] Eighty-two percent of the mosque leaders agreed that "American society is a technically advanced society that we can learn from." What can they learn? Apparently not the American Creed in which liberal theorists place so much hope for the salvation of our national unity. Only 35 percent of the respondents agreed that "America is an example of freedom and democracy that we can learn from." Worse, that disinclination to see much of merit in America's liberal political institutions apparently extends to American culture more generally. Sixty-seven percent agreed strongly or to some extent that "America is a corrupt, immoral society." Perhaps not surprisingly, these questions were not asked again in a 2004 follow-up study.[34] These figures and the sentiments they represent obviously have to be considered in the context of the September 11 attacks by extremist Islamic terrorists, and we shall do so when considering immigration and national security.

It seems clear that the double (American) hyphenation theory needs revision. Large numbers of new immigrants not only do not self-identify as double-hyphenated Americans; they do not even identify with a term that has American in it. And the actual level of attachment even in ethnic American identifications is wholly unclear. The problem with Walzer's indifference to which side of the hyphen, if either, Americans choose to live by and identify with is that increasingly many, including those who are citizens here, choose to do so in a way that gives little emotional weight to being an American.

Does Discrimination Cause Hyphenation?

An important, indeed central, question—given the evidence that some groups do not appear inclined to adopt an American identity—is very simply, Why? Critics of American political life believe they have found the answer: Discrimination. The researcher Hiromi Ono writes:

> A reported experience of discrimination and darker skin color are linked to three of the four types of ethnic identities. . . . Compared to respondents who do not report an experience of discrimination in the past, respondents who do report [such] an experience are approximately twice as likely to identify themselves as Mexicans. . . . A one-level increase in the darkness of skin color is associated with a 60 percent increase in the risks of identifying with Mexican [*sic*] and with multiple labels excluding American.[35]

Portes is convinced that "in America this process of acculturation carries the price of learning and introjecting one's inferior place in the social hierarchy."[36] Rumbuat emphatically agrees. In the conclusion to his study, he writes, "Those who have experienced being discriminated are less likely to identify as being American."[37]

This is a powerful indictment of America and Americans, *if* it is true. But is it? Widespread racism in America has certainly existed in the past. Stephan and Abigail Thernstrom point out that as late as 1954, the year Gunnar Myrdal's famous book on race, *An American Dilemma*, was published, only 45 percent of whites believed that blacks should have as good a chance as they had to get good jobs. Less than half of whites believed blacks were as smart as whites, and only a third thought blacks should attend the same schools as whites.[38]

But these statistics were almost completely transformed by the early 1970s.[39] For example, by 1972, 97 percent of whites believed blacks should have equal opportunities; 84 percent favored integrated neighborhoods, and 85 percent had no objection to a black neighbor of the same social class. Schulman and his colleagues state the case directly: "On questions concerning equal treatment of blacks and whites in the major public spheres of life (jobs, schools, residential choice, public accommodations, transportation), there has been a strong and generally steady movement of white attitudes from denial to affirmation of equality—so much so that certain questions have been dropped by survey organizations because answers were approaching 100% affirmation."[40]

These data deal with blacks, not with ethnic minorities like Hispanics or Mexicans. Perhaps Americans have simply transferred their old discriminatory views to newer ethnic minorities. But that is not the case according to recent survey data, which found that "stereotypes of Hispanics . . . though deeply rooted in the United States, seem to have become less negative over the years."[41]

Moreover, as a recent international study of forty-four countries by the Pew Foundation demonstrates, the United States is one of the most tolerant countries in the world. In the words of the survey report, "Americans express significantly more tolerance towards ethnic minorities than do Europeans. The U.S. public has overwhelmingly positive views of the country's two largest ethnic minorities—African Americans and Hispanics. . . . Western Europeans, by contrast, have a much more negative opinion of the ethnic minorities in their countries."[42]

One could argue that people may say one thing in surveys, but that actual behavior is another.[43] This might be one basis for the apparently wide-ranging discrimination—driven by a view of certain racial or ethnic groups as inferior—reported in the Rumbaut and Ono studies. But these studies are not necessarily reliable.

How did Rumbaut know that American non-identifiers had been discriminated against? He asked them. For Ono, the information was contained in a single straightforward question about having been discriminated against, although its exact phasing is not reported. The options were "yes" or "no." For the skin color question, interviewers coded the shade of the respondent's skin. The author noted, "In the United States, where non-Hispanic whites tend to have advantages, dark skin is probably a good proxy to capture a basis for ethnic/racial discrimination by others in competitive settings."[44]

No evidence is given for this bald statement. Darker skin color is simply assumed to be synonymous with discrimination experiences. The author could have presented the correlation between the question on experienced discrimination and skin color coding to buttress the point, but did not. Why not?[45]

The questions in both surveys are self-reports of experience that leave it up to the respondents to define the experience and the term. How does the respondent define discrimination—a look, a slur, not getting a job? We do not know.

The point is underscored by an incident reported by the Pulitzer Prize–winning reporter David K. Shipper.[46] He writes that Roger Wilkins, a black civil rights leader, approached Missouri senator John Danforth in a Senate office building. He introduced himself by saying: "Hello, Senator, I'm Roger Wilkins," to which Senator Danforth replied, "Hello, Roger."

Wilkins used the encounter to demonstrate to Shipper, who is white, the entrenched racist attitudes of condescension. Shipper countered that the senator may have just been informal and friendly. Wilkins replied that he would never have answered a white man that way.

A year later, Shipper attended another speech by Senator Danforth. At the conclusion, Shipper walked up to Danforth and introduced himself with his full name. "Hello, David," Danforth replied. When Shipper relayed this to Wilkins sometime later, Wilkins acknowledged that politicians use first names to decrease distance—but then argued that Danforth should have known better than to address a black man of his generation by his first name. He then went on to add that Danforth was obviously tone deaf on race, as evidenced by the fact that he had supported placing Clarence Thomas on the Supreme Court. With all that being said, was Danforth's earlier "Hello, Roger" comment truly race-based condescension? The answer is far from self-evident.

Who Discriminates against Hispanics?

Rubén Rumbaut's respondents did report discrimination, and it did correlate with the selection of a non-American identity. And many of the respondents to the Pew Hispanic survey did report experiences of discrimination.

The Pew survey asked a number of questions of Hispanics about their experiences with discrimination generally, and more specifically in the workplace and in school. They also asked about the form such discrimination took—being treated with less respect, receiving poorer service, or being called names and insulted. All these questions suffer from the same drawback of other self-placement questions. They depend on the perceptions and attributions of the respondents.[47]

Still, with that caveat in mind, their data are instructive. More than eight in ten of the Latinos surveyed reported that discrimination against Latinos is a problem that prevents Latinos from succeeding in the United States.[48] Asked whether discrimination was a major or minor problem, respondents said the following: in schools (major = 38 percent, minor = 37 percent), in the workplace (major = 41 percent, minor = 37 percent), and generally (major = 44 percent, minor = 38 percent). Interestingly, respondents who were "Spanish dominant" in their language use were much more likely (55 percent) than "English dominant" (29 percent) to report that discrimination was a major problem generally, in schools (48 vs. 25 percent) and the workplace (51 vs. 27 percent).

Clearly, there is a perception of a substantial amount of discrimination. But is this justified? For all the discrimination reported, only 15 percent of the sample said they had had a *personal* experience with discrimination of any kind, in any place.[49]

Any level of discrimination is too much. Yet theories that explain failures to identify as American with the experience of rampant discrimination have an obligation to be exceedingly careful with the nature and limits of their measures—which is not often the case.

Many will assume, without much further reflection, that the perpetrators of discrimination being discussed above are non-Hispanic whites. Certainly, the discussions by Ono and Rumbaut leave that distinct impression, and they may accord with the personal views of the authors.[50] Yet the Pew data suggest that there is a large and unexamined elephant in the room.

Perhaps because white prejudice toward blacks has been such a pervasive problem in the United States, many ignore the fact that minorities discriminate against minorities as well. Perhaps not so surprisingly, according to the Pew study, Hispanics also discriminate—against other Hispanics. Asked directly whether Hispanic discrimination against other Hispanics is a problem, 47 percent said it was a major one and 36 percent called it minor. Only 16 percent said it was not a problem at all. (Pew either did not ask or did not report whether respondents had a personal experience with Hispanic discrimination.) It is impossible to say with any precision how much of the general and personal discrimination reported is actually discrimination against Hispanics by Hispanics. Clearly, some portion of it is likely to be. And to the extent that it is, there is further cause to doubt that self-reported experiences of discrimination—presumably by whites—account for low levels of identification with an American identity.

In short, the easy answer that discrimination causes a lack of identification with American identity is suspect. We need to look elsewhere.

America's Ambivalent Support of Its National Identity

The attempt to consolidate and expand group identities in the United States owes a great deal to the actions of the American government. America gives its citizens and immigrants mixed signals regarding individualism and group attachment. On one hand, we laud the former; on the other, at the same time we encourage the latter. This encouragement takes many forms. In its most unexceptional form, it is reflected in the many public ethnic holidays and festivals throughout the year. A slightly more complicated manifestation is the attempt to instill ethnic pride as part of the public educational curriculum. More problematic still are the many ways in which ethnic identification is officially encouraged and rewarded by the many programs that count by race and ethnicity and the many more that emphasize retaining or enhancing ethnic languages.

Multiculturalism and Ethnic Counting

Almost from its inception, America has counted its citizens by race.[51] From the problematic "three-fifths" count of "freed men" in the Constitution to the infamous "one drop of blood" as a method for maintaining racial caste boundaries, racial counting has often been divisive and oppressive.

Modern racial counting, however, is not undertaken to exclude but to ensure racial inclusion, or so the argument goes. How could one know if discrimination existed without knowing anything about the numbers of people who belonged to various racial and ethnic groups and their representation in various occupation categories? Thus, beginning with the Richard Nixon administration, the government got into the ethnic/racial counting business in a large way.[52] Some liberals and conservatives agreed that America needed to count by race and ethnicity. However, the obvious questions are: How do we count it, and how do we use the information?

Race and ethnicity in the form of either an observer's ascription or a respondent's self-identification carry with them consequences. Both race and ethnicity are summary categories, like socioeconomic status, that carry within them many complex psychological and developmental processes. When we say that someone is in the middle class, we are also saying something about their motivation, their work habits, their educational history, and so on. Similarly, when we speak of a person's ethnicity, we are summarizing a complex amalgam of identifications and experiences.[53]

Former president Bill Clinton had warned that our growing diversity is "potentially a powder keg of problems, and heartbreak and division and loss."[54] Clinton concluded that how America handled diversity would be the biggest determinant of its future position in the world.[55] Three months later, the Clinton administration decided against adding a "multiracial" category to the 2000 census.[56]

What President Clinton did allow was the addition of a number of new classification categories and the option of allowing respondents to check more than one category. Is that not the functional equivalent of having a multicultural category? Yes, to some degree, but not in the way it was used. The multicultural category would have provided a nonspecific alternative to government-sponsored color coding of the population, a goal envisioned in the idea he adapted by using the phrase "One America" to describe his national conversation on race.[57]

Civil rights groups worried that a multicultural category would dilute their numbers and thus their clout. They raised reasonable concerns about the role that such a nonspecific category would have on the nation's ability to monitor its commitment to access and opportunity. How, exactly, would these numbers be counted?

A draft Office of Management and Budget (OMB) memo for the use of such numbers established that "responses that combine one minority race and white are allocated to the minority race."[58] In other words, for counting purposes, any person who checked the category "white," and any other minority box, would become a minority. Is an American born of an Asian and Italian mother and father a minority? Apparently so. Is an American born of a naturalized American father who traveled here from Spain who also has a mother who emigrated here from Morocco a minority? According to the OMB, yes.

This approach has the effect of adding minorities in need of special assistance and preference. In doing so, the Clinton administration preserved the increasingly divisive single race/ethnicity categories. And in the process, it took a step away from helping to nurture a "group that is quintessential American— emphasized the melting pot quality of the population rather than the distinctions"[59]—the very outcome that the president had said he championed.

Multiculturalism and English

The abilities to speak, read, and write English are tools for successful integration into American society. Yet functional English fluency has become part of the "contested discourse" of immigration. It would seem commonsensical to view English language skills as an important tool—not only for the economic advancement of immigrants (not to mention natives) but also to help integrate immigrants into American society.[60] Moreover, given the great weight given to "the American Creed"—a belief in and support of democracy and representative government—as well as the ability to take part in it, it would be hard to argue against the need for immigrants to learn as much English as they can, and as quickly as possible. But that is not necessarily the case.

Learning English is actually controversial. The Bilingual Education Act of 1967–68 developed by Texas senator Ralph Yarborough was specifically designed to increase English facility. It was not proposed or understood as an original-language maintenance measure, nor was its purpose to create or maintain language islands, or to create non-English dominant bilinguals.[61] Today that specific attempt to respond to Mexican American children who are educationally at risk has spawned a vast, invested bureaucracy supported by teachers' unions and by immigration advocacy groups like MALDEF and their political allies.

Some of the same players strenuously objected when, as part of the first large general amnesty for illegal aliens, the Immigration and Reform Control Act of 1986 (IRCA), the bill's sponsors tried to include English language and civics instruction for those who wanted to become legalized. A key sponsor of this legislation, Representative Jim Wright (D-Tex.), proposed a two-year waiting period before legalization, during which candidates could work but also learn English and civics.[62] Wright specifically eschewed the idea of a melting pot in which every different group would become mixed together in one undifferentiated whole. Rather, he wanted to give immigrants an opportunity to fit into American society in their own way. That argument won support from both liberals and conservatives and helped to break the legislative impasse that had stalled the bill. It passed Congress and was signed into law by President Ronald Reagan on November 6, 1986.

No sooner had the bill been signed than the agreements that had allowed it unraveled. Contentious debates broke out over the exact meaning of "civic instruction" for immigrants. The nature of the proposed education program and test sparked heated controversy. All questions concerning these understandings had been left to the Immigration and Naturalization Service. Money allocated for civic and language education was in turn made available to various governmental (schools, state offices) and nongovernmental (labor, religious, ethnic, and legal) organizations. Each hired its own teachers, who in turn initially determined the conditions for "satisfactory" progress and completion. Standards differed, to put it mildly.

After much debate, the content of the program was turned over to ethnic and immigrant advocacy groups.[63] Attendance, not demonstrated competence, warranted a certificate of satisfactory completion. What had started out as a minimum of 60 hours for completion of a proposed 100-hour program floundered—critics complained that such requirements were "excessive" and "burdensome." Immigration and Naturalization Service officials finally settled on 40 course hours of a 60-hour program. The full course of instruction had been reduced by 40 percent, and the amount of time necessary to attend in order to "pass" was reduced a further 20 percent. As Pickus notes, in an understatement, "The actual programs that developed [under IRCA] did not reflect Wright's goals."[64]

William Kymlicka, an advocate of a "multicultural nationalism" that features specific group rights for cultural minorities, notes that "the commitment to ensure a common language has been a consistent feature of the history of [American] immigration policy."[65] Yet he views that commitment as an insistence on "Anglo-conformity," a demand he believes should be resisted in the name of encouraging group cultural rights. Nor is he alone.

Peter Spiro, a law school professor, writes that "the requirement that naturalization applicants demonstrate English-language literacy presents for many the most formidable obstacle to the acquisition of citizenship."[66] He would like to lessen the requirement and really sees no need for it. How much of a barrier is it? Even though his own figures make this unclear,[67] Spiro claims that "naturalization law is a real instrument of exclusion and subordination."[68] But not much analytical traction is gained by using the term "subordination," which implies domination and illegal discrimination. If that were truly the case, the United States would have to adopt an open, unrestricted admissions immigration policy.

Just how important is English-language mastery to becoming an American? More than 36,000 students were interviewed in 1980 and again in 1982 to find out whether ethnic identifications persisted, and if so why. The findings are quite clear, "Persons for whom Spanish was an important communication tool almost never (1.1%) switched [away from an ethnic identification], while English-speaking monolinguals switched to a non-Hispanic Identity at a high rate (57%)."[69]

The same set of findings was repeated with a large survey of immigrants conducted in 1992. This survey found that among second-generation youth, those who spoke English very well were much more likely to choose a strictly American or hyphenated American identity. Those who used a language other than English with their parents or their friends were much more likely not to choose a strictly American or hyphenated American identity.[70]

In his major survey of adolescents, Rumbaut found that "respondents who prefer English and who speak only English with their close friends are significantly more likely to identify as American, and less likely to be defined by national origin. Conversely, youths who do not prefer English and who report greater fluency in their parents' native languages are most apt to identify by national origins."[71]

That relationship was confirmed by the Pew Hispanic study already discussed. They note that while time in the United States is associated with more of a likelihood to identify as an American, "it is only among Latinos whose families have been in the United States for multiple generations and among those who say that English is their primary language that a majority of respondents select the term 'American' as their primary identification."[72] In other words, speak English and you are likely to self-identify as an American; identify as an American, and you will most likely be speaking English.

Hyphenation Revisited

Hyphenation has a long history in the United States. It is a paradox of American ethnic identities that this country often provides more expansive identities than those with which immigrants arrived. The prototypical case is the Southern Italian worker who may have had little attachment to Italy—yet who developed that consciousness after arriving.[73] Less remarked upon is that the same was true, to some extent, of groups like Norwegians and Swedes.[74]

One contemporary example of this phenomenon is the designation of Latino/ Latina to cover anyone who speaks Spanish, regardless of the country and culture from which they arrived. Massey has argued, "There is no Hispanic population in the sense that there is a black population. Hispanics share no common historical memory and do not comprise a single, coherent community. Saying that someone is Hispanic or Latino reveals little or nothing about likely attitudes, behaviors, beliefs, race, religion, class or legal situation in the United States."[75]

Recall the voices from President Clinton's One America forums presented in the last chapter. Here is the voice of another immigrant, Anna Arroyo. She recalled her experience as a Puerto Rican in a college course on Latin America, indicating that her classmates thought that because of her origin she should be able to speak authoritatively on all Latin cultures. However, she said, "What people don't understand is that I'm not Peruvian; I'm not Mexican. I don't understand their culture. I'm Puerto Rican and all I know is Puerto Rico."

Group attachments have always been a vehicle for socioeconomic and political advancement. City Hall facilitated the upward mobility by the Irish in Boston. Koreans and others depend on their fellow group members for employment and advancement. Group solidarity among new immigrants is as American as individualism.

Why should this be a concern now? The answer lies in the different nature of American society then and now—and in the changed role of government and policy with regard to ethnicity and identification.

Researchers generally agree that ethnic labeling by government increases the tendency of individuals so categorized to so identify.[76] One obvious reason for this is that government commands power and prestige. If it is the government's official policy that you should consider yourself a particular kind of ethnic, then the government is sending a clear message that you should.

Immigrants can be excused if they are confused by a mixed message from the U.S. government. First, they are asked to take an oath of allegiance requiring them to renounce their former national allegiance. At the same time, they are asked to maintain their identity to their "home" country. Immigrants may well come to consider that in following the government's message to retain their group identity they are assimilating into American culture.

It is one thing for government to declare that ethnicity is acceptable and another to signal that it is preferable. American government at all levels, and many major private institutions in business and education, do more than facilitate pan-ethnic identifications—they encourage it. Many federal, state, local government, business, and education programs distribute resources on a preferential basis of ethnic and racial classifications. These include contracts, jobs, admissions to many public and private institutions, and stipends and fellowships. They thus reward individuals who make claims on the basis of group identity.

Yet it is not only the extensiveness of preferences that makes this issue different today than in the past. Now, group identifications are no longer viewed as transitional. Let us consider the Irish and other European (Eastern and

Western) ethnic groups. Yes, throughout their histories in the United States, individual members of these groups have banded together for comfort, information, and mobility. Yet as members of these groups began to branch out socially, economically, and interpersonally, through such mechanisms as cross-ethnic friendships and intermarriage, the old ties became more symbolic than practical. Today, European ethnics are more American than otherwise.[77]

There are many reasons to question whether today's immigrants will see the uses of group membership as a transition to a more clearly identified American identity. It is basic human psychology to prefer not to give up positions that confer an advantage. The incentive structures built into ethnic identifications are powerful, and they are maintained by numerous influential and prestigious American institutions. Moreover, no reasonable timetable has ever been given for ending them voluntarily. The answer to such questions is always: Not yet—or only when discrimination has been wiped out.

There is one further difference between then and now: the fact that the integration of ethnic groups in the United States is no longer solely a matter of domestic national policy or politics. The integration of immigrants today takes place in a context in which allegiances to extranational organizations, institutions, and other countries represent an unprecedented mix of additional and potentially dangerous complications. We turn next to them.

Notes

1. Nathan Glazer, *We Are All Multiculturalists Now* (Cambridge, Mass.: Harvard University Press, 1997).

2. Quoted by Tony Smith, *Foreign Entanglements: The Power of Ethnic Groups in the Making of American Foreign Policy* (Cambridge, Mass.: Harvard University Press, 2001), 137.

3. Michael Walzer, *What It Means to Be an American: Essays on the American Experience* (New York: Marisilio, 1996), 45.

4. In arguing for dual citizenship, Schuck and Spiro write: "We should encourage the assimilation of immigrants *who want* to become full Americans." Peter M. Schuck and Peter J. Spiro, "Dual Citizens, Good Americans," *Wall Street Journal,* March 18, 1998; emphasis mine.

5. Walzer, *What It Means to Be an American*, 45.

6. Ibid., 45; emphasis in original.

7. Ibid., 39. Miller calls Kallen the grandfather of multiculturalism; John. J. Miller, *The Unmaking of Americans: How Multiculturalism Has Undermined America's Assimilation Ethic* (New York: Free Press, 1998), 80.

8. Miller, *Unmaking of Americans*, 67.

9. Walzer approaches the idea that perhaps an American identity might be important. Writing of Kallen's support of the ways in which groups protected the "excellence

appropriate to their kind," Walzer wonders "what if the 'excellence' appropriate to 'our kind' is, simply, an American excellence?" Walzer, *What It Means to Be an American*, 40. Richard Rorty, "The Unpatriotic Academy," *New York Times*, February 13, 1994.

10. Ibid., 47.

11. My usage here departs from some traditional formulations of these terms. Gordon adapts the Social Science Research Council's mid-1930s definition of acculturation as the outcome of the meeting of two different groups in which each culture is influenced by the other. Milton Gordon, *Assimilation in American Life* (New York: Oxford University Press, 1964), 61. He goes on to list numerous definitions of assimilations (pp. 62–68, 71), before presenting his list of seven different forms of assimilation: cultural, structure, marital, identificational, attitude receptional, behavioral receptional, and civic. My use of the term "acculturation," denoting a surface accommodation, is consistent with Gans's useful term "symbolic ethnicity." Herbert Gans, "Symbolic Ethnicity: The Future of Ethnic Groups and Cultures in America," *Ethnic and Racial Studies* 2 (1979): 1020; see also Richard D. Alba, *Ethnic Identity: The Transformation of White America* (New Haven, Conn.: Yale University Press, 1990), 75–123.

12. Patrick. J. Blessing, "Irish," in *Harvard Encyclopedia of American Ethnic Groups*, ed. Stephan Thernstrom (Cambridge, Mass.: Belknap Press, 1980). Gordon, *Assimilation*, 86.

13. Alba, *Ethnic Identity*, 297.

14. Ibid., 294.

15. Pew Hispanic Center, "National Survey of Latinos: Summary of Findings," December 2002, http://www.pewhispanic.org, 9. Another way to look at these data is to ask if there are any generational effects, and there are. Figures for the first, second, and third generations and beyond showed the following: A total of 95 percent of first-generation Hispanics sometimes used a country-of-origin self-designation. That decreases to 82 percent in the second generation and 66 percent in the third. Eighty-five percent of first generation use a pan-ethnic identification, and that decreases—but less so over time, with 77 percent of second-generation respondents doing so and 72 percent of third-generation respondents doing so.

16. D'Vera Cohn, "Hispanic Growth Surge Fueled by Births in U.S.," *Washington Post*, June 9, 2005.

17. Pew Hispanic Center, "National Survey of Latinos: Topline Final," December 2002, 47, question 88; available at http://www.pewhispanic.org. It is unfortunate that the survey either chose not to ask or else report the same questions for native-born Latinos as it did for almost all the other questions it asked.

18. Ibid., 46, question 83.

19. Ibid., 44, question 83.

20. Samuel P. Huntington, "The Hispanic Challenge," *Foreign Policy*, March/April 2004, 1. See also Huntington, *Who Are We? The Challenges to American National Identity* (New York: Simon & Schuster, 2004).

21. Pew Hispanic Center, "National Survey of Latinos: Topline Final," 21.

22. Pew Hispanic Center, "National Survey of Latinos: Summary of Findings," 31.

23. Alexandro Portes and D. McLeod, "What Should I Call Myself? Hispanic Identity Formulation in the Second Generation," *Ethnic and Racial Studies* 19, no. 3 (1996): 523–47; the citation here is from table 1.

24. Rubén G. Rumbaut, "The Crucible Within: Ethnic Identity, Self Esteem and Segmented Assimilation among Children of Immigrants," *International Migration Review* 28, no. 4 (1994): 748–94. Rumbaut, "Assimilation and Its Discontents: Between Rhetoric and Reality," *International Migration Review* 31, no. 4 (1997): 923–60.

25. Rumbaut says that the last two categories (three and four) are exclusively identities "made in America," and that the last (four) represent "a denationalized identification with racial ethnic minority groups in the country of destination, and self-conscious differences in relation to the white [*sic*] Anglo majority population." "Crucible Within," 763. He then counts together those who select a plain American identification (11 percent) and those who select a panracial/ethnic identification (21 percent) because they are not connected to their origins but to their "American present" and both are "made in the U.S.A."

This is unwarranted. First, Rumbaut is certainly incorrect in not including a hyphenated ethnic American identity as "made in the U.S.A." and connected to their "American present." Where else would one learn or have such an identity? Second, the idea that "a dissimilative racial or ethnic pan identity" represents a self-conscious choice of identification taken to accentuate their differences with the "white Anglo majority population," is certainly a possibility, but no data are presented to support it. Furthermore, it is inconsistent with the fact that almost 70 percent of Hispanics choose "white" to designate their race on the 2000 U.S. Census.

26. Rumbaut, "Crucible Within," 765.

27. Ibid.

28. E.g., Hiromi Ono presents an extremely muddled conceptualization of identification that renders the article's findings essentially useless. Using data from a 1990 sample, some categories had to be combined because of small numbers in some cells. Hiromi Ono, "Assimilation, Ethnic Competition, and Ethnic Identities of U.S.-Born Persons of Mexican Origin," *International Migration Review* 36 (2000): 726–45. So, on p. 733 (emphasis mine), respondents were first divided into whether they use a single or two or more identities. American identities were then taken out of each category, leaving four: (1) single identification as an American, (2) single identification as a non-American, (3) multiple identifications *including American*, and (4) multiple identifications excluding American. We then learn the following anonymous fact. "Two categories—Mexican or Mexicano (*N* = 117) and Mexican American (*N* = 184)—account for approximately 75% of the cases that use a single identity other than American." How a hyphenated ethnic American identification can count as a case single identity is unclear.

29. R. E. Aguirre, Rogelio Saenz, and Sean-Shong Hwang, "Discrimination and the Assimilation and Ethnic Competition Perspectives," *Social Science Quarterly* 70, no. 3 (1989): 594–606.

30. Alba, *Ethnic Identity*, 41.

31. Rumbaut, "Crucible Within," 764, table 2.

32. Kambiz GhaneaBassiri, *Competing Visions of Islam in the United States: A Study of Los Angeles* (Westport, Conn.: Greenwood Press, 1997), 45.

33. Ihsan Bagby, Paul M. Perl, and Bryan T. Froehle, *The Mosque in America: A National Portrait* (Washington, D.C.: Council on American-Islamic Relations, 2001), available at httpı//www.cair-net.org.

34. Ihsan Bagby, *Detroit Mosques: Muslim Views on Policy, Politics, and Religion* (Clinton Township, Mich.: Institute for Social Policy and Understanding, 2004).

35. Ono, "Assimilation," 736–39.

36. Alejandro Portes, "Toward a New World: The Origins and Effects of Transnational Activities," *Ethnic and Racial Studies* 22 (March 1999): 463–77; the citation here is on 472. Elsewhere (p. 476), speaking of the United States, Portes states, "Discrimination and contempt are commonly found in the host society."

37. Rumbaut, "Crucible Within," 789. Note the slip from reporting on *perceived* discrimination—to simply saying, "Those who have experienced being discriminated are less likely to identify as being American." The correct phrase, of course, should be "those who say they have been discriminated against."

38. Stephan Thernstrom and Abigail Thernstrom, *America in Black and White: One National Indivisible* (New York: Simon & Schuster, 1997), 499–500.

39. Ibid., 500.

40. Howard Schuman, Charlotte Steen, Lawrence Bobo, and Maria Krysan, *Racial Attitudes in America* (Cambridge, Mass.: Harvard University Press, 1997), 191.

41. Lee Sigelman, James W. Schockey, and Carol K. Sigelman, "Ethnic Sterotyping: A Black White Comparison," in *Prejudice, Politics, and the American Dilemma,* ed. Paul M. Sniderman, Phillip E. Tetlock, and Edward G. Carmines (Stanford, Calif.: Stanford University Press, 1993), 104.

42. Pew Global Attitudes Project, "Views of a Changing World," available at http://people-press.org, 112.

43. R. La Piere, "Attitudes and Actions," *Social Forces* 13 (1934): 230–37.

44. Ono, "Assimilation," 735.

45. Rumbaut ("Crucible Within," 760) asks if the person has been discriminated against, and if so why, and by whom. He asks respondents to note how much they agree with the statement "no matter how much education I get, people will still discriminate against me." He reports the responses to these questions separately but there is a problem with the relationship between these two questions. People who believe they will always be discriminated against no matter what might well report more discrimination. He does not report that data.

46. David K. Shipper, *A Country of Strangers: Blacks and Whites in America* (New York: Vintage Books, 1997), 450–51.

47. Pew Hispanic Center, "National Survey of Latinos: Topline Final," 32–35, questions 57–66. E.g., respondents were asked if they had ever been denied a job or promotion because of their race or ethnicity (Pew Hispanic Center, "National Survey of Latinos: Summary of Findings," chart 4.4). Presumably, race or ethnicity was not the reason given by the employer, so the response obviously reflects an inference. Whether and to what extent alternative explanations were considered—another person better qualified, failings of respondent, etc.—cannot be ascertained from such inferences.

48. Pew Hispanic Center, "National Survey of Latinos: Summary of Findings," 72.

49. Pew Hispanic Center, "National Survey of Latinos: Topline Final," 34, question 60. Asked (in question 60) whether they or a member of their family had experienced discrimination during the last five years, 68 percent said no and 31 percent said yes.

50. I once attended a lecture at the New School by Rubén Rumbaut in which he casually characterized the United States as a racist society.

51. Melissa Nobles, *Shades of Citizenship: Race and the Census in Modern Politics* (Stanford, Calif.: Stanford University Press, 2000). Also see Nobles, "Racial Categorization and the Census," in *Census and Identity: The Politics of Race, Ethnicity and Language in Censuses,* ed. David I. Kerzner and Dominique Arel (New York: Cambridge University Press, 2002).

52. For an analysis of how racial categories came to be used and misused in the federal government's effort to count by race, see Peter Skerry, "Do We Really Want Immigrants to Assimilate?" *Society,* March–April 2000, 57–60. See also Nobles, *Shades of Citizenship;* Nobles, "Racial Categorization"; Joel Pearlman and Mary C. Waters, eds., *The New Race Question: How the Census Counts Multiracial Individuals* (Washington, D.C.: Brookings Institution Press, 2002); John D. Skrentny, "Reinventing Race," *The Public Interest* 145 (2001): 97–113; and Skrentny, *The Minority Rights Revolution* (Cambridge, Mass.: Harvard University Press, 2002). For a very thoughtful examination of classification systems, including racial ones, see Geoffrey C. Bowker and Susan Leigh Starr, *Sorting Things Out: Classification and Its Consequences* (Cambridge, Mass.: MIT Press, 1999).

53. As rates of intermarriage in the United States increase among almost all ethnic groups, it is important to consider the question of where "pure" race or ethnic categories are not only scientifically misleading but also politically injurious.

54. William J. Clinton, "Remarks and Question and Answer Session with the American Society of Newspaper Editors" (April 11, 1997), *Weekly Compilation of Presidential Documents* 33, no. 15 (April 14): 501–10; the citation here is on 509.

55. Ibid., 509.

56. Office of Management and Budget, "Recommendations from the Interagency Committee for the Review of the Racial and Ethnic Standards to the Office of Management and Budget Concerning Standards for the Classification of Federal Data on Race and Ethnicity, Notice," *Federal Register* 62, no. 131 (1997): 36844–946.

57. For an analysis of President Clinton's national race initiative, see Stanley A. Renshon, "Leadership Capital and the Politics of Courage: The President's Initiative on Race," in *One America? Political Leadership, National Identity, and the Dilemmas of Diversity,* ed. Stanley A. Renshon (Washington, D.C.: Georgetown University Press, 2001), 347–93. The earliest use of the phrase "One America" in the context of assimilation and integration issues that I been able to locate is in a post–World War II book extolling the contributions and problems of different racial and ethnic groups in American life: Francis J. Brown and Joseph S. Roucek, eds., *One America: The History, Contributions, and Present Problems of Our Racial and National Minorities,* rev. ed. (New York: Prentice-Hall, 1945). President Richard Nixon picked up the phrase for use in a radio address shortly before the presidential elections extolling the virtues of nondivisive campaigns. Richard M. Nixon, "Radio Address: One America," *Weekly Compilation of Presidential Documents,* October 28, 1973.

58. Office of Management and Budget, "Recommendations from the Interagency Committee for the Review of Racial and Ethnic Standards to the Office of Management and Budget Concerning Changes to the Standards for the Classification of Federal Data on Race and Ethnicity; Notice," *Federal Register* 62, no. 131 (July 1977): 36873–946; see also Office of Management and Budget, "Recommendations from the

Interagency Committee"; and Office of Management and Budget, "Draft Provisional Guidance on the Implementation of the 1997 Standards for the Collection of Federal Data on Race and Ethnicity," February 17, 1999.

59. Jerelyn Eddings, "Counting a New Type of American: The Dicey Politics of Creating a Multiracial Category in the Census," *U.S. News & World Report*, July 14, 1977, 22–23.

60. Peter D. Salins, *Assimilation American Style* (New York: Basic Books, 1996), 6.

61. Harold F. Schiffman, *Linguistic Culture and Language Policy* (New York: Routledge, 1996), 240; Heinz Kloss, *The American Bilingual Tradition* (Rowley, Mass.: Newbury House, 1997), 37.

62. An excellent analysis of this bill and the subsequent fate of its provisions can be found in Noah M. Jedidiah Pickus, "Truth, Faith and Allegiance: Immigration and the Politics of Citizenship," Ph.D. diss., Princeton University, 1995, 123–34. I draw here on that account.

63. Ibid., 131.

64. Ibid., 127.

65. William Kymlicka, *Multicultural Citizenship: A Liberal Theory of Minority Rights* (Oxford: Clarendon Press, 1995), 15.

66. Peter J. Spiro, "Questioning Barriers to Naturalization," *Georgetown Immigration Law Journal* 13 (1999): 479–517; the citation here is on 489.

67. Spiro, "Questioning Barriers," n. 33, drawing on a 1998 Price Waterhouse draft report on 7,843 naturalization filings, states that 34 percent of all failed efforts were due to the results on the English and civics test. Because no information is given, we cannot know what each contributed to those numbers. Spiro then quotes a release from the same company dated one year later that gives the combined figure as 10 percent for 1998.

We are then told that an initial failure results in the chance to take a retest and that of the 45 percent of cases that are continued (e.g., no final decision was made), 25 percent were because of a failed test. Is that 25 percent of 34 percent or of 10 percent? And if it is the former, why were not all 34 percent who failed the test given a second chance? How many applicants passed on their second or subsequent tries is not reported by Spiro. However, he does report the percentage of no-shows "which account for one-third for all denials." He "expects" that some of these no-shows are in fact a result of the testing requirement, and in this he is quite likely correct. Of course, the major issue is not the numbers that pass one or the other test on the first, second, or subsequent tests, but rather whether it serves public purposes to have them.

68. Ibid., 479.

69. Karl Eschbauch and Christina Gomez, "Choosing Hispanic Identity: Ethnic Identity Switching among Respondents to High School and Beyond," *Social Science Quarterly* 79, no. 1 (1998): 74–90; the citation here is on 83.

70. Portes and McLeod, "What Should I Call Myself?"

71. Rumbaut, "Crucible Within," 780.

72. Pew Hispanic Center, "National Survey of Latinos: Summary of Findings," 25.

73. Nathan Glazer, "Ethnic Groups in America," in *Freedom and Control in Modern Society*, ed. M. Berger and T. Abel (New York: Van Nostrand, 1954).

74. Andrew M. Greeley, *Why Can't They Be Like Us? America's White Ethnic Groups* (New York: E. P. Dutton, 1971), 21.

75. Espiritu has argued that pan-ethnic terms in the United States are largely a product of categorization. An imposed category ignores subgroup boundaries, lumping together diverse peoples in a single expanded "ethnic framework." Yen Le Espiritu, *Asian American Pan-Ethnicity: Bridging Institutions and Identities* (Philadelphia: Temple University Press, 1992), 6. Espiritu also argues that lumping together different nationalities and cultures "encourages individuals to broaden their identity to conform to the more inclusive designation" (p. 11). Also see Joanne Nagel, "Constructing Ethnicity: Creating and Recreating Ethnic Identity and Culture," *Social Problems* 41, no. 1 (1994): 152–76.

76. Nagel, "Constructing Ethnicity"; Espiritu, *Asian American Pan-Ethnicity*, 11.

77. Alba, *Ethnic Identity*.

PART III **Global Challenges to American National Identity**

CHAPTER 6

Transnationalism and National Identity

THE WORLD, WE ARE TOLD, IS INCREASINGLY A SMALLER PLACE. IN A number of ways—communication, transportation, and commerce—that is true. Yet whether it is a less divided one remains to be seen.

The reasons the world is seen as a smaller place generally is summed up in an amorphous conceptual term, "globalization," which is full of large meanings but little precision. Generally, it refers to the increasing interconnectedness and mobility of people, places, and ideas. Capital—human, financial, and intellectual—as often noted, is now free of the barriers and restraints that have formerly impeded its circulation. It is a force that many view as heralding a new age of boundary-less democratization. Others fear its tendency to treat people and local cultures as disposable commodities. And of course, the increasing permeability of international boundaries has implications for domestic national security—most specifically, but not only regarding, the successful conduct of terrorism.

That ambivalence is evident in national and international surveys. The Pew Global Attitudes Survey of forty-four countries found that in half the countries they surveyed, 60 percent thought globalization was at least "somewhat good."[1] Yet in many countries, large numbers of respondents offered no opinion, and in many others there was significant opposition to the process. One explanation for this opposition emerged when respondents were asked to respond to the statement "Our way of life needs to be protected against foreign influence." In every country surveyed, majorities agreed with that sentiment, an astounding uniformity.[2]

However, celebrants of globalized citizenship allege that Americans live in a new world, one in which the old boundaries and allegiances no longer apply. The two that most concern us here are the nation-state and the civic and emotional attachments that have accompanied them. Both, it is alleged, are passé at best and, worse, antidemocratic. According to Bosniak's telling characterization, "a handful of scholars and activists have announced the growing inadequacy of exclusively nation-centered conceptions of citizenship."[3] In its place, they have proposed the various forms of "flexible" or dual citizenship that were outlined in chapter 1. They consider themselves the vanguard of the new international cosmopolitans.

If multiculturalism represents the leading domestic challenge to an American national identity, international cosmopolitanism and transnationalism represent its global face.[4] The challenge from the new international cosmopolitans to an American national identity paradoxically both mirrors and inverts the challenge of domestic multiculturalism. Domestic multiculturalism seeks to deconstruct American identity into its constituent group parts.

The new international cosmopolitans also wish to transcend traditional American identity. However, their primary vehicle for doing so is not domestic ethnic group identity and autonomy but rather transnational attachments. Like multiculturalism, the new cosmopolitanism has both a weak and a strong form.

In its most obvious and unobjectionable form, transnationalism simply notes that some problems transcend boundaries.[5] "The air," writes Nussbaum, "does not obey national boundaries." Dealing with problems of pollution, food, supply, and so on will therefore "require global planning, global knowledge, and the recognition of a shared culture."[6] This is uncontroversial.

Equally unremarkable is the fact that with modern communications and transportation, many more people have increasing access to ideas and opportunities from other cultures and countries. As a result, they are able to develop new connections growing out of this contact or maintain old ones more easily.

The problems begin when these unexceptional facts are made the basis for some extraordinary and far-reaching proposals. These proposals share the paradoxical effect of dismantling the very national foundation that makes democratic progress on an extranational scale possible. Analyses of these new postnational arrangements, or proposals arising out of them, come in many forms. What they share is a conviction that the nation-state is on its way out and that new, transnational arrangements are the wave of the future, which ought to be hastened at every opportunity.

Consider an article written by Strobe Talbott, the former deputy secretary of state in the Bill Clinton administration. In a *Time Magazine* essay titled "The Birth of a Global Nation," he writes, "I'll bet that within the next hundred years . . . nationhood as we know it will be obsolete; all states will recognize a single global authority. A phrase, briefly fashionable in the mid-20th century—'citizen of the world'—will have assumed real meaning by the end of the 21st."[7] This is from the second-ranking official of the U.S. Department of State charged with protecting American national interests.

Why will this happen? Talbott views countries as basically "social arrange-ments," which like other such arrangements before them are "artificial and temporary." Recent developments—the European Community, the Interna-tional Monetary Fund, The General Agreement on Tariffs and Trade, the new legitimacy of "humanitarian interventions," and of course the U.N. Security Council—are among the examples he mentions.[8]

Echoing Nussbaum, he lauds the Rio de Janeiro Earth Summit as demon-strating "the transcending sovereignty of nature." The basic premise is that global problems require a global authority to deal with them. Moreover, the transition to global action and authority "will be easier to achieve in a world already knit together by cables and airwaves."

What will these developments mean for citizenship and national attach-ments? Presumably, these new "citizens of the world"—a phrase that parallels Bourne's call for Americans to become "international citizens"—would grad-ually trade their national attachments for international ones.[9] American national identity would presumably atrophy as other, international identifi-cations supersede it.

A New Global Transnational Order?

In this chapter, I approach the issue of transnationalism and American na-tional identity from two different but complementary levels. The first, and ultimately the least important and relevant of the two, is what might be called the "end-of-nations theory." Essentially, advocates of this position view the world as beginning to develop extranational institutions and associations that will render the nation-state obsolete. As a result, they believe, it is not too soon for Americans to turn away from their national identities and attach-ments to broader, more inclusive ones.

The second and more serious challenge to American national identity and attachments is international cosmopolitanism. Advocates of this view argue that in a world of increasing mobility—of capital, technology, and people—it makes little sense to root identity and citizenship within the boundaries of one nation-state. That being the case, attachments to other countries—particularly immigrants' home countries—is not only necessary but also desirable.

The arguments for a new world transnational order take several forms. They are found in the view that the "international community" is replacing the nation-state, especially when it comes to defining and enforcing individual rights. It is found in the view that transnational actors of various sorts, includ-ing terrorist organizations—have rendered the national state boundary obso-lete. And it is found in the view that international cosmopolitans, people at home in the world at large but not in a specific national place, are the wave of the future.

The Borderless World

Every year on July 4, the *Wall Street Journal*'s editorial page offers its view that the United States should adopt a five-word constitutional amendment: "There shall be open borders."[10] That view reflects the strand of libertarian thinking evident in some of the *Journal*'s emphases on "free markets and free people." The writer admits that such a proposal is "an ideal" rather than "an immediate policy prescription," and that "perhaps this policy is overambitious in today's world."[11] Nonetheless, he is willing to give it a try by suggesting that Mexico, Canada, and the United States—the signers of the North American Free Trade Agreement—open their borders to people as well as goods.[12] He is not alone.[13]

Borders serve a variety of functions—political, psychological, and cultural. In their most basic sense, they demarcate the boundary between here and there. In doing so, they also help to distinguish between members and nonmembers. Much has been made of the harm in such boundary-setting functions, but not all boundaries result in hate, prejudice, and discrimination. Moreover, boundaries are necessary for both individuals and countries that require connected and attached members to carry on the form of government its people have chosen. The United States is no exception.

Boundaries are also a key element in developing and maintaining a coherent personal identity. Psychologists have long established that separation and individualization are key and essential elements of human development. Symbiotic or enmeshed relationships are inconsistent with personal autonomy and independence.

This does not mean that everyone must become their own island. Obviously, others enter into our lives, and we share ourselves in a variety of circumstances. Still, the clinical point is clear: The ability to develop and maintain boundaries is a key element of personal identity and psychological functioning.

Boundaries also play a critical role in the development and maintenance of national identity. For those living within and identifying with a particular geographical space, boundaries are one element of the commonality that underlies a national culture and identity. That is one reason why you can live in either New Mexico or New Jersey and still consider yourself an American.

The rules of entry from outside to inside this boundary are obviously important. Critics focus on the fact that at different times and in different ways the rules of inclusion have been biased against certain groups. That is true.

Yet critics have failed to appreciate that on balance the rules of inclusion have not been inflexible and have changed periodically. One could ask, with equal relevance, how the United States discriminated against Eastern Europeans (or other groups) and why it no longer does so. Both are part of the American story.

But critics miss a larger point about restrictions. No society can maintain viable national identifications and attachments without having some guidelines about who is a member and who is not, and the basis by which the latter can gain entry. Boundary-less countries, like boundary-less persons, are a recipe for severe identity diffusion. And it is because of individuals' identity as Americans that they have been willing to undertake the hard but necessary tasks of citizenship that have enabled this country to survive.

The libertarian emphasis on freedom is not the only philosophical basis for advocating open borders. It can be justified by appeals to justice and fairness, at least according to the political philosopher Joseph Carens.[14] In his view, living in a Western democracy "is the modern equivalent of feudal privilege—an inherited status that greatly enhances ones life chances . . . and hard to justify when one is thinking about it closely."[15]

What of threats to public order from unimpeded mass immigration? Carens responds: "In ideal theory we face a world of just states, , , , Under such conditions, the likelihood of mass migrations threatening the public order of any particular state seems small. So there is little room for restrictions on immigration in ideal theory."[16]

One of the largest drawbacks of political theory for a reality-oriented scholar like me is that it makes ideal theory or human nature the basis for its theoretical arguments.[17] Yet deriving policy mandates from a personal, wholly constructed, and speculative view of ideal theory or human nature is often, from a psychological perspective, untenable. Who knows what people are truly like in a state of nature? Why are Carens's speculations about the ideal state any better or worse than any other such speculations? What do any of these speculations have to do with the psychology of people as they are and operate? Designing political arrangements for persons who do not exist seems like a dangerous and foolish prescription for the serious issues that face this country on immigration.

For all its power to elucidate, political theory lives in an "as-if" world.[18] The political theory equivalent of "as-if" psychology finds its voice in assumptions about the state of nature or ideal theory.

Carens grants that ideal theory is not wholly the same as real life. He is therefore willing to allow that a country is entitled to prevent "armed invaders and subversives" from entering—although this should not be overdone.[19] Yet what about the problem of sheer numbers? Carens admits that given the number of people from around the world that want to come to the United States, the numbers would be "overwhelming." He is willing to allow some very limited restrictions.[20]

Let us assume that Carens's ideal policy comes to fruition and that the United States either abolishes its borders or takes in not 1 million new immigrants a year but 5, 10, or even 15 million. Leaving aside severe issues of national security in the wake of the September 11, 2001, terrorist attacks, where would all these new immigrants get jobs? What will happen to the gap between the rich and the poor? How will they all get health insurance? If they do not, who will pay? Who will build all the new schools needed to accommodate their children? Who will pay for all the new teachers and multilingual instruction? What would it mean to the fabric of American democracy to have people arriving by the multimillions who want to make their fortune but who do not really call America home?

These questions are obvious. Such a scenario would bring about extraordinary and revolutionary changes in the United States. Curiously, for all the talk about the moral equivalence of each person, political theorists seem wholly uninterested in the 280 million people who live in the United States whose lives, prospects, freedom, and well-being would be severely disrupted. The surprise is that some people take these ideas seriously.

Global Individualism

Is national identity dying? Some think so. Zachary claims that "a fixed sense of belonging, based on shared conceptions of national traits is clearly dying."[21] He writes that "people increasingly construct themselves, piecing themselves together from diverse experiences, relying not only on their own kind, but also their knowledge of the wider world, their tastes and inclinations and the beliefs that work for them.[22]

Zachary's illustrations are a Ghanaian who chose to live and work in Iceland, a North Carolina native who spent two years in Macedonia, and a Scottish computer programmer who settled in Amsterdam—all people striving to live out some basic part of their psychology and aspirations in a larger world than the one where they started. These global hybrids, as he calls them, are hearty folk—able to forge new lives away from the comforts of their old ones. In Zachary's view, such people "no longer receive their identities; they take them and remake them. And they passionately connect not just with one ethnic national culture, but with many."[23]

How do such people construct their identities? According to Zachary, "Now identity depends more on what they've studied; where they've traveled; with whom they are friends; what they do for a living; whom they marry, and perhaps even what music they enjoy, what restaurants they eat in, style of dancing they prefer or books they read."[24] This list reflects something both obvious and limiting about what Zachary envisions. Most people do not define their identity by the music or restaurants they enjoy. The sum of that list is an upper-middle-class Western lifestyle available to very few people and not necessarily desired by all in those categories.

Interestingly, unlike other enthusiasts for a borderless world, Zachary does not view national governments as antithetical to, but rather *necessary* to, the development of global hybrids. "Only national governments," he claims, "can secure the conditions out of which hybridity springs. . . . Only nations can serve as a neutral arbiter required to ensure that the multiplicity of individual ties do not collapse in conflict."[25] In his preferred future, governments will be strong and farseeing enough to maintain and further develop the conditions by which to liberate their citizens from the ties that bind them. He appears to forget that it is these very ties that help to maintain the governments and the society that are instrumental to his proposal.

Is the International Community Replacing the Nation-State?

Some view the decline of the nation-state as a function of the development of supranational organizations, evolving human rights creeds, international treaties, and the extranational attachments that accompany them—in short, what many refer to as the "international community." Whether such a community exists and what its actual mechanisms are are matters of some debate. Let us examine these more carefully.

International Rights and the Global Community

Among the strongest statements of the international community view is found in Falk's assertion that it is "an array of transnational social forces, animated by environmental concerns, human rights, hostility to patriarchy, and a vision of human community based on the uniting of diverse cultures, seeking an end to poverty, oppression, and collective violence."[26] If in such a context the state is quickly becoming a historical curiosity, what will take its place? Soysal suggests it will be "a new and more uniform concept of citizenship . . . one whose organizing and legitimating principles are based on universal brotherhood rather than national belonging. To an increasing extent, rights and privileges once reserved for citizens of nations are codified and expanded as personal rights, undermining the national order of citizenship."[27]

In Soysal's view, universal personhood is eroding the basis for the nation-state. Her "post-national belonging" is based on universal human rights, as laid down in conventions and declarations of supranational bodies like the United Nations. Or as Falk puts it, "The spirit of global citizenship is almost completely deterritorialized, and is associated with an extension of citizenship as an expression of an affirmation of human unity."[28]

The problem here is threefold—definition, enforcement, and a narrow view of what nation-states actually provide. What do rights actually mean? Most international rights declarations and conventions are abstract and ambitious. They are a result of grand aspirations coupled with the more mundane need to draft a document that will satisfy the very diverse parties trying to reach agreement.

The more specific such conventions become, the more controversial the result, and the less likely that agreement can be achieved. So such declarations typically favor certain virtues without saying very much about how such conditions are to be achieved. And of course, it is states that draft such conventions, states that ratify them or not, and states that are charged with defining how and when they will carry out the general aspirations contained in these instruments.

This leads to the second problem. Many of the states that are involved in drafting and enforcing such international conventions of virtue are themselves the prime violators of these conventions. This is true as well of the international institutional machinery for these conventions, such as the United Nations Commission on Human Rights—in which dictatorships as well as democracies must be accommodated in a very diverse international community. Real democracies, located within specific countries, are much more likely to develop and enforce the virtues outlined in international treaties than other countries that sign them.

Last, there is the major problem of enforcement. Castles notes that Soysal's model of postnational belonging is based on international human rights declarations, "which are gradually being incorporated into the constitutions and laws of the specific nation-states."[29] This may be true, but the fact that they are being incorporated into the constitutions and laws of nation-states also means that it is *nation-states* that are doing it, not an international body. Two recent low-profile treaties that the United States signed illustrate the point.

In 2003, President George W. Bush consulted with other members of the international community and then submitted two treaties to the U.S. Senate. One contained amendments to the constitution and convention of the International Telecommunications Union (ITU), and the other a protocol for the Simplification and Harmonization of Customs Procedures.[30]

President Bush told the Senate, "Consistent with long-standing practice in the ITU, the United States, in signing the 1998 amendments, made certain declarations and reservations. . . . Subject to the U.S. declarations and reservations made above, I believe the United States should ratify the 1998 amendments."[31] Similarly, reservations were entered in his message to Congress on customs harmonization.[32]

Both of these transmission messages make clear that the United States will abide by some elements of the conventions but not others. The United States is not alone in doing so. The specific reservations themselves are less important than the fact that they are made, and that the treaty's enforcement and support are dependent on them. The dilemma is well summed up by E. J. Dionne: "Can a nation, even a nation as powerful as ours, protect its values and laws without engaging other nations in the effort? The answer is almost certainly no. Still, there is something about these non-democratic international institutions that even the most ardent internationalist will mistrust. Part of the answer is to make the institutions more open. But there are limits."[33]

Global Progressivism and the International Community

These limits are exactly what concern supporters of an American national identity and community. Just how democratic are international rights regimes? And, how democratic are the procedures used to arrive at them? The two questions are related.

International conventions that favor the expansion of rights are usually the outcome of conferences convened by organizations like the United Nations. They in turn extend invitations to various nongovernmental organizations (NGOs), individuals, and interested governmental parties. It is no secret that many member states of the United Nations are not democracies and are violators of the various rights regimes that have been passed. Yet they have full standing within these organizations.

So, too, many in the international rights community have expansive views of international rights regimes. But is this not an unalloyed virtue? After all, does not an expansionist view of rights reflect the higher aspirations of rights-based democracy? Are not rights to education, health, housing, movement, participation, and the rights of children, women, and minorities the foundation of democracy? In the abstract: Yes. However, rights are not practiced in a cultural, political, or a responsibility vacuum. They are practiced within countries that may have diverse views about what such rights mean and how they should be enacted. Such countries have their own cultural, historical, and political traditions as well.

The expansion of rights is not always clear-cut. It is a paradoxical fact that many of the countries most in need of an expansion of even basic rights are less the focus of rights regimes and advocates than those countries with long-standing and effective democratic institutions, traditions, and enforcement machinery. It would be useful to draw a strong distinction between those countries *introducing* basic rights and those *satisfying* them.

Whose International Community? The World Conference on Racism

One can see these distinctions by examining the United Nations World Conference on Racism, Racial Discrimination, Xenophobia, and Related Intolerance held in Durban in 2001. That conference was preceded by a series of regional preparatory conferences. At one of these, delegates to a Middle Eastern regional conference succeeded in pressing a "Zionism equals racism" plank for the conference's final agenda. This, and a demand from African delegates that the conference support reparations for past racism, were two of the most visible sources of contention. They were not the only ones. The *Washington Post* editorialized:

> The United Nations World Conference on Racism, which will take place later this month in South Africa, is one of those meetings that make people wonder about the usefulness of the U.N. Originally conceived as a forum to examine how to combat contemporary forms of racism, the meeting now threatens to dissolve into an unproductive debate about reparations payments for slavery, condemnation of Israel and such topics as whether the word 'Holocaust' should be capitalized. Analysts who had followed the pre-convention conference had observed that Arab and Muslim States, along *with radical Western non-governmental groups* [NGOs] had worked hard to promote their causes in preparatory meetings.[34]

Which NGOs sent representatives to the conference? Several were groups familiar in the United States and elsewhere—for example, Amnesty International and the NAACP. Others were less familiar, but more radical—the National Network for Immigrant and Refugee Rights, the Women's Institute for Leadership Development for Human Rights, and Third World Within (from the Bronx), among others.[35]

The United States and others, including UN secretary-general Kofi Annan, repeatedly tried to get the attendees to back away from, or compromise on, divisive issues. They failed. The conference opened with Yasir Arafat delivering a harsh denunciation of Israel as racist and practicing ethnic cleansing that was respectfully received by the assembled delegates. The United States' low-level observer mission walked out, as did Israeli delegates.[36]

The point of these examples is not to denigrate international rights efforts. They have been effective levers of change, for example, in the former Soviet Union and its former satellites. But I want to emphasize why the expansion of rights in the context of international conferences, protocols, statements of principles, and declarations is not an uncomplicated matter. Indeed, given their makeup, the delegate selection process, and the inclusion of many of the most radical advocates of various rights positions, such machinery cannot be considered representative or democratic.

Transnationalism and National Security

Transnational advocates base the decline of the nation-state on the rise of globalism in general and human rights covenants in particular. In doing so, they have chosen an exceedingly thin slice of the requirements for a truly global and effective international community. Whether one subscribes to "neo-realism" theory, which posits that nations act primarily defensively,[37] or "offensive realism" theory,[38] which views states as pursuing self-interest through assertion and, where necessary, aggression, the world is a dangerous place. There are failed states, rogue states, and aggressive states—and of course, catastrophic terrorism.

Transnational Terrorism: No State Needed?

At a recent conference on the George W. Bush presidency, two senior foreign policy analysts from the Brookings Institution, Ivo Daalder and James Lindsay, presented a critique of the Bush foreign policy. The authors wrote that "to believe that the state remains not just the primary, but the only relevant actors in international affairs is to ignore the vast changes in world politics that globalization has wrought."[39]

What are these changes? The Brookings analysts argued, "There is no doubt that transnational networks like al Qaeda benefit from state support whenever that is possible. But its power reaches beyond the state, and its existence does not depend on direct state support. The defeat of tyrants and regime change in rogue states, while perhaps helpful, is therefore no guarantee that terrorists will be significantly weakened."[40]

Daalder and Lindsay's critique of the Bush administration overstates its focus on states like Iraq and Syria. At the same time, they understate the extent to which the war on terrorism continues along with an emphasis on changing state behavior. Do transnational operations like al Qaeda reach "beyond the state," and does its existence "not depend on direct state help?" To some degree, the answer to both these questions is yes, but in a minimalist sense. Clearly, groups like al Qaeda can reach beyond states, and clearly such groups can exist without direct state support. Yet the more important question is: How well?

Supporters of the importance of transnationalism—whether political theorists like Nussbaum or foreign policy analysts like Daalder and Lindsay—considerably underestimate the significance of the state in facilitating the very transnational processes that they say reflect its demise. Groups like al Qaeda or Hezbollah have relied on states—Afghanistan in the first case, and Syria and Iran in the second—for a great deal of direct support that only governments can provide.

Terrorist training camps, for example, are located on land that is state territory—the Bakaa Valley in the case of Syria and Hezbollah, and the whole state of Afghanistan in the case of al Queda. Terrorists must buy weapons and pay recruits, and for that they need money. Certainly money can be raised in many ways and in many countries, but that money must be transported and bills must be paid. This usually means making use of banking and transfer systems, which are chartered and regulated by states.

Terrorists must travel. And to travel, they need passports—and issuing passports and entry visas is a state function and power. Terrorists, to succeed, must not get caught. Yet state intelligence and policy forces of many kinds pursue them using a variety of techniques that depend on state instrumentalities. Conversely, some states provide safe havens for terrorists.[41]

In short, terrorist groups can reach beyond single states and can exist without direct state support. Yet their capacity to function is enmeshed with structures of state institutions that regulate the very mechanisms that are so central to the execution of terrorists' purposes. A closer examination of transnational terror networks, far from demonstrating the irrelevance of states, actually underscores their continuing importance.

The International Community and National Security

Many advocates of expansive human rights theories make no mention of the current international system regarding community security. Yet as many historical circumstances (and much psychological theory) suggest, a basic structure of personal and community security is a foundation for the expression and application of individual rights.[42] Lawlessness, fear of attack, and other forms of psychological and physical insecurity are inconsistent with the enjoyment of rights. We can see these elements at work in the aftermath of September 11. Brownstein sums up the general response:

> At the moment the first fireball seared the crystalline Manhattan sky last week, the entire impulse to distrust government that has become so central to U.S. politics seemed instantly anachronistic. . . . Yet in the attack's dizzying aftermath, where did almost all Americans turn for answers if not to the federal government? That instinct extended far beyond the actual physical defense of the nation—a responsibility that almost all Americans, whether at the left, right or center, accept as a legitimate function for Washington. More telling has been the instant push in both parties for the federal government to replace the airlines in providing airport security. . . . It's times of tragedy that expose the hollowness of the manufactured disdain for government.[43]

We can see this in a number of more direct ways as well. After September 11 Americans, understandably, paid much more attention to news reports.

According to a *New York Times* / CBS News Poll, in April 1989 only 18 percent said they followed news about world affairs "very closely." By April 2003, that number was 41 percent. Those same polls also showed a "rally effect" around the president, which did not wholly recede as quickly as past "rally effects" had done. Before September 11, the president's approval rating was 53 percent and falling. After September 11, his approval rating hit 89 percent and seemed to find a plateau in the low to middle 60 percent range.

Major institutions, and particularly the military, have enjoyed a revival of public trust and confidence. In March and April 2002, the Institute for Survey Research found that 73 percent of the public had a "great deal" of confidence in the military, more than any other institution.[44] The *New York Times* reported on a Gallup Poll that showed confidence in the military rising from 58 percent in 1975 to 79 percent in 2003.[45] It can be seen in the surge of patriotic feelings after September 11. It can be seen in the number of initiatives that Americans have given wide support to that concern their domestic security. And it can be seen in support for the decision to go to war in both Afghanistan and Iraq. National communities, in Benedict Anderson's well-worn phrase, may be "imagined communities," but that does not mean that they do not have the most concrete consequences.[46]

Conversely, American confidence in the United Nations has markedly declined. The failure of the United Nations to stand behind its many resolutions demanding that Iraq and Saddam Hussein account for the weapons of mass destruction and then destroy them has sapped American confidence in the United Nations' ability to provide security in a dangerous world. The most recent Pew Global Attitude Survey asked individuals in forty-four countries (and the Palestinian territories) whether the United Nations was a good influence on their country. In 2002, 72 percent of Americans thought so, but just a year later only 43 percent did. Similarly, large drops were recorded in Canada, France, Germany, and the United Kingdom. Smaller but still significant drops were recorded in most other countries surveyed.[47]

The aftermath of September 11 makes it clear that it is a mistake to confuse Americans' laissez-faire stance toward government in calm times with the underlying assumption that the government can be and is counted upon to perform its basic functions. Indeed, it is precisely the latter that leads to the confusion with the former. At least in the United States and elsewhere as well, the rise of catastrophic terrorism in an already dangerous world has reinforced the nation-state—not contributed to its supposed demise.

Notes

1. Pew Global Attitudes Project, "Views of a Changing World," http://people-press.org, 84. They looked at a large range of globalization elements including cell

phones, the Internet, genetically altered foods, immigration, fast foods, the pace of modern life, and so on.

2. Ibid., 94.

3. Linda Bosniak, "Citizenship Denationalized," *Indiana Journal of Global Legal Studies* 7, no. 2 (2000): 447–58; the citation here is on 449.

4. As Faist points out, the two terms are not synonymous, with "globalization" being the more inclusive one. Thomas Faist, "Transnationalism in International Migration: Implications for the Study of Citizenship and Culture," *Ethnic and Racial Studies* 23, no. 2 (2000): 189–222; the citation here is on 192. Also see Jose Itzigsohn, "Immigration and the Boundaries of Citizenship: The Institutions of Immigrants' Political Transnationalism," *International Migration Review* 34, no. 4 (2000): 1126–54, esp. 1130.

5. Transnationalism as a field of inquiry is at a very early stage of development and can be characterized as a "highly fragmented, emergent field which still lacks a well defined theoretical framework and analytical vigor." Alexandro Portes, Luis E. Guarnizo, and Patricia Landolt, "The Study of Transnationalism: Pitfalls and Promise of an Emergent Field," *Ethnic and Racial Studies* 22, no. 2 (2000): 217–37; the citation here is on 218. Kivisto agrees and notes, "This concept suffers from an ambiguity as a result of competing definitions that fail to specify the temporal and spatial parameters of the term." Peter Kivisto, "Theorizing Transnational Immigrants: A Critical Review of Current Efforts," *Ethnic and Racial Studies* 24, no. 4 (2001): 549–77; the citation here is on 550. However, a thoughtful and helpful conceptual demarcation of the field can be found in Faist, "Transnationalism"; see also Steven Vertocec, "Conceiving and Researching Transnationalism," *Ethnic and Racial Studies* 22, no. 2 (1999): 447–62. My purpose here, however, is not to contribute to the conceptual delineation of this emergent field but to explore one particular slice of it—that dealing with the questions of transnational ties and citizenship within a national state milieu. (See Faist "Transnationalism," 197, 201–02, for a discussion from the standpoint of his conceptualization of the field.)

6. Martha Nussbaum, "Patriotism and Cosmopolitanism," in *For Love of Country: Debating the Limits of Patriotism*, by Martha Nussbaum (Boston: Beacon Press, 1996), 12.

7. Strobe Talbott, "Birth of a Global Nation," *Time Magazine*, July 20, 1992, 70.

8. Ibid., 71.

9. Randolph S. Bourne, "Trans-National America," *Atlantic Monthly* 118 (1916): 86–97; see also Richard Munch, *Nations and Citizenship in a Global Age: From National to Transnational Ties and Identities* (London: Palgrave-Macmillan, 2001).

10. Robert L. Bartley, "Liberty's Flame Beckons a Bit Brighter," *Wall Street Journal*, July 3, 2000; and Bartley, "Open NAFTA Borders? Why Not?" *Wall Street Journal*, July 2, 2001.

11. Bartley, "Liberty's Flame."

12. Bartley, "Open NAFTA Borders?"

13. Judith Shelton, "North America Doesn't Need Borders," *Wall Street Journal*, August 29, 2000.

14. Joseph H. Carens, "Aliens and Citizens: The Case for Open Borders," *Review of Politics* 49, no. 2 (1987): 251–73.

15. Ibid., 252. Carens's position rests on the philosophical underpinnings of Rawls and the admonition that "we must treat all human beings, not just members of our own society, as free and equal moral persons" (256). So if people were able to see out from the "veil of ignorance" imposed by their experiences and views, they would construct a just world in which one assumes the viewpoint of the ones who would be most disadvantaged by any rule. In matters of migration that is clearly the alien.

16. Carens, "Aliens," 259.

17. Tamir begins her analysis of liberal nationalism as follows: "My inquiry concerning the foundations of liberal nationalism begins with the basic methodological postulate of every political ideology, a portrait of human nature." Yael Tamir, *Liberal Nationalism* (Princeton, N.J.: Princeton University Press, 1993), 7; my emphasis. Rawls has his speculation of what people are really like behind the "veil of ignorance."

18. The term is borrowed from psychoanalytic theory and refers to people whose psychology proceeds on the assumption that things are as they wish them to be rather than as they are.

19. Carens, "Aliens," 260.

20. Yet he is willing to do so only on two conditions—first, that they be "much less restrictive than the one currently in force which is shaped by so many other considerations than the need to maintain the public order"; and second, that "the level of restriction be only that which is necessary to maintain public order."

21. G. Pascal Zachary, *Global Me: New Cosmopolitans and the Competitive Edge: Picking Globalism's Winners and Losers* (New York: Public Affairs, 2000), 5.

22. Ibid., 5.

23. Ibid., 6.

24. Ibid., 5.

25. Ibid., 111.

26. Richard Falk, "The Making of Global Citizenship," in *Global Visions*, ed. Jeremy Brecher, John Brown Childs, and Jill Cutler (Boston: Beacon Press, 1993), 39.

27. Yasemin Soysal, *Limits of Citizenship: Migrants and Postnational Citizenship in Europe* (Chicago: University of Chicago Press, 1994), 1.

28. Falk, "Making of Global Citizenship," 42.

29. Stephen Castles, "Multiculturalism Citizenship: A Response to the Dilemma of Globalization and National Identity?" *Journal of Intercultural Studies* 18, no. 5 (1997): 238.

30. George W. Bush, "Message to the Senate Transmitting Amendments to the Constitution and Convention of the International Telecommunications Union," *Weekly Compilation of Presidential Documents* 39, no. 18 (May 5, 2003): 509; and Bush, "Message to the Senate Transmitting Protocol Amendment to the International Convention of the Simplification and Harmonization of Customs Procedures," *Weekly Compilation of Presidential Documents* 39, no. 18 (May 5, 2003): 510.

31. Bush, "Message to the Senate Transmitting Amendments to the Constitution and Convention of the International Telecommunications Union."

32. His transmitting message to the Senate for the second contains these words: "I propose that the United States accept seven of the specific annexes in their entirety, but one each of two other specific annexes [A–E, G, and H, as well as chapters 1, 2,

and 3 of F and chapters 1, 3, 4, and 5 of J] and enter the reservations proposed by the bureau of customs and border Protection. . . . The provisions for which reservation is recommended conflict with current U.S. legislation or regulations." Bush, "Message to the Senate Transmitting Protocol Amendment to the International Convention of the Simplification and Harmonization of Customs Procedures," 210; emphasis mine.

33. E. J. Dionne, "Ways of the Patriots," *Washington Post*, July 3, 2001.

34. Quoted by Pamela Constable, "Mideast Dominates Racism Meeting," *Washington Post*, September 1, 2001; emphasis mine. It is worth asking who attended the conference. Constable, who was covering the conference for the *Washington Post*, also wrote: "The meeting's writ is so broad that it has attracted an extraordinary variety of minority groups, who traveled here to promote their causes. They include Indian untouchables, HIV/AIDS patients, South African Bushman, Tibetan refugees, Afro-Latinos and European Roma, or gypsies. . . . only a few heads of state are attending, mostly from African countries and many are from states that have questionable human rights records on discrimination and human rights. They include the leaders of Algeria, Togo, Rwanda, and Gabon as well as Bosnia and Cuba."

35. A more complete listing of radical groups in the context of the Durban racism conference can be found at http://www.antiracismnet.org/archive/index.html.

36. The underlying and fatal contradictions of this and similar conferences were pointed out by Bob Herbert, a columnist for the *New York Times*, and it is worth quoting at some length: "The truth is that the conference was doomed to irrelevance from its conception. The tragic problems of ethnic, religious, and gender intolerance have stained every region of the globe. They are much too big and much too complex and intractable to be seriously addressed by a U.N. conference. Making matters worse in Durban is the extent to which the conference was plagued by cynics chasing their own agendas and delegates befouled by their own bigotry. Some of the loudest attackers of Israel were from countries in which anti-Semitism is a way of life and proponents of civil or human rights are hunted down, imprisoned, tortured and sometimes killed. Some African countries represented at the conference have demanded apologies and reparations from Western countries formerly involved in the slave trade. But African delegates have been conspicuously quiet on the issue of present-day slavery in Sudan and Mauritania." Bob Herbert, "Doomed to Irrelevance," *New York Times*, September 6, 2001.

37. Kenneth N. Waltz, *Man, the State, and War* (New York: McGraw-Hill, 1979).

38. John J. Mearsheimer, *The Tragedy of Great Power Politics* (New York: Norton, 2001).

39. Ivo H. Daalder and James M. Lindsay, "The Bush Revolution: The Remaking of America's Foreign Policy," paper prepared for delivery at a conference on the George W. Bush presidency, an early assessment, Princeton University, Princeton, N.J., April 25–26, 2003, 29–30.

40. Ibid., 30.

41. Douglas Jehl and Eric Schmitt, "U.S. Suggests Al Qaeda Cell in Iran Directed Saudi Bombings," *New York Times*, May 21, 2003.

42. Abraham Maslow, *Motivation and Personality* (New York: Harper Brothers, 1954); Margaret S. Mahler, Fred Pine, and Anni Bergman, *The Psychological Birth of*

the Human Infant: Symbiosis and Individuation (New York: Basic Books, 1989); and John Bowlby, *Attachment*, 2nd ed. (New York: Basic Books, 2000).

43. Ronald Brownstein, "The Government, Once Scorned, Becomes Savior," *Los Angles Times*, September 19, 2001; see also Brownstein, "Both Parties Obliged to Reassess Washington Role," *Los Angeles Times*, October 15, 2001.

44. American Enterprise Institute for Public Policy Research, American Enterprise Institute Studies in Public Opinion, available at http://www.aei.org.

45. Robin Toner, "Trust in Military Heightens among Baby Boomer's Children," *New York Times*, May 27, 2003.

46. Benedict Anderson, *Imagined Communities*, rev. ed. (New York: Verso, 1991).

47. Pew Global Attitudes Project, "Views," 27.

CHAPTER 7

Why Not a Transnational American Identity?

Iɴ 1916, WRITING AGAINST WHAT HE SAW AS THE EXCESSES OF THE Americanization program for new immigrants, the journalist and cultural essayist Randolph Bourne called for a "transnational America." He envisioned us as a country populated by nationals with strong emotional ties to their countries of origin or, for immigrants, their home countries. In this new world, citizens would be united as Americans primarily by the fact that they were "international citizens." A look at the exploding numbers of dual-citizenship-encouraging countries detailed in chapter 1 suggests that Bourne's vision is being realized.[1]

Some contemporary theorists "have seized upon Bourne's 1916 essay 'Trans-National America,' as a multicultural manifesto for a new American national identity."[2] Aleinikoff, for example, specifically embraces Bourne's vision for the United States,[3] while another cosmopolitan advocate has called for dual or multiple citizenship to become a basic human right enforced by the United Nations General Assembly.[4] The question I raise in this chapter is whether Bourne's vision represents a dream to which we should give our support, or whether it is a utopian fantasy whose implications for this country have not seriously been thought through.

Dual Citizenship and National Identity

I would like to address this basic question, balancing between two positions: the enthusiastic, determined, and, I believe, naive embrace of massive dual-citizenship immigration as a matter of little consequence to us;[5] and the premature, but not unrealistic, concern of our potential evolution into a country in which separate psychological, cultural, and political loyalties trump a coherent national identity.[6]

Theory versus Advocacy

Liberal and postmodern theorists share a support for dual citizenship but base it on slightly different foundations. The first emphasize America's liberal tradition and our continued failure to live up to it. They see an America indelibly stained by its treatment of Indian tribes, people with darker skins or accents, women—and anyone else who challenges America's distribution of wealth, influence, and public attention and their share of them. Their common response is more emphasis on rights—group based, if necessary[7]—more emphasis on government guarantees of outcomes such advocates prefer, and more mandated measures to ensure that "recognition" is not trumped by any quirky individualism.[8] They welcome multiple citizenship because it represents a long step in the direction of ensuring more democracy, defined as parity for diverse cultural traditions regardless of their degree of fit with already-existing ones.[9]

The second group of theorists, the postmodernists, have a partially correct insight that social organization is a by-product of intent and is thus, to use their term, "constructed." From this they conclude that no social form has any intrinsic or functional value, except those they advocate. They have little, if any, regard for America's cultural and political traditions, which they see as inherently racist, xenophobic, and anachronistically nationalistic. Their remedy is to welcome, and where possible to further, the demise of American national culture and to substitute "larger loyalties," which in their view are more "democratic" and conducive to strong "multicultural" identifications.[10] They welcome multiple citizenship because they believe that it weakens ties to the "hegemonic" capitalism of which the United States is their chief exemplar.

Unlimited Identities: A Narcissistic Conceit

The problem with most theoretical discussions of multiple citizenships is that they go well beyond most solid substantive or theoretical grounding and are often personal or political views masquerading as political theory. Consider the question of multiple loyalties and national identity. Some subscribe to the "Why not one more?" theory. We are reminded that we are, as in my own case, sons, husbands, and fathers.[11] We are labeled as Caucasian and Western. We are working class by background and upper middle class by socioeconomic status. We are Jewish and reformed; and New Yorkers, Manhattanites, and Upper West Siders. We are professors, scholars/writers, psychologists, psychoanalysts, and neo-Freudians. We are economically progressive, politically moderate, and culturally conservative. And we are Americans.

Postmodern theorists see us comprising a virtually unlimited and replaceable set of selves that can be enacted or abandoned at will.[12] Liberal political theorists and their allies count up all the categories by which we may be understood and conclude that adding one more, say, Mexican or Indian nationality, will make little if any difference.[13]

The first fallacy of these arguments is that core identity elements are infinitely malleable. They are not. The second is that all identifications have equal weight. They do not.

In clinical work, diffused, dysfunctional, or incoherent identities are always a matter of psychological concern.[14] Politically, therefore, this state hardly seems a worthy candidate for our national aspirations. Moreover, the fact that we can have many elements in our complex modern identities does not negate the need to integrate them into a coherent and functional package. It only makes that required task more difficult. Finally, the "Why not one more?" theory fails to distinguish between the elements of personal identity that form a central core of one's psychology and those that are more peripheral. I am much more a father than a Caucasian, much more a political moderate than an Upper West Sider, and definitely more of an American than most of the categories in my list.

Consider in this context Aleinikoff's contention that multiple attachments do not produce "anomie or post-modern neurosis."[15] Indeed, he argues that "on the contrary, it appears that human beings are rather adept at living in more than one world, bring the insights of one to bear on the other, or compartmentalizing their lives into separate spheres." He then gives as evidence the case of his friends who adopted a Russian baby and held a dual ceremony at which the baby both received a Jewish ritual circumcision and was naturalized as an American citizen, with the parents reciting the oath of allegiance for him. This, in his view, "shows that the opposite of a single fixed identity is not necessarily a loss of bearing or radical personal conclusion. The two identities—Jew and U.S. citizen—are deeply significant to their relevant communities; but the assembled friends and family did not see a contradiction (or even a tension) between them."

Of course they did not. The parents were presumably native born, or had lived here long enough to be naturalized Americans. The baby would therefore be raised by parents who were themselves a product of many years as Americans, with all that entails. They would speak the same language and have the same cultural patterns and outlooks, and the baby would grow up with the connection to its new country as a very early and primary experience. That these two adults chose to adopt a baby reflects the fact that what they shared was more powerful than the possible nationality–religious tensions between them.

Holding multiple identifications, even those with deep significance, does not mean they must be, or are, equal. Consider that it is certainly permissible for our political leaders to have, and even to express, a commitment to their faith that has deep meaning to them. However, as discussions surrounding John F. Kennedy's Catholicism in 1960 and Joseph Lieberman's Judaism in 2000 make clear, we also expect that identity as, and commitment to, being an American will take precedence.

As a practical matter, however, why expect tension at all when the categories of religion and national identity have become essentially fused? As Herberg pointed out almost fifty years ago, the religion of America is Americanism.[16] Or to put it another way, religion in the United States has become secularized and, to the extent that it has, Americanized. There is very little tension present in contemporary American society, especially that part of it that is highly educated, affluent, and occupationally well placed, in being both an American and a Catholic, a Protestant, or a Jew.

No sensible person argues that people cannot function with multiple commitments—wife and mother, Catholic and professor, a child's parent and some parent's child. Most often in the United States, these commitments are tensionless, and even when they are not, they do not call into question fundamental values or ways of being in the world. In short, there is an important distinction between core elements of our identity that (1) we acquire early and shape other important identity elements that develop later and (2) are acquired and maintained with little trouble and less commitment.

We must be clear about what it takes to develop and maintain a national identity that is coherent and integrated. And we must be clear about how personal and national identity functions to support the cultural and political arrangements that underlie this fabulous experiment known as America.

Metaphors and Muddles

Such understandings may help us make less of a muddle of our metaphors. For example, dual citizenship is often compared to bigamy.[17] However, that analogy is deficient. Marriage is a voluntary union between two adults searching for intimacy, companionship, and partnership. It is based on a combination of similarity, complementarity, practicality, and the hope for wish fulfillment.

Nationality, conversely, is that combination of national identification, psychology, and outlook that begins with the earliest experiences of language, family, custom, and parental psychology. I want to underscore the word "outlook" in this list, because culture is deeply embedded in not only *what* we think but also *how* we do so. Cultural frames are not interchangeable.

Furthermore, this early foundation generally develops within a relatively consistent institutional, cultural, and psychological setting that is not freely chosen, nor easily abandoned.[18] In these and other ways, nationality and national identity are quite the opposite of marriage.

Another marriage-framed metaphor compares dual citizenship to relations with one's family and one's in-laws. Advocates who use this metaphor agree that conflicts can arise but believe you can still be loyal to both. There is of course much that lies behind the word *can*, as in the phrase "can still be loyal."[19] In some societies, the wish of the elders takes precedence over the wishes of the couple, if they differ. In American society, it is easier to be loyal because the preferences of the couple are expected to outweigh the wishes of the parents. Yet there is a more basic question here.

What happens when both parties feel very strongly about an issue? How does one resolve and maintain fidelity to dual loyalties in those circumstances? Not every issue between two countries will involve irreconcilable principles and policies. However, they might well arise.

What are the effects of siding with your family at the expense of your spouse? What are the effects on your relationship with the spouse whose views were trumped by the partner's family? Translated into the concerns here, what is the effect on the United States and the immigrants it seeks to integrate when they, as dual citizens, give substantial weight to the policy preferences of their "country of origin"?

Nationality and national identity, therefore, seem closer to family than married life.[20] Is it possible to have equally full, deep, and enduring relationships with two spouses? I doubt it. However, if the family metaphor is more apt, it is more accurate to begin with a basic fact and then ask some different questions.

That basic fact is that the pattern of post-1986 U.S. immigration has resulted in substantial immigrants flows from countries with non-Western cultural and political traditions. Given this fact, questions framed through the lens of the family metaphor might be: Is it possible to have two different sets of parents—with sets of different core psychologies, different sets of values, different sets of beliefs, and different world views—along with the information and experiences that support them all? Is it possible to give equal weight to all these elements that help form one's central emotional attachments? No, not without an extremely shallow foundation for one's identity. Such an identity is more likely to be conflicted than functional.

The idea that individuals can integrate multiple, conflicting, basic orientations toward life may well prove a form of cultural conceit. It is apparently easier for some to disregard the primary attachments that most citizens have to their own countries. In so doing, they appear to have confused sophistication with a new form of modern rootlessness. Such people may go anywhere but belong nowhere.[21]

Dual Citizenship and American Democracy

This orientation is the polar opposite of civic engagement. The American ideal of civic republicanism is, after all, the citizen not the subject. Citizenship in a democracy—especially one facing complex, divisive issues arising from its increasing diversity, and which is located in a world in which the same is true—requires much of those who enjoy its benefits. In such circumstances the costs of dual citizenship to a country integrating large numbers of immigrants from diverse cultures may be high indeed.

Advocates consistently minimize the difficulties of being fully engaged, knowledgeable, and effective citizens in one political system, much less two. For example, Spiro argues that "the retention of previous nationality does not necessarily detract from participation in one's newly adapted polity even if the individual remains politically active in her country of origin."[22] What evidence is presented to support this assertion?

Spiro presents no evidence on levels of participation by dual citizens who are or are not active in their "home" countries. Indeed, he presents no evidence on the participation of dual citizens in this country. And he presents no evidence on the levels of understanding and attention paid to the American political process by dual nationals regardless of their engagement in the politics of their home countries. The evidence that does exist suggests that declarative certainty on this point is premature.

Spiro further argues that "political engagement in one polity should not preclude similar commitment in another at least to the extent that rules of political engagement in them are compatible. This possibility is most clearly evidenced by the internal American construct of dual sovereignty in which citizenship in one's state is held concurrently with U.S. citizenship."[23]

This is hardly a convincing or reassuring argument, and elsewhere in the same article Spiro appears to take the opposite position. He allows that, "as for commitment, it may be difficult fully to engage in the civic activity of more that one polity."[24] Yet the problem with equating dual citizenship with the American federal system goes beyond Spiro's apparent agreement with both sides of the argument. The comparison of American federalism and dual citizenship between two or more different cultures and countries simply does not hold up. Any American state in relationship to the national system shares critical and fundamental basic attributes. The language spoken is the same; the common culture is shared as well; the overall framework is unitary; and one system is fully incorporated into the other. They operate on parallel time sequences, with parallel ranges of expected behavior, have had a long history of parallel and integrated historical experience, and so on. Does any one seriously believe that Washington State and Washington, D.C., do not have more in common with each other than either has with India, Mexico, the Philippines, the Dominican Republic, Vietnam, Jamaica, El Salvador, Haiti, Pakistan, Colombia, Russia, Ukraine, Peru, Bangladesh, Poland, and Iran—to name sixteen of the top immigrant-sending countries (to the United States) that encourage dual citizenship?

Spiro then endorses Sandel's view that whether one chooses to carry out one's commitments as an American citizen or the citizenship responsibilities of another country is a matter of personal moral reflection and choice.[25] This is an appealing position, but one with the most profound consequences for what has been for 230 years the foundation of American republican democracy: an informed and engaged citizenry.

Knowledge of Two Cultures?

The informed citizen is the basic foundation of the democratic process.[26] If citizens do not know or will not learn the nation's history and do not understand the policy dilemmas they face, a linchpin of democratic government has been lost. Widespread ignorance or historical amnesia is all the more dangerous at a time when the United States and its citizens must address the complex domestic issues of diversity and the dangers of catastrophic terrorism.

What do citizens of this country need to understand and appreciate? It would be helpful if they had some knowledge of the ways in which the ideals of personal, religious, political, and economic freedoms motivated those who founded this country and those who followed. It would be useful if they were familiar with the courage, determination, self-reliance, optimism, and pragmatism that accompanied those motivations. And it would be necessary to have some knowledge of the country's struggles to realize these aspirations. It would then be possible for immigrants to link their struggles as new Americans who carry the experiences of generations of new arrivals who also have struggled for and found their place in American life.

These are important matters. They apply equally to current as well as to prospective citizens. Yet we are failing badly in both groups on these matters. The "test" for citizenship requires knowledge of a number of disjointed facts requiring little, if any, knowledge of the traditions, both political and psychological, that have shaped this country. Many thousands become citizens and require translations of ballots on which they cast their vote. It is hardly likely that these citizens have followed the complex pros and cons of these policy issues because they do not adequately understand the language in which these debates are conducted.[27] More likely, they gain their information from advocacy groups with a very particular point of view, but one certainly not based on a dispassionate presentation of the issues so that new voters can make up their own minds.

Advocates of multiple citizenship argue that it is possible—indeed desirable—for Americans to be well versed in the culture, history, language, and political debates of other countries. Like many other such statements that have been examined above, this one is also obvious and uncontroversial. As a general aspiration, this is certainly uncontroversial. The problems arise because there is overwhelming empirical evidence that American *and* immigrant children are not learning very much about their own country. Both citizens and immigrants fail badly on indicators of deliberative knowledge. This leads some to ask whether it is legitimate to hold immigrants to a standard unmet by citizens. Many studies underscore that question.

Consider that the Pew Research Center for the People and the Press reported that in 1999, "one-quarter of those they surveyed said they learned about the presidential campaign from the likes of [Jay] Leno and David Letterman, a figure rising to 40 percent among those under 30."[28] Not surprisingly, perhaps in view of those figures, other national studies show that American schools are losing ground in what might well be considered one of the most basic tasks in preparing young persons for their role as citizens: having a foundation of knowledge about the country in which they live and the political institutions that are the foundations of its freedom and way of life.[29] For instance, a survey conducted by the National Constitution Center found that "only 6 percent can name all four rights guaranteed by the First Amendment; 62 percent cannot name all three branches of the Federal government; 35 percent believe the Constitution mandates English as the official language; and more than half of Americans don't know the number of senators."[30]

The National Assessment of Educational Progress (NAEP) Civics Report Card is a major test of subject knowledge for three grade levels (fourth, eighth, and twelfth graders). The 1998 NAEP national surveys and Civics Report Card divided scores on knowledge and proficiency into four groups: below basic, basic, proficient, and advanced. At each of the three grade levels tested, "basic" was defined as having "partial mastery and skills that are fundamental to proficient work at each grade," whereas "proficient" was defined as representing "solid academic performance."

How many students at each grade level were proficient or, even better, advanced? Not many. In fourth grade, only 25 percent scored as proficient or advanced. In eighth grade, the figures were 24 percent for proficiency or advanced competence; and in twelfth grade, the figures were 30 percent for the two categories. These are composite scores and do not directly report the disparities by race and ethnicity that are, if anything, even more troubling.

Is it legitimate to hold immigrants to a standard unmet by citizens? It would seem that ignorance among the latter is not a good reason to allow the same among the former. Certainly, there is a legitimate case to be made for asking those seeking citizenship to be conversant with the traditions and practices of the country to which they are asking for entry. Yet the implications of these data are troubling for Americans and immigrants alike.

Americans do not have and are not acquiring the levels of basic information and understanding that are essential to living in, becoming attached to, and supporting a democratic republican form of government. These deficiencies apparently extend from our most average students to our "best and brightest." They raise severe questions about whether American children will have the tools to shoulder the responsibilities of helping to guide the United States through the dangerous and difficult times we face. And they certainly do not give much comfort to those who believe it is no difficult matter to be sufficiently versed in the history, politics, and political debates of two cultures. Evidence keeps mounting that doing so even in one country is a task beyond the reach of increasing numbers of U.S. citizens.

This fact, however, does not argue for lower standards. On the contrary, the informed exercise of citizenship plays a central, critical role in this democratic republic. Therefore, it is extremely inconsistent for advocates to push more liberal dual-citizenship policies in the name of furthering democracy, while at the same time pushing for standards of knowledge and commitment that undermine it. These dilemmas are well captured by David A. Martin:

> Democracy is built on citizen participation, and its ideal is meaningful participation—of an engaged and informed citizenry. This presupposes a certain level of devotion to the community enterprise, to approach public issues as a unified community, even while leaving much to individual choice in deciding on the aims the politic should pursue or on the specific policies to address specific public issues.[31]

Although Martin at first shows some sympathy to dual citizenship, he goes on to say quite directly that

> it must be conceded that the claims made, . . . if pushed to their limits, would argue strongly against dual nationality in the first place. If focusing on primary political activity in this fashion [by allowing the right to vote in only one place] carries such benefits for solidarity, democratic engagement, and civic virtue, how much more could these goods be expected to flow from channeling *exclusive* political activity? And the point is even stronger if the person, by surrendering, or being required to renounce, all other national ties, has thereby forsworn the use of the exit option when policies do not turn out as she favors.[32]

Promoting Democracy Abroad?

Dual-citizenship advocates routinely tout the beneficial effects of dual citizens living here on democratizing the politics of their home countries. However, a review of the evidence suggests that this is not necessarily the case. Americans who vote in foreign elections do so to further what they see as their own self-interest. Itzigsohn argues after reviewing the evidence that "transnational elites often challenge the existing sociopolitical order, *but theirs are demands for inclusion and recognition as part of that order, not for its radical change.*"[33]

It is quite possible, of course, that leaders aspiring to gain or keep power will promise reforms that benefit those dual citizens abroad who support them. In return, those dual citizens might well support those who favor a broadening of *their* rights—economic or political. This narrow form of self-interest, however, is surely not what advocates have in mind when they discuss the virtues of multiple voting and allegiances. "Self-interest" is not necessarily synonymous with "widening democracy."

Moreover, the idea that immigrant communities will necessarily foster democracy overlooks the fact that *many* political parties and interests in the "home country" are now seeking to organize their nationals abroad. Some of these groups are democratic, as most Americans understand that word; however, some are not. During the civil war in El Salvador, the Marxist guerrilla group FMLN "organized the Salvadorian communities abroad for solidarity and support activities."[34]

Sometimes, we simply do not know which side of the democratic–versus–traditional elites voters line up to support. In the June 2005 Iranian vote, U.S. citizens of Iranian descent were allowed to vote. Their choices were to boycott the vote, as had been urged by Iranian reformers eager to delegitimize the election; to vote for Ali Akbar Hashemi Rafsanjani, the former hard-line president of Iran; or to vote for a reform candidate. The *Washington Post* described several such voters, all of whom eventually decided to vote, thus choosing not to protest by abstaining.[35] Of course, these two examples tell us nothing about how U.S. citizens of Iranian descent actually voted. There is no basis for assuming that the reform candidates received the most votes, or that voting at all was necessarily better than abstaining. Immediately after the vote in Iran, the third-place reform finisher said that the voting had been rigged.[36] We cannot simply assume that voting by Americans in foreign elections furthers democracy.

Dual Citizenship and the Integration of Immigrants

What are the implications of changes in American national culture and psychology for the very large number of dual-citizenship immigrants entering the country in the middle of a forty-plus-year culture war? Two consequences seem clear. First, the cultural stability of the receiving country makes a critical difference in its ability to integrate immigrants into its national community. Immigrants, whether from countries that allow or discourage multiple citizenship, enter into different cultural circumstances in countries where the primary culture is stable and secure and where it is not.

Conversely, multiple citizenship has different meanings and implications in these two different circumstances. Immigrants entering into a country whose cultural assumptions are fluid and contested will find it harder to integrate, even if they wish to do so. A critical question is: Into *which* America should immigrants try to integrate? Is it the traditional America of personal responsibility and initiative, hard work, and an eye on the future? Or is it the America of easy narcissism, self-indulgence, and entitlements? Both Americas exist. Cultural conflict increases the likelihood that immigrants will maintain attachments to their "home country" and put at risk the development and consolidation of newer cultural and country identifications.

Further, a country where the very legitimacy of the integration of immigrants is under attack is substantially different from one where it is not. In the past, assimilation was both an expectation and a reality.[37] Today, neither is true. Assimilation is equated in some quarters with forced and unnecessary demands for conformity to a culture that some feel has little legitimate basis for asking for it.[38]

The Cultural Context of Immigrant Integration

The impact of multiple-citizenship immigrants coming into this country varies as a function of the context in which their older and newer attachments unfold. When more than 85 percent of the very large number of immigrants that the United States admits each year are from dual-citizenship-allowing countries, it is surely time to carefully consider the implications. When immigrants enter a country where the assumption that they should adapt to the values and traditions of the country they have freely chosen is fiercely debated, dual citizenship in America is indeed truly an issue of vast proportions and broad significance.

The American Trade-Off: Instrumentality versus Attachment

It is easy to see the United States instrumentally. It is a place of enormous personal freedom and great economic opportunity. America has always recognized that many arrive seeking these treasures, which are in such short supply in other countries. The fear that self-interest will trump appreciation and genuine emotional connection to the country has, I think, always been the subtext of attempts to ensure that new arrivals became "American."

That has been the trade-off. America takes the chance that it can leverage self-interest and transform it into authentic commitment. Immigrants agree to reorient themselves toward their new lives and away from their old ones. This involves some basics—learning to be at home with English, understanding the institutions and practices that define American culture, and reflecting on the ways in which their search for freedom and opportunity fits in with the history, with all its vicissitudes, that has shaped the idea and promise of

America. It is only at that point that immigrants can make the transformation from self-interest to a genuine emotional connection to their new home.

Bourne's Vision Revisited

The recourse to "common values" as the glue that holds America together is directly contrary to Bourne's vision of a "transnational America."[39] According to Bourne, hyphenated Americans would retain and develop their ties to their countries of origin or home countries and that would make each group more "valuable and interesting to each other." Moreover, these sustained and enhanced national origin differences would spur the development of an "intellectual sympathy," which gets to the "heart of different cultural expressions," and enables each person in one group to feel "as they [the other group members] feel." That, in Bourne's view, would be the basis of the new cosmopolitan outlook, the transnational identity that he favored. Americans would be bound together by the sum of their differences, a remarkable psychological assertion. Such an "intellectual internationalism," he claimed, "will unite and not divide."

There are several problems with Bourne's vision. An "intellectual sympathy" that "gets to the heart of different cultural expressions" and allows one to feel as the other group members feel is inconsistent with psychological theory. Empathy is primarily an emotional attunement, not an intellectual one. The idea that "I know how you feel because of how I would feel if I were in a parallel circumstance" is simply unfounded. It assumes that you are just like me.

Bourne's enthusiasm for his vision is understandable. He was a social critic and advocate. Moreover, he wrote well before advances in the understanding of human psychology. The same, however, cannot be said for his contemporary champions.[40] No psychological theory of identity with which I am familiar finds that the more deeply immersed and central your own cultural identity becomes, the more open you are to incorporating other equally strongly held, and very different, identities.

The literature is unequivocal. People who hold deeply held convictions, an identity based on common values, cultures, psychologies, and worldviews, are much more likely to take their identities as given—as the way things are and the way they ought to be. There is no evidence historically or empirically that taking your Japanese identity seriously makes you more open-minded toward Africans, or that growing up with a strong identity as an Italian or Moroccan makes you better able to feel what it is like to be an Israeli. When cultural identities are "contested," a lack of sympathy and empathy can easily turn into hostility and hatred.

In a country where citizens are drawn from every part of the world, is it realistic to believe that Somalians will learn about and empathize with Italians, who will in turn do the same with Filipinos? Simply to state that is to underscore the limits to such a vision. There are cognitive, emotional, and practical limits and barriers to the amount of information one can take in and make use of, even if one is inclined to—which is another large presumption of Bourne's theory.

The evidence so far is that most groups are more interested in being understood than understanding. Moreover, it seems naive to presume that people can or will take the enormous time required, along with making the huge emotional and informational effort, to develop real empathy for all the many different cultures and groups that now populate America. What is more likely is the kind of superficial avoidant tolerance that does not require much of people except a disinclination to make judgments.

Primary Culture Revisited: An Illustration

Whose view prevails when different understandings of "intellectual internationalism" are at issue? Who gets to decide? This is not a matter of an abstract and ethereal belief that differences rooted in basic cultural experiences and views "will unite and not divide." These matters come up routinely in newly multicultural societies with democratic traditions. For example, should a democratic country committed to the equality of women allow what, to some groups, is the accepted cultural practice of female circumcision or polygamy?

Parekh has thoughtfully tried to square this intellectual circle. However, like all such attempts at theoretical alchemy, there is a large element of substantive evasion of the basic realities. He lists five possible resolutions of these dilemmas: (1) the hope for universal values, which will eventually transcend differences (moral universalism); (2) the primacy of core values, which allows a society to distinguish those it will and will not tolerate (core values); (3) the view of society as so deeply split among class, gender, and other lines that no values can hold and the uniting principle must be "do not harm"; (4) human rights as the ultimate value, a combination of 1 and 4; and (5) the encouragement of an "open-minded and serious dialogue with minority spokesmen and to act on the resulting consensus" (dialogical consensus).[41]

He concludes that none of these views is "wholly satisfactory."[42] Nonetheless, choices must be made—for example, whether a democracy should allow the cultural practice of polygamy. Parekh favors "dialogical consensus." The only problem here is that conflicting, deeply held beliefs may generate more talk than agreement. What then is to be done?

Minorities whose beliefs run directly counter to the premises on which the society operates must acquiesce. Or to put it in Parekh's more gentle phrasing, "Since deep disagreements cannot be always satisfactorily solved, . . . if the majority remains genuinely unpersuaded [after serious dialogue], its values need to prevail."[43] Why? The reason, he claims, is that every society develops "operative public values, those that they live by and which are embedded in their institutions, practices, and moral understandings." They are "the only moral standpoint from which to evaluate minority [cultural/social] practices."[44]

Parekh goes to great lengths to urge a real dialogue with those whose practices are inconsistent with "operative public values," and he gives a good accounting for the arguments for and against the practice of polygamy.[45] Yet in the end, he is both judge and jury. For example, the demand from some quarters to ban arranged marriages because they are coercive is "unjustified" because the practice, "while it has no religious or cultural basis . . . means a great deal to Asians."[46]

And what of a request for circumcision from an adult female? She "should be at liberty to demand any circumcisions she prefers," he claims, even with "complicating factors."[47] And polygamy? After rehearsing the arguments that Muslims might make in favor of that practice, Parekh pronounces them "unconvincing." Assigning his own weighting system to the arguments he presents in favor of banning the practice, he says they "ought to go a long way in convincing the Muslim clerics of the value of monogamy. Western society, then, has the right to ban the practice of polygamy."[48] Perhaps. However, it is quite unlikely that a devout Muslim would weight the arguments as has Parekh. He concludes:

> *If* the current inequality of power and status, self-esteem, and the like between men and women were to end so that women could be depended upon to make equally uncoerced choices, *if* a sizable section of society were free to opt for polygamy, and *if* the latter could be shown not to have the harmful consequences mentioned earlier, there would be a case for permitting it. Since this is not the case today, we are right to disallow it.[49]

Parekh's willingness to entertain the practice rests on what can only be called a wholesale and fundamental transformation of the very culture and its practice that give authority to the claim. He is essentially saying that polygyny would be allowed when the culture reaches the stage where it no longer wishes it. One is reminded here of Stanley Fish's complaint about "boutique multiculturalism": "A boutique multiculturalist may honor the tenants of religions other than his own, but she will draw the line when the adherents of a religion engage in the practice of polygamy. In . . . these cases (and in many analogous cases that could be instanced), the boutique multiculturalist resists the force of the appreciated culture at precisely the point at which it matters most to the strongly committed members."[50]

Exactly. And does it not have to be exactly that way for a coherent, integrated, and functional culture? I will return to that central question as the conclusion of this analysis.

Many Cultures, One Nation

America reached its present state of political, economic, and social development by providing enormous personal freedom and abundant economic opportunity. In doing so, it has leveraged personal ambitions as a tool to transform the social and economic circumstances of individuals. In the process, it has helped to develop and reinforce psychological elements that are consistent with personal success and civic prudence in American democracy—among them an emphasis on hard work, the delay of immediate gratification, prudence, pragmatism, and optimism.

In return, the United States has asked of immigrants that they learn the country's language, culture, and political practices. Thus oriented toward their new home, immigrants can become part of the fabric of American cultural and political life. Leaving a life behind, even one that one wanted to leave, was of course difficult. Yet generations of immigrants have thought the sacrifice worthwhile.

Multiple citizenship, with its associated splitting of attention and commitment, challenges that traditional and successful recipe. Immigrants increasingly come from countries that encourage dual citizenship. Their purposes in doing so are primarily self-interested. It may be to ensure the continued flow of financially critical remittances from those working in the United States. Or it may be to organize their nationals to further their home country's policy preferences, for example, amnesty for those who enter the country illegally or the support of bilingual language policies that help to maintain and facilitate ties to the "home" country. It may take the form of making U.S. citizens and resident aliens sources of financial support for political leaders or parties in the home country. Whatever the specific purposes, sending countries are increasingly mobilizing to retain immigrants' emotional attachment and to further develop a commitment to the home country from which they emigrated.

These developments set the stage for a direct conflict of interest among new immigrants' and citizens' new and old attachments. Given the geographical distribution of such immigrants, it is possible that whole states and certainly some localities will contain a substantial portion of dual citizens with active and deep connections to their country of origin. They will be asked to put aside these experiences and connections in favor of America's national or community interest. Whether that is possible as a matter of psychology or politics remains to be seen.

Dual Citizenship and Narcissistic Expectations

Dual citizenship seems well suited to an age in which advocates, theorists, and politicians tell us that there are no limits to what we should expect to have, and no costs involved in having it. Yet for a democracy—especially one facing issues of cultural coherence and emotional attachment—the costs of admitting and allowing large numbers of dual citizens with multiple loyalties are substantial. In a time when we worry about the decline of social capital and its implications for American civic life, the split attachments of large numbers of dual citizens is not a salutary development. Reforming dual citizenship in the United States is certain to be controversial. It will be politically difficult. This country provides so much freedom and opportunity to those fortunate enough to call it home. Asking citizens to have a primary and relatively uncontested interest in its affairs and a concern for its welfare seems a small and legitimate sacrifice to ask of those who also share its treasures.

Helping Immigrants Feel More at Home: But Whose?

Making immigrants feel welcomed and at ease in their new surroundings is important. Yet there are valid questions regarding different forms that welcoming can take, and whether some forms do not damage the very outcomes of integration they seek to foster. Recently, for instance, a Denver public high school whose student body is 84 percent Hispanic decided to hang the Mexican national flag alongside the American flag in the school lobby and in the social studies classroom. Both the school principal and the teacher involved defended this decision on the grounds of making their Hispanic students feel more "welcomed."[51] They were apparently unfamiliar with a number of studies that have documented the strong role that symbols such as the flag play in the development of American national identity, and their importance in public school classrooms.[52]

Do we foster attachment to American citizenship and its ideals by devaluing it? If we allow or, as some would have us do, encourage an immigrant's loyalties to his or her home country, do we not put at risk their involvement with and connection to American society and culture, which have traditionally been the hallmarks of other immigrants groups?

Schuck and Spiro argue that "we should encourage the assimilation of immigrants who want to be full Americans, but who naturally retain familial, emotional, and economic interests elsewhere."[53] The view that we can encourage immigrants to be "full Americans," while at the same time encouraging them to develop and consolidate their attachments to their home countries, is psychologically and politically contradictory. And given that the governments of these home countries are mounting increasingly sophisticated efforts to strengthen these attachments, the view that we can do both seems determinedly problematic.

Schuck and Spiro's apparent solution to this dilemma is also questionable. They report with apparent approval that "the hyphenated Americans may also be acquiring an ampersand: Irish & American, rather than Irish-American, Dominican & American, rather than Dominican-American. But mostly, Mexican & American." In other words, in place of the now common, bifurcated attachments to this country—Italian Americans, Hispanic Americans, and the like—they suggest that we embrace the development of citizens whose ethnic ancestry equals or trumps their identifications as Americans. If we follow this advice, we will arrive at a most paradoxical situation: a United States devoid of Americans.

No country, and certainly no democracy, can afford to have large numbers of citizens with shallow national and civic attachments. No country facing divisive domestic issues arising from its increasing diversity, as America does, benefits from large-scale immigration by those with multiple loyalties and attachments. And no country, striving to reconnect its citizens to a coherent civic identity and culture, can afford to encourage its citizens to look elsewhere for their most basic national attachments.

The Fundamental Question

The question that America faces in the twenty-first century is whether its cultural, psychological, and political diversity will lead to a fragmented and thus dysfunctional national identity. When he ran for president in 1992, Bill Clinton understood this basic public dilemma.[54] As cited earlier, in a talk with reporters, he said that "it is really potentially a great thing for America that we are becoming so multi-ethnic. . . . But it is also potentially a powder keg of problems and heartbreak and division and loss. And how we handle it will determine, really—that single question may be the biggest determination of what we look like fifty years from now . . . and what the children of that age will have to look forward to."[55]

Is the only alternative to fragmentation Anglo-Western "domination?" No, even to raise this question is to inflate a caricature. If "Anglo-conformity" truly dominates, what accounts for America's pluralism?[56] There have indeed been pressures for immigrants to conform, but this conformity has been toward national political values more than parochial cultural ones. Moreover, some of the pressure to conform to "Anglo values," as for example in the case of learning English, has much more to do with wanting newcomers to become integrated into the society in which they have chosen to belong—not with subjugating them. This has been true throughout U.S. history. A common language was one way the new American republic helped to unite a diverse people.

Must America insist on being the *dominant* culture for its citizens? Perhaps a better question is whether, in a democratically pluralist country like the United States, it is still important to have a *primary* culture.

Notes

1. This chapter builds on Stanley A. Renshon, "American Identity and National Character: The Dilemmas of Cultural Diversity," in *Political Psychology: Cultural and Cross Cultural Foundations*, ed. S. A. Renshon (New York: Macmillan, 2000).

2. Richard Wrightman Fox and James T. Kloppenberg, "Randolph S. Bourne," in *A Companion to American Thought*, ed. Richard Wrightman Fox and James T. Kloppenberg (Cambridge, Mass.: Blackwell, 1995), 85.

3. Alexander T. Aleinikoff, "A Multicultural Nationalism?" *The American Prospect*, January–February 1998, 80–86; also see Spiro 1992.

4. Patricia McGarvey-Rosendahl, "A New Approach to Dual Nationality," *Houston Journal of International Law* 8 (1985): 305–26; the citation here is on 305, 321–25.

5. Peter J. Spiro, "Dual Nationality and the Meaning of Citizenship," *Emory Law Journal* 46, no. 4 (1997): 1412–85; Peter M. Schuck and Peter J. Spiro, "Dual Citizens, Good Americans," *Wall Street Journal*, March 18, 1998.

6. Georgie Anne Geyer, *Americans No More: The Death of Citizenship* (New York: Atlantic Monthly Press, 1996).

7. William Kymlicka, *Multicultural Citizenship: A Liberal Theory of Minority Rights* (Oxford: Clarendon Press, 1995).

8. Charles Taylor, *Multiculturalism and the Politics of Recognition* (Princeton, N.J.: Princeton University Press, 1992).

9. Jürgen Habermas, "Citizenship and National Identity: Some Reflections on the Future of Europe," *Praxis International* 17 (1992); for a cautionary note, see Rogers M. Smith, "The 'American Creed' and American Identity: The Limits of Liberal Citizenship in the United States," *Western Political Quarterly* 41 (1987): 225–51.

10. John Isbister, *The Immigration Debate: Remaking America* (New York: Kumarian Press, 1996); Isbister, "Is America Too White?" in *What, Then Is the American, This New Man?* ed. E. Sandman (Washington, D.C., Center for Immigration Studies, 1998); and Dale Maharidge, *The Coming White Minority: California's Eruptions and America's Future* (New York: Times Books, 1996).

11. For an eloquent formulation of this view, see Sanford Levinson, "Constructing Communities through Words That Bind: Reflections on Loyalty Oaths," *Michigan Law Review* 1440 (1986): 1463–70.

12. Kenneth J. Gergen, *The Saturated Self* (Cambridge, Mass.: Harvard University Press, 1998).

13. David A. Martin, "New Rules on Dual Nationality for a Democratizing Globe: Between Rejection and Embrace," *Georgetown Immigration Law Journal* 14 (1999): 1–34; the citation here is on 8–9.

14. Erik H. Erikson, "The Problem of Ego Identity," *Journal of the American Psychoanalytic Association* 4, no. 1 (1956): 58–121.

15. The quotations in this paragraph are drawn from T. Alexander Aleinikoff, "Between National and Post-National: Membership in the United States," *Michigan Journal of Race and Law* 241 (1999): 9453.

16. Will Herberg, *Protestant, Catholic, Jew: An Essay in American Religious Sociology* (Garden City, N.Y.: Doubleday, 1955).

17. Geyer, *Americans No More*, 68. Martin points out that the bigamy metaphor was made in the context of dual-citizenship debates in the early nineteenth century; "New Rules," 8, n. 24.

18. Martin begins his discussion of dual citizenship by informing the reader that he will use the terms citizenship and nationality interchangeably and elsewhere refers to "mere nationality." He terms the distinction between citizen(ship) and national(ity) a "technical one," which is "rarely important for my purposes"; "New Rules," 8–11. He then goes on to discuss the issue of multiple and conflicting loyalties in which, of course, the distinctions between nationality and citizenship are central, not mere technicalities.

19. Aleinikoff, "Between National and Post-National," 39.

20. The metaphor linking family life and national identity suggests certain parallels. There are, of course, differences as well. The nation is not a parent writ large. Nor does it have the primary responsibilities for nurture, guidance, and socialization. Conversely, like a nation, the family is present from the child's earliest experiences. It is to be found in language, cultural practices, and national cultural identifications of the parents. However, it is also the consistent context in which a child's development unfolds and provides the institutions (e.g., schools, civic, and community experiences) and objects (flags and rituals like the pledge of allegiance) through which the child's personal and national identity becomes fused at an early age.

21. Walzer notes that "in immigrant societies people have begun to experience what we might think of as a life without clear boundaries and without secure singular identities." Michael Walzer, *On Toleration* (New Haven, Conn.: Yale University Press, 1997), 87.

22. Spiro, "Dual Nationality," 1468.

23. Ibid., 1469.

24. Ibid., 1478.

25. Michael J. Sandel, *Democracy's Discontent: America in Search of a Public Philosophy* (Cambridge, Mass.: Belknap Press, 1966), 343.

26. Dennis F. Thompson, *The Democratic Citizen* (New York: Cambridge University Press, 1970).

27. What Martin refers to as "simple voting" ("New Rules," 31) is in fact anything but simple; see Stanley J. Kelley and T. Mirer, "The Simple Act of Voting," *American Political Science Review* 68 (1974): 572–91.

28. Quoted by Howard Kurtz, "Americans Wait for the Punch Line on Impeachment as the Senate Trial Proceeds, Comedians Deliver the News," *Washington Post,*

January 26, 1999; see also Michael X. Delli Carpini and S. Keeter, *What Americans Know about Politics and Why It Matters* (New Haven, Conn.: Yale University Press, 1996).

29. John J. Patrick, "Political Socialization and Political Education in School," in *Handbook of Political Socialization: Theory and Research*, ed. Stanley A. Renshon (New York: Free Press, 1977); Judith Torney-Purta, "Education on Multicultural Settings: Perspectives from Global and International Education Programs," in *Toward a Common Destiny: Improving Race and Ethnic Relations in America*, ed. W. D. Hawley and A. W. Jackson (San Francisco: Jossey-Bass, 1995); Torney-Purta, "Psychological Theory as a Basis for Political Socialization Research: Individuals' Construction of Knowledge," *Perspectives on Political Science* 24 (1995): 23–33; and Richard Neimi, *Civic Education: What Makes Students Learn?* (New Haven, Conn.: Yale University Press, 1999).

30. Cited by M. S. Branson, *The Role of Civic Education* (Los Angeles: Center for Civic Education, 1998), available at http://www.civiced.orglarticles_role.html.

31. Martin, "New Rules," 13. It was Martin who first emphasized the importance of a "common life"—in David A. Martin, "The Civic Republican Ideal for Citizenship, and for Our Common Life," *Virginia Journal of International Law* 301 (1994): 301–19—and then later ("New Rules," 4–14) said he was persuaded to support dual citizenship, albeit subject to limits.

32. Martin, "New Rules," 27.

33. Jose Itzigsohn, "Immigration and the Boundaries of Citizenship: The Institutions of Immigrants' Political Transnationalism," *International Migration Review* 34, no. 4: (2000): 1126–54; the citation here is at 1146.

34. Ibid., 1144.

35. Caryle Murphy, "D.C. Area Iranians Cast Ballots, Debate Boycott," *Washington Post*, June 18, 2005.

36. Michael Slackman, "Iran Moderate Says Hard-Liners Rigged Election," *New York Times*, June 19, 2005.

37. This is the immersion into the "melting pot," which colors the myths of both assimilation's advocates and critics. The former see that process as natural and desirable, and the latter see it as little better than the cultural rape of immigrant identity. On assimilation's discontents, see also Peter Skerry, "Do We Really Want Immigrants to Assimilate?" *Society*, March–April 2000, 57–60.

38. Ronald Takaki, *A Different Mirror: A History of Multicultural America* (Boston, Little, Brown, 1993).

39. Randolph S. Bourne, "Trans-National America," *Atlantic Monthly* 118 (1916): 86–97.

40. T. Alexander Aleinikoff, *Between Principles and Politics: The Direction of U.S. Citizenship Policy* (Washington, D.C.: Carnegie Endowment for International Peace, 1998); and Aleinikoff, "Multicultural Nationalism?"

41. Bhikhu Parehk, "Minority Practices and the Principle of Toleration," *International Migration Review* 30, no. 1 (1996): 251–87; the citation here is on 254–55.

42. Ibid., 255.

43. Ibid., 259.

44. Ibid., 261.

45. Ibid., 265–83.

46. Ibid., 267.

47. Ibid., 271.

48. Ibid., 282.

49. Ibid., 283; the emphasis is mine.

50. Stanley Fish, "Boutique Multiculturalism," in *Multiculturalism and American Democracy*, ed. Arthur M. Melzer, Jerry Weinberger, and M. Richard Zinman (Lawrence: University of Kansas Press, 1998), 69–70.

51. Valerie Richardson, "Denver Schools Will Replace Mexican Flags," *Washington Times*, August 19, 2004.

52. See the discussion of these studies in chapter 3.

53. Schuck and Spiro, "Dual Citizens."

54. I have described the basic public dilemma as a fundamentally unresolved question concerning public psychology and governance facing the president on taking office elsewhere: Stanley A. Renshon, *High Hopes: The Clinton Presidency and the Politics of Ambition* (New York: Routledge, 1998), 3–33. It is not a specific question about public policy but rather the public's psychological connections to its institutions, leaders, and political process. This unresolved public concern underlies and frames more specific policy debates.

55. William J. Clinton, "Remarks and Question and Answer Session with the American Society of Newspaper Editors" (April 11), *Weekly Compilation of Presidential Documents* 33, no. 15 (1997): 501–10; the citation here is on 509.

56. Harold J. Abramson, "Assimilation and Pluralism," in *Harvard Encyclopedia of American Ethnic Groups*, ed. Stephan Thernstrom (Cambridge, Mass.: Harvard University Press, 1980); see also Paul Gleason, "American Identity and Americanization," in *Harvard Encyclopedia of American Ethnic Groups*.

PART IV The Development of National Identity

CHAPTER 8

Do Multiple National Attachments Equal Conflicted National Loyalties?

It seems clear that the acquisition of multiple national identifications is both legal and technologically feasible. But is this advantageous
or even desirable for the relatively small number of Western industrial democracies, most notably the United States, that are being called upon to accept
and embrace them?[1]

Attachment to and identification with a country are complex amalgams of
psychology and experience. In this chapter, I distinguish between primary and
secondary attachments. I then present some evidence from studies of the acquisition of national identity and attachment in children that suggests that
early attachments are not so easily discarded or modified. These data present
a cautionary message to those who argue that many important identity elements can easily coexist with the same psychology.

The question of how individuals integrate or fail to integrate multiple identity elements is not solely a matter of interior psychology. The individual's
loyalties, attachments, and identifications unfold in the context of the society
and culture where he or she develops. A changing national psychology or a
changing national culture provides the basis for a different configuration of
identity.

I also focus here on another feature of the current international and American environment: the strategic decision of other national governments to recognize and make use of international migration patterns for their own state
and political purposes. As Portes points out, "The mobilization of Third
World governments in pursuit of the economic and political benefits of transnationalism has taken several forms that range from the creation of a specialized ministry or government departments, the granting of dual citizenship
and the right to vote in national elections . . . and new legislation allowing the

election of representatives of the Diaspora to the national legislature."[2] Mexico provides a useful case study of why such developments might be of concern for the American national community.

What evidence is there that foreign governments wish to make use of their dual-citizenship nationals? What evidence is there that if they are so inclined, they are successful? Again, the case of Mexican Americans is instructive, and I examine data relevant to this question. Finally, advocates of multiple nationalities and loyalties ask a fair question: What is different now? Have not Americans of different national descent, such as the Irish and the Jews, lobbied in favor of their particular home countries throughout American history? Obviously, the answer is yes.[3] So why should it be more of a concern now? I present five answers to that question.

Dual Citizenship and Political Conflict

According to Peter Spiro, who argues that we should "embrace dual nationalism":

> The prospective spectacle of millions of Mexican-American dual nationals lining up at their consulates to vote in Mexican elections, on the one hand, and the possibility of their voting in high concentration in some U.S. elections, on the other, suffice to justify the enterprise [e.g., reappraising dual nationality]. . . . However, the oddity of these developments should not by itself provoke resistance. In fact, under the standard of earlier times, dual nationality now poses little threat to the polity.[4]

What are these standards of earlier times to which Spiro refers? The fact that now "democracies rarely make war on each other" and, it was war "that ultimately made dual citizenship so problematic in a hostile world. In a malign incarnation they could undermine from within by doing the command of their other allegiance, threatening the polity at a fundamental level."[5] Actually, however, the problem is a good deal more complex than Spiro allows.

Spiro is raising the specter here that dual citizens might be treasonous because of their mixed loyalties in wartime, but he asks us not to worry about this because democracies now rarely go to war. This is an extremely odd argument for an advocate of dual citizenship to make. If mixed loyalties are so dangerous to this republic that treason is a major issue—and I am *not* arguing that it is—then the fact that we rarely go to war with other democracies is small comfort.

The fact of the matter is that many of the 150 immigrant-sending, dual-citizenship-encouraging countries are not democracies. Of the top twenty immigrant-sending countries to the United States that account for 85 percent of its total number of immigrants each year, only three—Canada, the United Kingdom, and India—are mature democracies. Most are not democratic (e.g., Iran, Pakistan, and Vietnam), and the rest are fledgling democracies that often have deeply rooted authoritarian strains (e.g., Mexico, the Dominican Republic, Russia, and Ukraine).

Moreover, democracies do still have armed conflicts with nondemocracies. And as David Martin points out, "If relaxed rules on dual nationality are adapted or expanded over the coming decades, persons with such a mix of citizenship (one democratic and one non-democratic) will doubtlessly make up a significant percentage."[6] He also notes that an "especially worrisome cloud" is the rise of ethnic tensions and identity politics, which increase the structural fault lines in a large number of what he terms "polyglot nations," of which the United States is surely now one.

Martin is not wrong to worry. In Santa Ana, California, former Vietnamese communists and their noncommunist counterparts scuffled during a protest against an art show's positive depiction of the communist regime.[7] In another similar incident, the decision of a Vietnamese immigrant to drape a communist flag across the front of his store sparked thousands to protest.[8]

In the Elian Gonzalez case, residents of Miami, backed by their local government, said they would defy federal orders to hand the boy over to immigration authorities. The *New York Times* reporter who covered the story wrote:

> To many people here, some who cheered and some who shuddered, it was a declaration of independence for a part of the country that is, increasingly, a nation apart. People have even begun to greet each other with: "Welcome to the Independent Republic of Miami." Latin Americans make up the overwhelming majority, and English has faded from homes, offices, and stores. But it is the Cuban exiles who drive the county's economy, politics and culture, and it is Cuba's flag, not the United States', in the windows of shops, on car antennas and on the mural behind the Chevrolet dealership on Le Jeune Road.[9]

Do Multiple Loyalties Equal Conflicted Loyalties?

Loyalty is a complex emotion. Psychologically, it is an attachment to, a sense of identification with, and feelings toward a person, place, or thing.[10] These can run from the shallow to the profound, from the episodic to the immutable, and from the singular to the diverse.

Recall from the studies reviewed in chapter 3 that our primary nationality, the one that we are born into, begins to take root very early—indeed, before the child is born. The history and practices that brought a particular couple together are themselves influenced by the cultural expectations and understandings that they acquired while growing up in their country and culture. How they prepare for their child and how they relate to him or her is also conditioned by the same realities. And of course, the parents speak to the child in their own language, soon to be his. As he grows, they are the guides and interpreters of the culture that he must learn and transverse. The process of becoming embedded in and attached to one's country of origin begins early.

Loyalty to a nation and the feelings of attachment begin at a primal age and become increasingly consolidated as the child develops. That is why people are willing to die for their country, why great national accomplishments bring pride, and why the symbols of a country—the flag, the constitution—carry such great emotional weight and political power.

It is why a *New York Times* reporter, covering the attitudes of African immigrants to this country, could write: "Many African immigrants say that whether they stay here for 2 or 20 years, Africa is, and always will be, home."[11] It is why Funeraria Latina—owned by the funeral industry giant Service Corporation International—transports 80 percent of its bodies out of the United States.[12]

The *New York Times* also recently published a story on the funeral practices of different South American groups. Employees at the large R. G. Ortiz funeral parlor chain noted that while it was also common for other groups to send their dead back, Mexicans were the most adamant about it. About half the funeral home's Puerto Rican clients and three-fourths of its Dominican and Ecuadoran clients wanted bodies sent back to their homelands. For Mexicans, the figure was closer to 95 percent. Some put the figure higher, at about 99 percent. In contrast, Father Grange of Saint Jerome's Roman Catholic Church in the Mott Haven section of the Bronx was quoted as saying, "When the Irish came to stay, the first thing they did was to buy a grave," he said. "For the Mexicans, home is not here yet. In 10 years maybe New York will be home, and they'll start to bury their dead here."[13]

Or consider the reactions of some Mexican Americans interviewed about whether they would apply for U.S. citizenship in light of Proposition 187. Some of the answers were: (1) "Never, I was born in Mexico, raised in Mexico, and I want to die in Mexico. (2) Giving up my Mexican citizenship is like giving up a child of mine. (3) It's as though I'm betraying my country, my people and my culture."[14]

The point here is not that immigrants are disloyal. They are, however, conflicted. And increasingly, governments of dual-citizenship, immigrant-sending countries are taking steps to ensure that the loyalties and attachments that many immigrants feel for their country of origin are maintained and even stimulated. A good illustration is Mexico and its immigrant nationals in the United States.

Mexico's Dual-Citizenship Decision: A Mix of Self-Interested Motivations

Mexico shares a long border with the Southwest and Western United States and is the single highest immigrant-sending country to the United States. The latest official estimates (2000) of the number of foreign-born persons, of whatever legal status, living in the United States is almost 26 million. The number of immigrants for the last few years of the decade stretching from 1990, coupled with the total number of immigrants in the previous decade, adds up to the largest consecutive two-decade influx of immigrants in the country's history. Half the foreign-born population is from Latin America, and more than a quarter (28 percent) is from Mexico.

Or consider that in 1960, 1970, 1980, and 1990 Mexico was one of the top ten countries that sent immigrants to the United States. In 1980 and 1990, it was *the* immigrant-sending country. In 1980, there were 2.1 millions Mexicans living in the United States. By 1990, that figure had doubled to over 4.2 million. By 1994, it had jumped to 6.6 million.[15] And by 1997, it had jumped to over 7 million.[16] By 2000, that number was approaching 8 million.[17]

Mexican Americans have particularly high birthrates. The Census Bureau estimates that the proportion of the foreign-born population is likely to increase in future years, given that group's relative youth and high fertility rates.[18] This prediction proved accurate. Census figures from 2004 found, "in another contrast to the 1990s, births have overtaken immigration this decade as the largest source of Hispanic growth," and that "one in five children under 18 is Hispanic."[19] Mexicans are thus poised to have a greater and greater demographic, political, and cultural significance in the United States. These facts have not been lost on the government of Mexico, which has been changing its laws accordingly. As Gutierrez points out, "The dual nationality amendments radically depart from Mexican tradition and laws."[20] The legal changes have required three articles of the Mexican Constitution to be amended and at least fifty-five secondary laws to be repealed or revised. This enormous undertaking has represented "a sharp reversal after decades in which successive governments either ignored Mexican expatriates or referred to them as *pochos*, or cultural traitors."[21] What changed?

The full story of that change has yet to be written, but it will surely entail self-interested strategies on the part of the ruling Mexican party, the opposition party, and a growing chorus of Mexican Americans who want to further their economic, political, and cultural claims in their country of origin. Each of these parties has its own versions of self-interest, but when these strategies are considered, the interests of the United States are clearly absent.

And what are these calculations? Mexico has always depended on the northward movement of immigrants into the United State to reduce population and economic pressures, and the political consequences that flow from them. Encouraging northward migration operates as a "safety valve" for Mexican society and, not incidentally, for its governing elites.

Mexico, like other immigrant-sending countries, benefits economically from sending many of its nationals to the United States to work. The reason is that Mexican nationals working in the United States are a key source of national income, which helps to relieve economic and thus political pressures on the governing elites. A recent study on the binational impact of Latino financial remittances found that because of "the very large number" of new arrivals from Latin America remittances have "dramatically increased" and "represent a substantial contribution to the national economies of the receiving countries."[22]

The specific figures for Mexico are themselves startling. For example, in 1990 the five countries that the study examined (Colombia, Dominican Republic, El Salvador, Guatemala, and Mexico) received over $1 billion in remittance income; however, "remittances to Mexico account for over half of the total amounts sent to the five countries combined." As the study points out, the World Bank figures it uses are "conservative estimates, and others indicate that Mexican remittances account for between $2 to $4 billion." Moreover, Mexico was one of three countries in which the increase in remittance rates was greater than its immigrants' income. Finally, the amount of remittances to all five countries exceeds the official aid of the United States. This is true even for countries like El Salvador, which received the largest amounts in the 1980s.

A 2003 survey by the Inter-American Development Bank found that Mexicans sent back home $14.5 billion in remittances, making it the second largest source of funding in the Mexican economy.[23] As part of that analysis, a survey was conducted that suggested that a significant percentage of Hispanics, particularly Mexicans, are interested in moving to the United State: A total of 19 percent of Mexican adults, or about 13.5 million people, said they were thinking of migrating here.[24] In recent years, Mexican and American authorities have made it easier and more affordable to send money back to their "home" countries, "and American banks have begun allowing illegal immigrants to open accounts so relatives at home can withdraw funds from automatic teller machines."[25] So, as this survey makes clear, economic incentives stimulate immigration, much of it illegal, while the U.S. government and banking institutions increase the incentives to migrate here.

From the standpoint of Mexican economic incentives, the advantages of dual citizenship and its attachments to Mexico are clear. The closer the ties to the "homeland" can be encouraged and stimulated, the more stable the flow of remittances will be and the more likely they are to increase over time. At the same time, the promises of making more money and sending it "home" will operate as a powerful magnet to large numbers of Mexicans and other Central and South Americans to migrate to America, mostly illegally.

The Mexican government aids this cycle of self-interest in a number of ways. Recently, the Mexican government admitted for the first time that it "has not done enough to stop the flow of illegal aliens across the U.S.–Mexico border, particularly non-Mexicans who first illegally cross Mexico's southern border."[26] The admission concerned the rise in border crossings by "other than Mexicans" into the United States, a national security issue for the United States. U.S. officials had said that their Mexican counterparts must take unspecified "confidence-building measures" to prove that they are "serious" about reducing illegal immigration.

Perhaps one place to start would be for the Mexican government to cease publication of the booklet *Guide for the Mexican Migrant.* According to the *New York Times*, it "instructs migrants how to safely enter the United States illegally and live there without being detected. . . . It also counsels migrants to keep a low profile once in the United States, advising, for instance, that they stay away from loud parties or discos that might be raided by the police and stay out of domestic disputes, which might lead to an arrest. Finally, it lists what rights migrants have if caught, among them safe transport home, medical care, food and water."[27]

Removing barriers that keep Mexican Americans alienated from their home country is another plus from this standpoint. Dual-citizen Mexican Americans can now send their money home and have use of it when they spend time, retire, or even die there. From the self-interested economic perspective of Mexican Americans, this is a positive development.

Yet however powerful the economic incentives, and they are substantial, it would be an error to underestimate the political importance of Mexican Americans to the Mexican government. Spiro has argued that "Mexico and other countries would have no concrete means to use their nationals as instruments, at least not consistent with international law." I am not sure what international law making use of multiple loyalties is inconsistent with, but it is clearly part of the strategic thinking of Mexican leaders.[28]

In a private meeting with U.S. Latino leaders in 1995, former Mexican president Ernesto Zedillo said that his government would support the then-pending constitutional and other legal changes, allowing dual citizenship to "increase the political clout of Mexican Americans."[29] Why was he interested in doing that? For one reason: because his goal was to "develop a close relationship between his [Mexico's] government and Mexican-Americans, one in which *they could be called upon to lobby U.S. policymakers on economic and political issues involving the United States and Mexico.*"[30]

Or, as Vargas notes, the many recently developed Mexican government programs that are now reaching out to the Mexican American community in the United States have a clear purpose: "The government of Mexico is investing in Mexican Americans now with the plans to collect tomorrow. Recognizing their political and economic power in the United States, but aware of the familial and spiritual links that they continue to maintain with Mexico, the country of their ancestors, the Mexican government is hoping to contribute to the development of a powerful and effective lobby ready to represent and defend the interests of Mexico in this country."[31]

Or, consider the rather direct candid comment of Juan Henandez, a Mexican American who was recently appointed to the Cabinet of the president of Mexico. Hernandez's role is to organize and mobilize Mexican Americans in the United States. What is he mobilizing them to do? In an interview with Ted Koppel on *Nightline*, he made it quite clear: He wants Mexican Americans in the United States to think "Mexico First. . . . I want the third generation, the seventh generation, *I want them all to think 'Mexico first.'*"[32] Americans on the other hand might well be excused if they wonder why one of their fellow citizens is legally entitled to work in and for a foreign government advocating that Americans put another country first.

Mexican Americans living in the United States are well aware that the Mexican government has changed its approach—and they understand why as well. Raul Izguirre, the president of the National Council of La Raza, said in a 1996 interview, "For many years there was an aversion by Mexico to deal with our community. Now they realize we represent a long-term interest."[33] What interests are these? Writing before the changes became law, Vargas explained:

> Mexicans with dual nationality would raise an array of novel and delicate questions in the United States. Such questions may address international law in general and specific areas of domestic legislation of these two countries. Taxation, labor issues, acquisition of real estate and other business transactions, inheritance, domicile, military service, family law and minor's rights, deportation and other immigration law aspects, political rights and diplomatic protection may be among the long list of technical legal questions directly affected by this contemplated legal change.[34]

To this list, one might add current Mexican president Vicente Fox's call for essentially open borders between the two countries.[35] Because almost all the traffic would go in the south to north direction, this suggestion would appear to be highly advantageous to Mexico. It would ensure that more Mexican

Americans would send more remittances, further aid the Mexican population, and relieve economic and social pressures. The overall benefits for the United States appear economically modest; politically, it is potentially destabilizing.

The Mexican president remarked to the Mexican Federal Congress in May, 1995: "The Mexican nation goes beyond the territory contained by its borders. Therefore an essential element of the 'Mexican national program' will be to promote the constitutional and legal amendments designed for Mexican to retain their nationality."[36] There is certainly enough additional evidence to support this view that many Mexican immigrants already retain an important attachment to their country of origin.[37]

The Mexican government is not alone in trying to make use of its nationals in the United States. Itzigsohn writes of the Dominican Republic:

> The Dominican government and the Dominican parties are actively encouraging Dominican immigrants to adopt American citizenship and participate in the American political process. The Dominican government hopes that stabilizing the legal situation of immigrants will guarantee the continuous flow of remittances. It also hopes that the Dominican leadership in the United States will lobby for the Dominican government on issues ranging from [the North American Free Trade Agreement] to regulating the deportation of Dominicans jailed in the U.S.[38]

Indeed, Itzigsohn makes the point that all the Latin American immigrant-sending countries he studied "have an interest in improving the socio-political position of immigrants in the United States, believing that this will guarantee the flow of remittances and provide them with a lobbying base of support in the American Congress."[39]

More recently, Leonel Fernández, the president of the Dominican Republic, visited New York to address an audience of Dominican Americans. Among the ideas he was there to discuss was "a Dominican Peace Corps that would bring young Dominican Americans back to their roots . . . and institutional alliances that would help increase the political profile of Dominicans in New York, where they are rapidly overtaking Puerto Ricans as the city's largest Hispanic group."[40] The Dominican president was said to see the Dominicans as one people living in different parts of the globe, much as the Mexican president saw his nationals.

Some insist that the whole problem is overblown and dismiss concerns about other countries organizing their former nationals in defense of policies they favor. Martin and Aleinikoff believe that dual nationality poses "few risks." Why? Because worries about dual citizenship will fade, "if a state did not extend citizenship to future generations abroad then a family loses all connections with the country of origin."[41] That *if* is a pretty big one; and as we have seen, there are many strong incentives for countries to do precisely the opposite.

O'Brien argues, for example, that "it is difficult to imagine a manner in which the Mexican government could formulate 'Mexican interests' in a way that U.S., Mexicans dual citizen voting patterns could manipulate towards the attainment of particular goals in the United States."[42] Actually, it is not difficult at all to imagine how this would be done. Generally, they rely on appeals to nationalism; pride in one's former and, with dual citizenship, present country; and a politics of grievance. They also have a variety of tools at their disposal to do so.

There are, of course, local newspapers on the World Wide Web, beamed television from home countries, the use of societies that are organized in part by the government to further their countries' nationals, and increasing political campaigns that spill over into the United States. The reach of "home countries" and the ambition to use it have reached unprecedented levels.

In November 2002, almost 500,000 Salvadorans in the United States received a recorded message from the president of that country, urging them to meet a deadline the next day to extend U.S. work permits they received through an emergency program.[43] The George W. Bush administration had granted temporary protected status to many Salvadorans in March 2001, arguing that they should be allowed to stay here and work legally because their country had just been shattered by two earthquakes, and was extending it for one year. As Sheridan notes,

> To spread that message, the Salvadoran government is reaching directly into homes here—a sign of how politics is stretching beyond borders as immigration increases. El Salvador's campaign has gone well beyond TV ads. Videos shown on its national airline, TACA, describe the work-permit program so that travellers will inform their relatives. In the United States, workers have handed out letters from the Salvadoran president at soccer games and at parties held to help immigrants re-register. In the most ambitious initiative, the long-distance phone company Americatel, agreed to send a recorded message from the Salvadoran president into the homes of 750,000 U.S. clients in its database who had called El Salvador.[44]

Another example concerns the political outreach efforts of the Mexican government to its nationals in the United States. One reporter notes that several Americans are running for seats in Mexico's Congress. If elected, "their priorities include streamlining the process of sending money to Mexico, making it easier for Mexicans abroad to invest in their hometowns, and influencing United States drug and immigration policies."[45]

Mexican American Dual Citizens: Ambivalent Attachments

On many empirical measures, Mexican Americans stand apart from traditional or even contemporary patterns of integration into American society. We have already noted in chapter 5 the major study of immigrant identification and integration into the American national community carried out by Rubén Rumbaut. Recall that he found an "assimilative trend in the form of a hyphenated American identity over time for the groups he studied, with the exception of Mexicans."

Moreover, among second-generation Mexicans, "a very substantial number identified as Chicano, virtually all of them U.S. born and all of them in California; in fact a quarter of all second-generation students of Mexican descent self-identified as Chicano, a historical and problematic identity unique to that group." In other words, compared with other second-generation immigrant children (e.g., Asians), Mexicans were far more likely to select a pan-racial/ethnic identity that did not include some American component.

The same kinds of differences showed up in language use—one of the key elements of integration into a new society. Rumbaut measured language facility by relying on self reports, a method ripe for methodological errors like those brought about by social desirability factors.[46] Even so, he found a difference: "Three quarters of the total sample preferred English, including substantial majorities in every group. . . . The single exceptions are the Mexicans who are the most loyal to their native tongue, although even among them 45 percent preferred English. More than one-third speak English only with their parents, although, interestingly, a smaller proportion speak English only with their close friends (who are also children of immigrants)."[47]

And finally, when one examines the rate of naturalization for those qualified to seek it, Mexicans again stand out. The proportion of naturalized citizens among the foreign-born population in 1997 was 53 percent for those from Europe, 44 percent for those from Asia, and 24 percent for those from Latin America. Why are the Latin American naturalization rates so low? Primarily, according to the U.S. Department of Commerce, "because of the low figure for the population from Mexico (15 percent)."[48]

Does dual citizenship inhibit naturalization in the United States? Hispanic advocacy groups argue that it does not. De la Garza and his associates compared a group of Central and Latin American countries that do and do not grant dual citizenship and ask whether dual citizenship affects naturalization rates.[49] They conclude that it does not. However, they erroneously include six countries that *do* grant dual citizenship (Bolivia, Chile, Guatemala, Costa Rica, Ecuador, and Brazil) in their list of ten that do not.[50] Moreover, they are only able to conclude that there is no difference by excluding the single largest immigrant-sending country with (at the time) no dual-citizenship provisions—Mexico—from their analysis.

A more careful analysis of the impact of dual citizenship on naturalization rates was undertaken by Yang as part of a large empirical analysis of naturalization using national census data. He notes, "The odds of naturalization for immigrants from countries which recognize dual citizenship are about 20 percent ($-0.201 = 0.799 - 1$) smaller than the odds for those from countries which do not."[51]

The ambivalence that immigrants feel because of the pull of dual loyalties can be resolved in several different ways. The pull of the old country can recede, and the attachment to the newer one can grow. The pull of the old country can retain its original strength and even grow, given modern technology and/or efforts by the "old country" to stimulate them. Or the immigrants can continue to have strongly mixed feelings, essentially making them feel never truly at home.

Multiple Attachments, Then and Now

We are now in a better position to answer a question that arises in connection with the spread of dual citizenship. Other immigrants have come to the United States and established themselves and yet still retained an active interest and involvement in the affairs of their home countries, even after several generations. Irish Americans and Jewish Americans come easily to mind here.

Certainly many Irish Americans were concerned with "the troubles" in Northern Ireland, and some provided financial support for the positions they favored. In the annals of lobbying, the efficacy of those lobbying for the state of Israel is legendary and a model for those who wish to use their dual citizenship to emulate it. So why is what is "good" for Irish Americans and Jewish Americans not equally good for Mexican dual nationals? There are several differences between then and now. Let us look briefly at each.

American Culture in Transition

As I suggested above, American culture has been going though a difficult and contentious period. American culture has been through forty-plus years of cultural warfare that shows no signs of abating. These contentious debates have permeated almost all our major cultural and political institutions and issues. A partial list includes marriage, the military, schools, abortion, the debate over inclusion versus performance, and bilingual education. It is a small wonder that immigrants might be confused over exactly with what parts of our culture they are expected or might wish to identify.

Yet the issue is deeper and more pronounced than a list of our cultural battles might indicate. Some parts of our cultural wars affect immigrants' integration into the American national community more dramatically than others. Same-sex marriage debates are much less likely to retard immigrant attachment than are debates about what should be taught in school about American civics and history. Debates about the proper roles of women and mothering are less likely to impede attachment than are debates about whether assimilation is a racist plot to strip immigrants of their ethnicity and home attachments. These more harmful debates center on our core institutions and concepts that help immigrants to bridge the gap between their lives and attachments to their country of origin with their lives here, which makes them the most damaging.

These debates do not take place in a vacuum. They take place in the context of a public that is timid about asserting its clearly stated belief in public opinion polls: that immigrants should take steps to become incorporated into American life and culture. They take place in a context in which the government sends mixed and sometimes counterproductive signals regarding what is expected of immigrants. Even that word "expected" is almost never heard in immigration debates.

The use of that term would mean that there were steps to take toward a good-faith effort to become part of your new home community. It would also carry the implication that there would be some measure of dissatisfaction if the steps were avoided. Americans might be forced to make an assessment— even a judgment. And as noted, the research strongly suggests that Americans have become very reticent to make judgments about others' choices—even those, as with immigrant integration, on which they hold strong views.

Elite Laissez-Faire and Public Concern

Public leadership sets the tone of debate about immigration. In the last great wave of debate, the public and its leaders were of one mind about immigrants: They ought to assimilate. The public expected it, leaders expected it, and institutions reflected it. Henry Ford set up his model housing projects where immigrant workers learned to be American. Schools and other major institutions pitched in to do their share to bring immigrants into the American community.[52] Theodore Roosevelt used his "bully pulpit" to extol the virtues of 100 percent Americans. To repeat, leaders and the public were united in the question of how to integrate immigrants into the American national community.

Heavy handed? Perhaps a bit. But as Glazer and Moynihan demonstrated, the so-called melting pot hardly erased ethnic identities.[53] Whether this was a heavy hand or a helping hand depends on your perspective, but the result cannot be denied. Tens of millions of immigrants and their families found their footing in the United States.

Today the government has gone from a helping hand to a missing hand. Though there are a number of its actual policies and a number of policy areas where it chooses not to act, the government now sends very mixed signals to immigrants. Since the sea change brought about by the 1965 immigration law, the government has provided little in the way of orientation to American life, though the Bush administration has begun to reinstate efforts in this area with a new and helpful welcoming guide.[54] The government does little to help immigrants learn English, a single powerful key to becoming more integrated into American society. It continues to take no position on foreign governments' attempts to bind their nationals to the "home country." It takes no position on immigrants voting in foreign elections or holding two passports. Indeed, it continues to operate as if the integration of waves of new immigrants in the early part of the century happened by magic and not through the concerted effort of government, civic, and business organizations, buttressed by the overwhelming support of the American people.

Today, the American government does not lead the charge to foster immigrants' integration and attachment. It shrinks from these responsibilities. Can you imagine any modern president referring to "100 percent Americans?" I am not arguing in favor of doing so; strong and primary attachments to this country can easily leave room for other attachments as well. I simply want to underscore how far we have wandered from the idea that the integration of immigrants into our national community is desirable for the country and for immigrants. At the turn of the century, elites and the public were united in their view that this was a fair expectation. No longer.

Consider the number of legal immigrants entering this country every year, which has averaged close to 1 million. The Chicago Council on Foreign Relations polled both the public and a wide-ranging leadership on a number of issues including immigration, and it found a serious disconnect there. Of the public sample, 54 percent wanted to reduce present levels of immigration, while only 10 percent of the leadership sample did. While 31 percent of the public want to keep immigration levels the same, 50 percent of the leadership sample wanted to keep immigration levels the same (ranging from 46 percent among Bush administration officials to 73 percent among Democratic Party staff members). And 33 percent of the leadership sample actually wanted to increase immigration levels, while only 11 percent of the public wishes to do so. In a further illustration of the mismatch between public and leadership views on this issue, only half the leadership sample correctly estimated public views on this issue.[55]

American political and civic leaders are hesitant to take the small necessary steps to help immigrants integrate (in some cases, they are opposed). Many leaders at all levels of government share the discomfort in expressing, through law or policy, any expectations regarding immigrant integration. Whether it is developing a civics curriculum that manages to be honest and informative while providing a bridge between immigrant and national experience or making a serious and sustained commitment to integrating the many millions of new immigrants rather than repeatedly calling for the "regularization" of illegal immigrants, the government has failed in a core responsibility: making us truly One America.

The timidity and failure of civic and political leadership in this area has many causes, including a failure to appreciate the central stakes involved, a disinclination to take stands that might result in being the target of advocates' attacks, and a focus on small constituent interests rather than national ones. Ethnic advocates may want wider open doors for their illegal compatriots, but most Americans do not. Those who can hire them may want more housekeepers and better-kept lawns, and big business may prefer fraudulently documented cheap labor, but most Americans do not.

Of course, it is true that culture is always in transition. Ongoing and expected cultural evolution and development, which builds on and refines basic cultural and political institutions, is one matter. Building on the ruins of what was previously accepted is another. When Irish Americans and Jewish Americans expressed and acted on their continuing interests in their "home" countries,[56] they did so in a context in which one set of basic elements of an American identity—a commitment to its core institutions and cultural arrangements and their desire to be part of them—was not in doubt.

Changes in American National Psychology

The term "American national psychology" does not mean that there is one American psychology or an indelibly etched American "national character." It does reflect the fact that the blend of opportunity and freedom framed by a constitutional republic created a group of citizens who were determined to realize their ambitions and make use of their opportunities. American cultural practices and institutions have developed over the past 200-plus years in response to these facts.

Obviously, not every American has displayed these characteristics. However, America would not have been built without these qualities. American public psychology has, of course, evolved over the past 200 years. We are no longer a nation of rugged individualists surging westward, although those characteristics remain a clear national presence. But alongside modern individualists, there are many who prefer not to stand out or apart.

American national psychology can be traced to two modern trends, the rise of "other-directedness" and the rise of the culture of narcissism. David Riesman argued that in response to anxiety about the vicissitudes of mobility in a society dominated by large institutions, Americans began to train their children to "fit in" and "get along,"[57] Of course, to get along, one must go along—hardly a recipe for stand-apart individualism.

That formula's by-product could be found in the "live-and-let-live" cultural code. As Yankelovich put it, "Traditional concepts of right and wrong have been replaced by norms of 'harmful' or 'harmless.' If one's action are not seen as penalizing others, even if they are 'wrong' from the perspective of traditional morality, they no longer meet much opposition."[58] Unlike the 1960s, when counterculture adherents dismissed traditional values as bourgeois and confining, this live-and-let-live approach to personal values and convictions has led to a new ethic that can be summed up by what has become almost an eleventh commandment, "Thou shalt not judge."

The "non-judgmentalism of middle class Americans" in matters of religion, family, and other personal values emerges as the major finding of Wolfe's in-depth interviews with mainly suburban clusters of Americans across the country.[59] He attributes it to an emphasis on pragmatism rather than on values in making tough personal decisions, a reluctance to second-guess the tough choices of other people, and ambivalence or confusion as the default moral position. There is an important distinction to be drawn between being slow to judge and being averse to making judgments.

These cultural and psychological currents are the framework within which the cultural wars of the past forty years have taken place. Not surprisingly, they have affected Americans' understanding and expectations regarding immigrations. Assimilation? Maybe, as critics argue, it is an ugly process meant to strip immigrants of their cultural heritage. Maybe it is better not to expect that new immigrants will become part of the American national community beyond taking advantage of the economic opportunities here. Patriotism? Maybe it is more welcoming to not do anything to interfere with immigrants' right to retain and further develop strong emotional ties to their "home country" and their home country's attempt to foster it.

In the past, whatever interests Irish Americans and Jewish Americans had in their respective home countries were filtered through the lens of a more widely shared national psychology and culture that did not shy away from independent-minded judgments. They also lived in a period when patriotism and attachment to the American national community were not contested. Irish Americans and Jewish Americans became integrated into the American national community at a time when becoming American was an aspiration and when institutions and those who led them were not ambivalent about the value of having immigrants integrate.

Multiple Loyalties, Then and Now: The Psychology of Identity Primacy

Consider the hyphenated Irish American identity. Does that mean such a person is an *Irish* American, an Irish *American*, an *Irish American,* or an *American* of Irish descent? As I noted, each of these permutations reflects a psychological identification with, and arrangement of, some of the basic building blocks that form our identity.

It seems very unlikely that for most Irish Americans and Jewish Americans, their home country identifications were neither equal to nor more important than their American identity. Moreover, had any of their fellow nationals suggested that they should be, most might well have responded clearly, straightforwardly, and without much self-doubt: No. They might be interested in some aspects of their home countries, but most, if not all, would say they were American first and primarily.

Consider further the hypothetical case in which the Irish American and Jewish American equivalents of "black" or Chicano (Hispanic) were available. Let us call them "white" and "European." Of course, those terms were available but had never been embraced by Irish and Jewish Americans. Such an embrace would effectively decouple one's identity from any specifically stated identification with America.

Can anyone seriously argue that such an identity would be chosen, as Rumbaut found was the case in second-generation immigrants from Mexico?[60] He found that almost half select a pan-racial/ethnic identity, or that another 8 percent of such adolescents would select an identity exclusively allied with national origin. Would a random sample of Irish American or Jewish American second-generation children show over 50 percent whose *selected* self-identification did not include an American element? I think not.

One Hundred Fifty and Rising Fast: The Problems of Scale

The number of countries encouraging multiple citizenship has risen dramatically. There are relatively few countries left that do not have some form of dual citizenship. Yet there is an asymmetry in the movement of immigrant populations. The flow is from economically struggling, often less republican political countries to more economically secure liberal democracies. The weight of cultural, economic, and political adjustment falls on the latter, not the former.

Few Americans who are not of Mexican origin seek to become nationalized there. And if they did, they would learn that Mexico, unlike the United States, requires those who would do so to renounce their former citizenship—and is serious about it. If the foreigner makes such an affirmation but does so in a "fraudulent manner or without true intent *to be definitely and permanently obligated by them*," the result can be a stiff fine.[61] Who decides when and whether the taking of an oath is done in this matter? The issue is "exclusively dependent on the absolute discretionary powers of the Mexican authorities."

Moreover, the Mexican government does not even issue birth certificates for the children of non-Mexicans born in Mexico.[62]

Even if Mexico were to liberalize its nationalization laws for other than its nationals living abroad, it would have little discernible impact on the nature of their political, cultural, and social institutions. The same cannot be said of the United States.

The United States takes in the greatest number of immigrants, from more countries, than any country in the world. It is also the destination of substantial numbers of illegal immigrants, now estimated to be closer to 8 or 10 million rather than the 5 to 6 million previously thought.[63]

These three facts, coupled with the reality of 150 immigrant-sending countries that encourage dual citizenship for their nationals (but not necessarily for the nationals of other countries), leads to one inescapable conclusion: No other country in the world has so many dual citizens, many with multiple loyalties.

In the past, Irish Americans and Jewish Americans, to the extent that they had interests and some level of attachment to their home countries, were the numerical exception, not the rule. Today, with 85 percent of the large number of immigrants we have accepted in the last four decades from dual-citizenship-encouraging countries, the situation is fast being reversed. Dual citizens are increasingly becoming the rule, *not* the exception, in the United States.

Compatibility of Interests, Then and Now: Some Distinctions

Immigrant involvement in "homeland issues," as Harrington terms them, is not new.[64] The Irish in the United States made U.S. relationships with Ireland's archenemy England a campaign issue as far back as the 1840s.[65] Ancestral quarrels like those between Greece and Turkey have periodically spilled over into American legislative politics. Yet is it accurate to say, as Spiro does, that a "dual Mexican American who advocates policies that benefit Mexico, is little different from a Catholic who advocates policies endorsed by the church or a member of Amnesty International who writes his congressman at the organization's request"?[66]

Any American citizen who espouses a policy position is likely to be in accord with the views of one advocacy group or another. Does the citizen who agrees with Amnesty International's position define himself or herself as a "world citizen" and not a U.S. citizen? Or is he or she an American citizen who supports the position of an international organization? Is every American citizen who supports the work of the United Nations an example of one with dual loyalties? Obviously not. Neither Amnesty International nor the United Nations is a home country with all the emotional attachments that follow from such a relationship.

What of Catholics voting in accordance with the Vatican's position on a political or legal issue? Though this gets us closer to the issues raised by dual loyalties, it still is not analogous. Few if any Americans were born and raised in and then emigrated from the Vatican. As a result, whatever doctrinal beliefs learned in church were also learned in an American community, embedded in American cultural and social institutions, and these individuals were surrounded by others with the same core American experiences. Moreover, policy positions of whatever sort are primarily *cognitive*, while attachments to one's country more fully *affective*. Policy preferences are not often deeply held, and even when they are, they rarely organize the person's sense of core identity.

Moreover, the Vatican has never sought to substitute its positions on, say, birth control for the more general, fundamental, and important set of beliefs that constitute the American Creed. One can easily be an American Catholic who supports the Vatican's position on a particular issue or an American Catholic who does not—the Vatican's long-held opposition to abortion and capital punishment are good examples—but one will remain, above all, an American.

Still, is it not the case that Irish Americans and Jewish Americans lobby on behalf of what is, in fact, a foreign government or group? Yes, but one can make distinctions. The Irish have certainly successfully lobbied to involve the U.S. government in solving the "troubles" in Northern Ireland. And Jewish Americans have lobbied the U.S. government to support the establishment of and the continued existence of Israel.

These do not, however, constitute lobbying for policies that are against the interests of the United States. Resolving tensions between the Irish and America's historical allies, the British, is not against U.S. interests. Nor is supporting the right of existence of a democratic state of Israel.

The same cannot be said of organized efforts for major amnesty programs that subvert the attempt to make immigration an orderly, fair, and supportable policy. The same cannot be said of organized efforts in support of open borders with countries that stand to reap many more advantages from that policy than the United States. The same cannot be said of organized efforts to make the United States a multilingual country in which a common language can no longer be assumed. Does it not matter that the results of such policies, if successful, would change the basic cultural, psychological, social, institutional, and political organization that has been the foundation for this country's republican democracy for 230 years? Of course it does!

War, Then and Now: Some Distinctions

Advocates of dual citizenship and multiple nationalities look to the past and reassure us that we are unlikely to go to war over dual citizenship as we did with the British in 1812.[67] That conflict arose when the British, then following the "perpetual allegiance" theory of citizenship, forcibly tried to repatriate American citizens at sea. It is hardly imaginable that we would go to war with any country over their claim on any citizens who happen to have more than one nationality. Neither would we use forceful coercion to require Israel to return one of its dual citizens who committed a murder in the United States and fled the country. It is a fact of contemporary international politics that democracies rarely go to war with each other.[68]

Still, that does not end the matter. If multiple citizenships and loyalties no longer raise the prospects of war between countries, that is not the same as saying that they raise no troubling conflicts. And if war between democracies is unlikely, this does not mean that war or armed conflict between democracies and states organized on other political principles are still not possible. Finally, even if war between states of whatever political persuasion is unlikely *over* these issues, this does not mean that such concerns do not raise profound domestic concerns for the countries so affected.

The chief change in the international and domestic environment in that regard is the rise of catastrophic terrorism. Large immigrant populations from countries in which anti-Western and especially anti-American feelings are strong represent a new and present danger. The attachments and integration of immigrant communities from such countries is a different matter than it was in the past.

The numbers of such individuals may not be large. However, that is not the point. They need not be. Developing and maintaining national attachments and helping to ensure the successful integration of all the diverse groups the United States now takes in is no longer a matter of sociology, but of life and death.

Notes

1. This chapter builds on Stanley A. Renshon, "American Identity and National Character: The Dilemmas of Cultural Diversity," in *Political Psychology: Cultural and Cross Cultural Foundations*, ed. S. A. Renshon (New York: Macmillan, 2000).

2. Alejandro Portes, "Toward a New World: The Origins and Effects of Transnational Activities," *Ethnic and Racial Studies* 22 (March 1999): 463–77; the citation here is on 467.

3. James F. Smith, "Mexico: In Zacatecas State, Development Projects Seen as a Key to Keep People from Fleeing to U.S.," *Los Angeles Times*, August 20, 2001.

4. Peter J. Spiro, "Dual Nationality and the Meaning of Citizenship," *Emory Law Journal* 46, no. 4 (1997): 1412–85; the citation here is on 1460, and also see 1468, n. 246.

5. Ibid., 1461.

6. David A. Martin, "New Rules on Dual Nationality for a Democratizing Globe: Between Rejection and Embrace," *Georgetown Immigration Law Journal* 14 (1999): 1–34; the citation here is on 8, n. 23.

7. "Exhibit of Vietnamese Art Arouses Immigrant Anger," *New York Times*, July 7, 1999.

8. Rene Sanchez, "Days of Rage in Little Saigon: Portrait of Ho Chi Minh Incenses Vietnamese Immigrants," *Washington Post*, March 5, 1999. During the recent outbreak of violence in the Middle East, large groups of anti-Israeli/pro-Arab demonstrators held noisy protests, at which several were arrested. Amy Waldman, "New Yorkers Stand Out in Protests over Vieques," *New York Times*, May 5, 2000; see also Dan Barry and Nichole M. Christian, "Thousands March to U.N. to Support Palestinians," *New York Times*, October 14, 2000. During this period, several synagogues were vandalized; C. J. Chivers, "Police Investigating Vandalism at Door of Bronx Synagogue," *New York Times*, October 9, 2000.

9. Rick Bragg, "Stand over Elian Highlights a Virtual Secession of Miami," *New York Times*, April 1, 2000.

10. In psychoanalytic theory, the term that would cover all three is "object," which can refer to concrete (specific people, places) and categorical entities (like nation or America).

11. Amy Waldman, "Killing Heightens the Unease Felt by Africans in New York," *New York Times*, February 14, 1999.

12. Bruce Finley, "Hearts Torn between Old, New Worlds," *Denver Post*, August 23, 1998.

13. Tripti Lahiri, "In Death Homeward Bound," *New York Times*, June 26, 2003. Alejandro Ruiz—who left Mexico and began work on landscaping crews around Denver, became a U.S. citizen, and raised ten children, forty grandchildren, and three great-grandchildren here—can still say he wants to be buried at "home," meaning Mexico. He says, "My heart is here, but it's also there. Even though here I made money, enough to feed my family—it was easier for me to make a living here—I will go back to Mexico. When I die, I must go back to Mexico." See Finley, "Hearts Torn."

14. Alfredo Corchado and K. Anderson, "Mexican's Interest in Citizenship Up as Proposition 187 Prompts Increase," *Dallas Morning News*, December 1, 1994.

15. Rodolfo de la Garza, Mannuel Orozoco, and Miguel Barona, *The Bi-National Impact of Latino Remittances* (Los Angeles: Tomas Rivera Center, 1997). U.S. Bureau of the Census, *Profile of the Foreign Born Population in the United States: 1997*, Current Population Reports Special Studies (Washington, D.C.: U.S. Government Printing Office, 1997), 13, table 3–1.

16. U.S. Bureau of the Census, *Profile of the Foreign Born Population*, 23–195; the citation here is on 12.

17. U.S. Bureau of the Census, "Coming to America: A Profile of the Nation's Foreign Born," *Census Brief: Current Population Survey*, February 2002.

18. E.g., so the average foreign-born household had larger numbers of children under eighteen than native born household (1.02 vs. 0.067). Or, to put it another way, 60 percent of those with at least one foreign-born householder had one or more children under eighteen compared with 45 percent of native households. Foreign-born

households were more likely to have two (44 vs. 36 percent) or more (16 vs. 9 percent) children than native-born households. Twenty-five percent of families with a foreign-born householder from Latin America had three or more children, and among married couples, with householders from Mexico, this figure is 79 percent.

As Holmes points out in his analysis of the 1998 National Center for Health Statistics study, "Much of the increase in Hispanic-origin births is a result of high fertility rates among Mexican Americans, particularly recent immigrants, about 70 percent of the babies born to Hispanic women 1995—up from 61 percent in 1989—were born to women of Mexican heritage. . . . The study provides further evidence that people of Mexican heritage have an increasing demographic significance in American society." Steven A. Holmes, "Hispanic Births in U.S. Reach Record High," *New York Times*, February 13, 1998.

19. D'Vera Cohn, "Hispanic Growth Surge Fueled by Births in U.S.," *Washington Post*, June 9, 2005.

20. Paula Gutierrez, "Comment: Mexico's Dual Nationality Amendments: They Do Not Undemine U.S. Citizens' Allegiance and Loyalty or U.S. Political Sovereignty." *Loyola L.A. International and Comparative Law Journal* 19 (1997): 999. Also see Jorge A. Vargas, "Dual Nationality for Mexicans?" *Chicano-Latino Law Review* 18, no. 1 (1996): 1–58; the citation here is on 7–10.

21. Sam Dillon, "Mexico Wants to Make Dual Citizenship Legal," *New York Times*, December 11, 1995.

22. The data given in this and the next paragraph are from De la Garza, Orozoco, and Miguel Barona, *Bi-National Impact*, 1–4. These researchers also argue that remittances to "home countries" benefit the United States nationally. Their argument is based on the fungibility of financial figures. Thus if country X buys products from the United States and its immigrants abroad send money home, this money can be viewed as helping to pay for such imports.

However, the researchers do acknowledge that the vast majority of remittances come from five states where such immigrants are generally located (California, Texas, Florida, Illinois, and New York) and they are substantial. The researchers estimate (p. 8) that more than $3.1 billion in remittances were sent home by immigrants from these five states. They note: "Clearly, constitute a major resource, which if invested locally [in the United States] could significantly improve state and local economies in general, and the personal conditions in which these immigrants live in particular" (p. 8).

23. Ginger Thompson, "A Surge in Money Sent Home by Mexicans," *New York Times*, October 28, 2003.

24. Sergio Bustos, "Hispanics Send Billions to Kin: Could Prompt More Migration to U.S.," Gannett News Service, November 25, 2003.

25. Thompson, "Surge in Money Sent Home by Mexicans."

26. Steven Dinan, "Mexican Officials Take Blame on Aliens," *Washington Times*, June 14, 2005.

27. James C. McKinley Jr., "Mexican Manual for Illegal Migrants Upsets Some," *New York Times*, January 6, 2005.

28. Peter J. Spiro, "Dual Nationality and the Meaning of Citizenship," *Emory Law Journal* 46, no. 4 (1997): 1412–85; the citation here is on 1470.

29. Quoted in Vargas, "Dual Nationality," 3. Vargas is of Mexican nationality and was formerly a professor of law in Mexico City and then a visiting professor at the University of San Diego Law School.

30. Alfredo Corchado, "Mexican Study Dual Citizenship: Implications of an Idea Intriguing to Many," *Dallas Morning News*, July 15, 1995; emphasis mine. Also see Vargas, "Dual Nationality," 3.

31. Vargas, "Dual Nationality," 9. These include aggressive government strategies to develop and maintain contact with important groups of Mexicans abroad, the creation and proliferation of sixteen Mexican Cultural Institutes and Centers, a promotional campaign in favor of the North American Free Trade Agreement, a considerable increase in the number of Mexican Consulates, the development of special programs to provide legal and diplomatic protection to both documented and undocumented migratory workers, and the publication of a new bilingual newsletter, *La Paloma*.

32. Juan Hernandez, interview by Ted Koppel, *Nightline*, ABC Television, June 7, 2001 (emphasis mine).

33. Quoted by Alfredo Corchado, "Zedillo Seeks Closer Ties with Mexican Americans," *Dallas Morning News*, April 8, 1995; see also Vargas, "Dual Nationality," 7, n. 23.

34. Vargas, "Dual Nationality," 3.

35. Mary Jordan, "Mexican President Touts Open Borders," *Washington Post*, August 25, 2000; Ginger Thompson, "Fox Urges Opening of U.S.-Mexican Border to Build New Partnership," *New York Times*, August 14, 2000; and Jerry Sepen, "Mexican Official Seeks Open Border," *Washington Times*, September 27, 2004.

36. Quoted in Vargas, "Dual Nationality," 5; emphasis in original.

37. Vargas, "Dual Nationality," agrees, noting (p. 10) that one set of "sociological" arguments in favor of dual citizenship for Mexicans is that, "Mexicans are very proud of their culture. In principle, any Mexican is a true nationalist. They love their history, culture and traditions, and especially they love their beautiful country. Accordingly Mexicans remain Mexicans anywhere they are."

38. Jose Itzigsohn, "Immigration and the Boundaries of Citizenship: The Institutions of Immigrants' Political Transnationalism," *International Migration Review* 34, no. 4 (2000): 1126–54; the citation here is on 1133.

39. Ibid.,1142.

40. Nina Bernstein, "Dominican President Visits, Reaching Out to Diaspora," *New York Times*, December 5, 2004.

41. David Martin and T. Alexander Aleinikoff, "Double Ties: Why Nations Should Learn to Love Dual Nationality," *Foreign Policy*, November–December 2002, 81.

42. Jeffrey R. O'Brien, "U.S. Dual Citizenship Voting Rights: A Critical Examination of Aleinikoff's Proposal," *Georgetown Immigration Journal* 13, no. 533 (1999): 573–95; the citation here is on 579.

43. Mary Beth Sheridan, "Calling All Salvadorans," *Washington Post*, November 11, 2002.

44. Ibid.

45. Pam Belluck, "Mexican Presidential Candidates Campaign in the U.S.," *New York Times*, July 1, 2000.

46. There are reliability and validity problems with such data as well. E.g., Rumbaut, "Crucible Within," 760, reports correlations of the respondents' self-reports with performance with the objective Stanford reading achievement test score. He reports there was a "strong correlation" of .42 ($p = .0001$). What these numbers do not reveal is that in a sample of over 5,000 respondents, it is fairly routine to get findings of such magnitude and reach "statistical significance." Moreover, a correlation of .42 sounds high, but it means that of all the variance in the relationship between self-report and object test measures, only 16 percent is actually explained. Or to put it another way, the objective test results explain 16 percent of the level of proficiency reflected in the self-report; 84 percent is unexplained.

47. Rubén G. Rumbaut, "The Crucible Within: Ethnic Identity, Self Esteem and Segmented Assimilation among Children of Immigrants," *International Migration Review* 28, no. 4 (1994): 748–94.

48. U.S. Bureau of the Census, *Profile of the Foreign Born Population*, 20.

49. De la Garza, Orozoco, and Miguel Barona, *Bi-National Impact.*

50. They base their list on a publication by Blaustein and Flanz titled *Constitutions of the World* but give no date for the publication.

51. Philip Q. Yang, "Explaining Immigrant Naturalization," *International Migration Review* 28, no. 3 (1994): 449–77; the citation here is on 473–74. He continues, "Perhaps, immigrants may . . . have confusion about and difficulty in maintaining dual allegiances to both the country of origin and the host country. Thus, immigrants may be reluctant to identify themselves with Americans and are therefore much less likely to naturalize."

52. For an early analysis of Americanization efforts that detailed serious deficiencies, see Howard C. Hill, "The Americanization Movement," *American Journal of Sociology* 24, no. 6 (May 1919): 609–42. For a more recent analysis, see John J. Miller, *The Unmaking of Americans: How Multiculturalism Has Undermined America's Assimilation Ethic* (New York: Free Press, 1998), 22–63.

53. Nathan Glazer and Daniel Patrick Moynihan, *Beyond the Melting Pot: The Negroes, Puerto Ricans, Jews, Italians, and Irish of New York City*, 2nd ed. (Cambridge, Mass.: Harvard University Press, 1970).

54. See http://uscis.gov/graphics/citizenship/welcomeguide/index.htm.

55. Chicago Council on Foreign Relations, "Global Views: 2004," 53, 54; available at http://www.ccfr.org/globalviews2004/sub/pdf/Global_Views_2004_US.pdf.

56. Of course, the number of immigrants from Israel to the United States is low, both in numbers and percentages in comparison to, e.g., Mexico or the Philippines. The dual citizenship / loyalty issue arises primarily because of the historical circumstances preceding the establishment of the state of Israel and the fact that the 'law of return" promises any Jew Israeli citizenship on immigration. So, for most American Jews the question is not returning to a state from which they once lived, but emigrated, but rather their attachment to the existence of a Jewish homeland after a 2000 years of the Diaspora.

57. David Riesman, with N. Glazer and R. Denny, *The Lonely Crowd: A Study of the Changing American Character* (New Haven, Conn.: Yale University Press, 1950).

58. Daniel Yankelovich, *New Rules: Searching for Self-Fulfillment in a World Turned Upside Down* (New York: Random House, 1981), 88.

59. Alan Wolfe, *One Nation After All* (Chicago: University of Chicago Press, 1998).

60. Rumbaut, "Crucible Within," 764, table 2.

61. Vargas, "Dual Nationality," 32–33; the emphasis is mine.

62. Ibid., 35.

63. D'Vera Cohn, "Illegal Residents Exceed Estimate: Experts Analyzing New Census Figures Say 6 Million May Instead Be 9 Million," *Washington Post*, March 18, 2001; Cindy Rodriguez, "The Impact of the Undocumented," *Boston Globe*, February 6, 2001.

64. Mona Harrington, "Loyalties: Dual and Divided," in *Harvard Encyclopedia of American Ethnic Groups*, ed. Stephan Thernstrom (Cambridge, Mass.: Harvard University Press, 1980), 680–86.

65. Ibid., 682.

66. Spiro, "Dual Nationality," 1477.

67. Spiro, "Dual Nationality," 1422–23; see also Martin, "New Rules," 20.

68. Bruce Russett, *Grasping the Democratic Peace: Principles for a Post–Cold War World* (Princeton, N.J.: Princeton University Press, 1993).

Reforming Dual Citizenship: Some Proposals

MULTIPLE ATTACHMENTS ARE A FACT OF LIFE. SO, NOW, IS DUAL CITI-zenship. Yet as I have argued, dual citizenship—especially when it entails active participation in the political life of an immigrant's home country—leads to conflicts of interest, attention, and attachment. Of course, immigrants have feelings regarding their countries of origin, but they owe the country that is now their chosen home their primary focus and commitment. And the United States, in turn, owes them the effort to ensure that they become integrated into the American national community.

In this and the following chapter, I outline two general sets of policy recommendations to further those critical purposes. The first, in this chapter, outlines a series of recommendations for reforming some elements of the growing incidence of dual citizenship in this country, along with a rationale for each proposal. The second set of recommendations, in the chapter that follows, focuses on more general strategies to integrate new immigrants and those who are already Americans more fully into our national community.

The four recommendations outlined below are meant to be viewed as a package. The number of dual citizens affected by each varies. More dual citizens vote in foreign elections than serve in the offices of a foreign government or fight abroad in another country's army. Even though the numbers vary for each, it is important for the United States to send a coherent and uniform signal if it expects immigrants and citizens alike to give it primacy in their civic responsibilities.

Paradoxically, the reform of dual citizenship in the United States actually has two elements: one foreign, the other domestic. The first concerns the relation of potential or actual dual citizens to the political process to their "home" countries. What ought to be done about American citizens voting, holding office, or serving as advisers to a foreign government?

The second asks what we might do in relation to a potential or actual dual citizen *in* the United States in relation to the American political community.

What should be done regarding Americans who maintain dual citizenship but serve in public service or policymaking capacities in this country? Should a dual national be allowed to serve as president of the United States or as a Supreme Court justice? While the idea may seem novel, it is not at all far-fetched. As more and more dual citizens find a place in American society, it is more and more likely that they will find their way into positions of responsibility and power. This issue has been raised indirectly by attempts to amend the Constitution to allow naturalized citizens to run for president. In fact, the questions raised by multiple national attachments in American political life are much more pervasive than a single office. It is preferable to give this matter some thought before it becomes a matter of national urgency.

As Peter Schuck points out, "Americans seem to worry much more about the divided loyalties of those who are nationals of other states and wish to naturalize in the U.S. than they do about the loyalty of American citizens who choose to naturalize in other countries while retaining their American citizenship (as other states increasingly permit them to do)."[1] In reality, both sides of that coin are an issue.

The foreign dimension of dual citizenship raises three critical public policy issues for Americans: First, should American citizens be able to vote in foreign elections? Second, should American citizens be able to serve in, represent, or advise a foreign government? Third, should American citizens be permitted to serve in foreign military forces? As of today, all three are legal in the United States. Whether, given the worry over integrating unprecedented numbers of new immigrants every year into the American national community, they are advisable is another matter.

What Other Countries Do about Dual Citizenship

The two sets of questions—domestic and foreign—raise similar, yet slightly different, questions. Yet, before getting into specifics about what the United States might do, it is instructive to take a brief look at what other countries do when they are faced with the same circumstances.

Most countries strongly regulate the rights and responsibilities of dual citizenship without outlawing it. They do so, no doubt, for the same reasons that lie behind my suggestions—concerns with the attachments to, and integration of, *their* national communities.

Many countries allow *their* citizens to become dual citizens but balk at allowing immigrants to their country to do so.[2] For example, within the European Union countries, Austria, Denmark, Finland, Germany, Luxembourg, Spain, and Sweden do not allow immigrants who become naturalized citizens to keep their prior citizenships. Yet Germany, Luxembourg, and Sweden allow their nationals to keep their citizenship when they become naturalized abroad—as do France, Greece, Ireland, Italy, Luxembourg, the Netherlands, Portugal, and the United Kingdom. Spain allows neither or both, depending on whether the person is of Spanish heritage.

New Zealand now permits dual nationality unless, in a specific instance, it "is not conducive to the public good."[3] The French Civil Code formerly provided that any adult who voluntarily accepted another nationality would automatically forfeit French citizenship, but this provision was amended in 1973 so that now "any adult, habitually residing abroad, who voluntarily accepts another nationality will only lose the French nationality if he expressly so declares." Some dual-citizenship-granting countries, like France and Algeria, have worked out accommodations on such issues such as required military service in one or the other country. Others have not.[4]

Scandinavian countries—Sweden, Denmark, Norway, and Finland—grant foreign residents voting rights in local and regional elections. Some countries, like the United States, reserve voting rights for citizens. Irish citizens in the United Kingdom may vote and sit in Parliament. The Irish Constitution was changed in 1984 to permit Britons living in the Republic of Ireland to vote in elections to the lower house of the Irish national Parliament. Spain does not permit those who hold other Latin American citizenships to vote or stand for election.[5] Peru, Argentina, and Columbia allow absentee voting by their dual-citizen nations. El Salvador, Panama, Uruguay, and the Dominican Republic do not.[6]

The recent Mexican citizenship law creates dual citizenship (but not nationality) and regulates it. Holders of the Declaration of Mexican Nationality identification cards, even if citizens of another country like the United States, can cast their votes in Mexican elections, so long as they are physically in Mexico. New laws are being considered that will allow dual citizens abroad to vote in Mexican elections without returning to their "home" country. Mexican citizens living abroad who are also citizens of another country are, however, not able to serve in the Mexican armed forces or to work aboard Mexican-flagged ships or airlines.[7] The new Iraqi government has passed a nationality law allowing dual citizenship, which lets the country's nationals abroad, including those in the United States, vote in its 2005 national elections.[8]

This brief survey is meant to underscore one important point: Countries that allow multiple citizenship vary substantially in the specific ways and the extent to which they encourage or limit the responsibilities and advantages of their multicitizenship nationals. It is possible to both permit and regulate dual citizenship. Most countries that allow dual citizenship also restrict and regulate it—but not the United States. The United States is surely among the most, if not *the* most permissive on these issues. It has no restrictions whatsoever on any of the wide range of practices that other countries regulate. As is generally the case with modern American immigration policy, this practice seems not to have been much a matter of conscious public debate or political choice.

It is certainly possible to regulate multiple citizenships without outlawing them. Outlawing dual citizenship would be unnecessary, impractical, and ineffective. Nor would I suggest that immigrants who continue to take up the responsibilities of citizenship in their "home countries" lose or be denied their American citizenship. In addition to being unnecessary, such a law would also be illegal, according to the Supreme Court case of *Afroyim v. Rusk* (387 U.S. 253, 1967).

That ruling held that there must be persuasive evidence establishing that the action taken by the citizen was accompanied by an "affirmative intention"[9] to transfer allegiance to the country of foreign nationality, abandon allegiance owed to the United States, or otherwise relinquish U.S. citizenship.

So taking an oath of allegiance to another country is no longer taken as firm evidence of intent to give up U.S. citizenship, even if that oath includes a renunciation of that citizenship. Serving in a foreign government or in a foreign army or voting in a foreign election are not grounds for losing one's U.S. citizenship, unless the individual goes through a detailed process of renunciation. That can easily be avoided by a public declaration. Thus Raffi Hovannisian, an American citizen who became foreign minister of Armenia, stated publicly: "I certainly do not renounce my American citizenship," and thus closed off any legal challenge to what he had done.

There is another, more basic psychological reason why outlawing multiple citizenship or taking away the American citizenship of dual citizens is ill advised. Multiple attachments are a basic fact of everyone's psychological life. It is simply impossible to legally mandate a severing of important emotional ties. Nor would it be in the best interests of the United States to do so. It is better to foster attachment than to mandate it.

Yet, having said that, it cannot be emphasized too strongly that there is a very important difference between the psychological fact of multiple attachments and the specific ways in which individuals and groups arrange these attachments. It is entirely consistent to recognize the reality of multiple attachments and also to develop policies that encourage American national community attachments to be primary and other attachments to be less central.

America's laissez-faire approach to multiple citizenship can be reformed in ways consistent both with the psychological fact of multiple attachments and with fostering primary ties with the American national community. It can be reformed in ways that do not deny immigrant feelings for their homeland countries but also do not negate the importance of developing strong integrated and emotionally connected ties to this country.

Voting in Foreign Elections

Dual citizenship raises three critical public policy issues. First, should American citizens be able to vote in foreign elections? Second, should American citizens be able to serve in, represent, or advise a foreign government? Third, should American citizens be permitted to serve in a foreign military force? As of today, yes—all three are entirely legal in the United States. But whether that is advisable is another matter. Here, then, are four recommendations.

RECOMMENDATION 1: **American citizens should be actively discouraged from voting in foreign elections. This discouragement should take the form of making such a prohibition a stated condition of citizenship applications, including such an affirmation as part of the oath of citizenship, and placing pressure on foreign countries not to make efforts to enroll American citizens in foreign voting. It might well also include congressional legislative action proscribing such behavior.**

There are many ways to see how seriously voting is taken in the United States. Voting has been enshrined by the Courts and the Constitution.[10] The expansion of voting rights has been a critical element of American democratic practice, beginning with the country's earliest history of expanding the right to non–property holders through struggles for women's suffrage and more recently the post–Fifteenth Amendment struggle for African Americans. It is a centerpiece of the study of political science both in this country and abroad. It can also be seen in the process through which immigrants become citizens. We ask immigrants to await an application and review process and a five-year period in this country before they can exercise the right to vote. Voting could hardly be more central to membership in the American national community.

Bruce Fein writes that "approximately 60 countries permit expatriates or migrants to vote via absentee ballots, including Venezuela, Columbia, Brazil and Honduras."[11] Immigrants from these countries to the United States number in the tens of millions. However, not everyone thinks that having Americans vote in foreign elections is a problem. In an otherwise thoughtful analysis, Schuck argues that it is "unproblematic . . . so long as this participation does not embroil the U.S. in unwanted disputes with the other country that involve situations in which the voter subordinates the interests of the U.S. to the other country."[12] Schuck does not specify the kind of circumstances he has in mind, but they presumably involve situations where the United States and country X have a disagreement and American nationals from that country vote consistently with their home country's interests and not those of the United States.

The basic problem with Schuck's position is that the conflicted attachments that underlie his concern that American citizens voting in foreign elections would lead to conflicts has equally worrisome implications for American domestic politics and the community attachments that underlie them: American citizen nationals from country X may be tempted to vote in ways consistent with their home country's interests in measures or votes brought before the American people for resolution. Country X, for example, may want its language to be the language of instruction at school, whereas it is in the American community's interest for all its members to be fluent in English. Multiple and conflicted attachments are a problem at home as well as abroad.

Voting is a critical and basic right, but with it comes great responsibility. Citizens are asked to give their informed choice, not just their vote. Many citizens do not live up to this ideal, but that has not diminished the importance of trying to ensure that they do so.

Should American dual citizens be allowed to vote in foreign elections? It is said that allowing American citizens to vote abroad will encourage democracy. Yet as noted in chapter 7, a review of the evidence suggests that this is not necessarily the case. Americans who vote in foreign elections do so to further what they see as their own self-interest. Moreover, the idea that immigrant communities will necessarily foster democracy overlooks the fact that *many* political parties and interests, some democratic and some not, in the "home country" are now seeking to organize their nationals abroad.

It is said that it is possible to be a fully informed citizen of two countries. However, this is among the weakest of the arguments in favor of multiple voting. There is no evidence that immigrants have mastered the information necessary to exercise responsible citizenship and voting in two cultures. Indeed, there is a great deal of evidence that was reviewed in chapter 7 to suggest just the opposite—that it is increasingly difficult even for Americans to be considered informed citizens in their own country. It is much less likely that they would be well-informed about two countries.

E. J. Dionne characterized the results as "a national scandal." But it is worse than that: "When the country began establishing public schools in the last century, the whole idea was that freedom depended on an educated citizenry. Civics wasn't an add-on. It was the whole point."[13] Historical amnesia and civic ignorance are dangerous to democracies that depend on their citizens' knowledge, perspective, and judgment.[14]

The following questions could be asked of immigrant and citizen alike, with sobering consequences. Did you pay close attention to the campaign? Did you read the news analyses? Have you heard or followed the debates? Are you familiar with the details of the candidates' positions? Have you looked into the major issues themselves and not just depended on candidates' views of them? As the *Washington Post* put the matter, "It is fair to ask whether the desired quality of a citizen's genuine commitment to this country can be reinforced by anything short of a full and undivided political allegiance to one sovereign, as expressed by the solemn act of voting."[15]

Some people argue that immigrants follow the elections in their home countries as much as Americans do in theirs—which is to say, they follow them somewhat, but not a lot. Others point to the low level of information that Americans bring to their election choices and ask why immigrants should be held to a higher standard. The first argument is not convincing. The question is not whether immigrants have the same level of understanding of their home-country politics as Americans have of theirs but whether it is possible to have good enough knowledge of two different political systems, America's and the immigrant home country's.

The second argument is also unpersuasive but for different reasons. Here, the unstated premise is that low levels of understanding are fine for *both* immigrants and Americans. That is hardly an effective point in favoring American dual citizens to vote in foreign elections. The point is not whether immigrants are as ill informed as Americans but whether it is possible to be well informed about two different electoral systems and contents and whether—given limits of time, attention, and understanding—we ought to prefer *all* Americans to be knowledgeable first about their own system of government and election issues.

There is one other difference between native-born and immigrant Americans that is relevant to this particular argument but rarely mentioned. Being born and raised in a culture gives one a foundation of understanding. The average ill-informed American college student has nonetheless lived in the country for twenty years, been exposed to its political culture for those years, and lived through numerous local, state, and national elections and the events and issues that have been a part of them. It is likely that immigrants who come here as young or older adults do know more about their home country's politics and culture, which is not essential here. The politics of the Dominican Republic or of India is not a necessary or even useful template for American politics. In some ways, immigrants must learn not to interpret what they see in frames of references they are used to. They must unlearn their past as well as acquire new and more appropriate frames for their new country's politics.

Elections as Emotional Bonding Mechanisms

Advocates argue that the United States ought to encourage dual citizens to vote in the elections of their "homeland country." This, it is said, is one way for America to be more welcoming of new immigrants. The question is whether this is the kind of intense attachment that the United States ought to encourage.

Before addressing that question, it is worth considering why participation became so central to the American republic. One clue is found in the fact that it was not only the lack of *representation* that caused the rupture with England but also the lack of *participation*. One could, of course, have representation without participation. England's appointed viceroys and governors were examples. Early Americans, however, wanted participation to lead to representation, not have one without the other.

In trying to separate representation from participation, England made a strategic mistake of the first rank. Participation not only reflects attachments; it also creates them. Taking part in a collective civic exercise sanctioned— perhaps "idealized" is a better word—by the national community is part of a shared experience that helps to generate and maintain ties to that community.

Empirical evidence of the effects of participation is found in an analysis of a national survey data examined in 1968 and 1972 by Ginsberg and Weissberg.[16] They tested the proposition that one function of voting is to generate support for the government, independent of particular policies or whether a person's preferred candidate won or lost. They found that participation itself was strongly associated with an improvement in the extent to which citizens view the government as responsive—even if their candidate did not win.[17] They conclude: "Though elections are usually conceived as instruments of popular control, we have seen that American elections can also serve to mobilize citizen support for leaders and the regime itself. It is in the area of regime support that we find the clearest impact of elections."[18]

The emotional bonding function of participation underlies the arguments that were made for expanding suffrage over the course of American history. Not being a full citizen who could vote was viewed and experienced as unfair and alienating, as well as being morally, politically, and ethically suspect. Anger and alienation, of course, do not facilitate but impede attachment. However, participation is emotionally bonding. Those able and willing to participate feel more closely connected with the political community and the way of life that supports it.

This is, not incidentally, the same reasoning that has led observers in Iraq to propose that, even though the Sunni Muslims chose not to take part in the early national elections, they should still be brought into the political process in the allocation of parliamentary seats and the writing of the new Iraqi Constitution. The psychological principle underlying both examples is quite clear. Participation as a legitimate member of a community develops and reinforces the ties to that community. The mechanism is the same whether we are speaking of new citizens and the American community, Sunnis and the new Iraqi national community, or American dual citizens and their countries of origin.

Countries that send immigrants to the United States wish to benefit from that phenomenon. The sociologist Alexandro Portes has written:

Consulates of Mexico, Columbia, El Salvador, Guatemala, and the Dominican Republic in areas of their concentration of their respective nationalities in the

United States have taken to promoting the acquisition of U.S. citizenship or at least permanent residence of their nationals. From these policies, it is clear that sending governments do not want their immigrants to return, but rather to achieve a secure status in wealthy nations . . . from which they can make sustained economic and political contributions in the name of patriotism and home town loyalty.[19]

Those countries realize that voting is one principal way of organizing and extending their influence. The act of voting is of course preceded by a campaign. When Mexico was considering whether or not to encourage dual citizenship for its nationals abroad, primarily in the United States, it conducted a study of the possible benefits. That study envisioned a scenario in which "thousands of Mexican election officials have fanned out across the United States to supervise the balloting, which caps a campaign in which candidates have barnstormed through Mexican population centers, lambasting United States immigration, narcotics, and other policies unpopular in Mexico."[20]

While the numbers are not yet as high as the Mexican government study scenario envisioned, there is no doubt that the United States has become a campaign arena for foreign governments. According to the *Washington Post*, "Eager to reach their countrymen living in the United States, Mexico's two main opposition presidential candidates are barnstorming through Southern California as if it were Mexico's 32nd state."[21] This has increasingly meant that the candidates of other countries actually campaign in the United States for financial and other kinds of support. When Vicente Fox campaigned for the Mexican presidency, he campaigned in Mexican communities in the United States.[22] In 2002, Francisco Labastida, the candidate of the Institutional Revolutionary Party (PRI) for president, appeared on the *Washington Post*'s live Internet question-and-answer session to campaign among his fellow nationals in the Washington area.[23]

For Mexican politicians, this process has even spread to the state and local levels.[24] In 1998 two candidates, Ricardo Monreal and Jose Olvera—rivals for the governorship in the Central Mexican state of Zacatecas—campaigned in California, where thousands of their fellow citizens live and work.[25] That same year, Cuauchtemoc Cardenas Solorzano, the mayor of Mexico City, was in Chicago to inaugurate the first U.S. branch of Mexico's Revolutionary Democratic Party.[26] A coalition—"Mexicans Living Abroad"—brought together Mexicans living in California, Texas, Iowa, and Illinois to press the Mexican government for the right to vote in Mexican elections.

Moreover, governments are increasingly taking affirmative steps to ensure that their nationals abroad vote. In Mexico's 2000 presidential campaign, Vicente Fox's National Action Party and Cuauchtemoc Cardenas Solorzano's Party of the Democratic Revolution sponsored caravans to take Mexicans who qualified to vote from cities as far-flung as New York and Yakima, Washington.[27]

These initiatives are not confined to Mexico. In the 1999 Israeli elections, both parties chartered jets to fly dual citizens to the polls in Tel Aviv.[28] Elsewhere, more than 50,000 Dominican immigrants, many of them U.S. citizens, are registered to vote in the Dominican Republic. In May 2003, they were able to do so for the first time in their adopted homeland, forming long lines at the sixteen polling booths set up in New York alone.[29]

Dual Votes without Dual Responsibility

David Martin points out: "As the globe shrinks and international cooperation increases, political decisions made by other nations have an increasing effect outside their own borders. . . . Human beings are represented in these settings by elected national political leaders, or their delegates. A person who has a say in selecting two or more sets of leaders . . . secures an advantage."[30]

These issues go deeper than whether select groups have a larger voice through multiple voting. There is also a large issue of who bears the consequences of second, foreign votes—certainly not the dual citizens who continue to live in the United States while voting abroad.

Israel is a good example. In its 1999 elections, the two parties stood for very divergent policies with regard to the security of the country. Yet not a single American Jew who voted in that election, whether on the left or right, would be in Israel for the consequences. It was in effect a free ride from the real responsibility that comes in living where the consequences will be most directly felt. Living with the consequences of your choice is one mechanism that helps to ensure focus and perspective.

This issue is not only confined to foreign elections that have life-or-death implications. In June 2003, Americans of Polish descent went to the polls to vote on the issue of whether or not Poland should join the European Union. One local observer of the Chicago Polish community wrote, "Some wish that residents with Polish roots would show the same enthusiasm about Chicago elections as they have about this one."[31] That article continued, "Polish names once figured prominently in city politics. 'Polish mothers don't raise their children to be aldermen,' said Aurelia Pucinski, a former clerk of Circuit Court in Cook County. Among the best known was Dan Rostenkowski, the former House Ways and Means Committee chairman. But that clout is waning as local Poles move to the suburbs and focus their attention on money instead of politics. Unlike other ethnic groups, the political process is not something they see as important in their lives. That has not been true with this issue."[32]

One might reasonably ask why Americans of Polish descent who have been in this country for generations are voting on policy in a country on another continent. A likely answer is: Because they have an interest in and connection to their former communities. Yet the response to that is to ask whether it is possible to have an interest and a connection without voting in another country's elections. Of course it is.

The increasing use of the United States as an election arena for foreign nationals and nations is a growing problem. It drains attention and attachment away from immigrants becoming more integrated into the American national culture. The Mexican presidential election was held in 2000, the very year that the United States held a presidential election. Did dual-national voters pay equal attention to both? Did they spend the time necessary in both elections to exercise an informed vote? Is it possible to do so? Is it desirable?

What to Do?

Some find the idea of American citizens voting in foreign elections and otherwise associating themselves with foreign governments contrary to America's best interests and want to take strong remedial steps. Bruce Fein, a constitutional lawyer, argues that "Americans who vote in a foreign election, occupy any office in a foreign state, enlist in a foreign army, attempt to overthrow the U.S. government, or otherwise affirm allegiance to a foreign nation should forfeit their citizenship."[33] The problem with that approach is that the Supreme Court ruled 5–4 in *Afroyim v. Rusk* (1967) that an American could not lose his or her citizenship for voting in a foreign election. Fein's solution: "Congress should either propose a constitutional amendment to overcome *Afroyim*; or, enact legislation that deletes the specific intent requirement in the expectation that the high court will reconsider the precedent."[34] The problem with this approach is that passing a constitutional amendment is difficult at best, and one can anticipate howls of outrage at what will be argued is a punitive, anti-immigrant measure. Having Congress pass a measure specifically framed to have the Supreme Court reconsider its opinion depends upon the makeup of the Court.

Some, recognizing that voting in foreign elections is damaging to the interests of the American national community, suggest a "split the difference" approach. Aleinikoff proposes that the United States negotiate a series of bilateral agreements with foreign countries whereby their former nationals be given a choice of whether to vote in the United States or not.[35] An American dual citizen domiciled in a foreign country would have to return to this country a year before the election in which he or she wished to vote or not be able to do so. This would involve the United States in arduous and, I think, unnecessary negotiations with 150 countries.

Not only is this clumsy, but there are a number of constitutional barriers to such a proposal.[36] These include the difficulty of establishing a "compelling federal interest," the problem of overcoming the strict scrutiny standard that would most likely be applied (because American dual citizens domiciled abroad would not be able to vote by absentee ballot), and the question of whether such a proposal is sufficiently narrowly tailored, among other things.

O'Brien suggests several alternatives.[37] One is to repeal the Absentee Voting Act, a modification of Aleinikoff's proposal, whereby only those who have voted before in foreign elections are given the choice, or establishing a universal "vote where domiciled" rule. Each of these also has problems. Doing away with absentee ballots would disenfranchise all Americans living abroad, included those serving in our military. The modification O'Brien proposes creates an incentive for dual citizens to get more quickly involved with their former home-country elections so as to preserve their options. And the search for a universal rule, vote where domiciled, forces Americans who live abroad not to vote in their own elections.

These problems pale, however, before their most basic and fatal flaw: They are trying to accommodate the voting of American citizens in foreign elections. There is no compelling reason to allow this, and certainly none to encourage it. What the United States should be doing is encouraging immigrants, their families, and their descendants to consider America their "homeland." This is less likely to happen if there are continual pressures and incentives to look toward a foreign country from which they originally emigrated.

Given the importance to the American national community and the republican democratic system that is an integral part of it, it seems prudent to do everything possible to encourage attachment to this community and to take steps to lessen the incentives for connections to other countries and their national communities. U.S. law cannot of course mandate what other countries choose to do or not to do with their former nationals, but it can be made clear in a variety of ways that recruiting American citizens to vote in foreign elections is not looked upon with favor by the United States.

Holding Office in or Serving a Foreign Country

RECOMMENDATION 2: U.S. citizens should be actively dissuaded from seeking or serving in elective or appointive offices abroad. Americans should be actively discouraged from serving on the policymaking legislative or executive government entities of foreign governments.

**This discouragement should take the form of making such a prohibi-
tion a stated condition of citizenship applications, including an affirmation to this effect as part of the oath of naturalization, making
it a finable offense while an American citizen and placing pressure
on foreign governments not to make efforts to enroll American citizens in standing for or serving in the governments of foreign countries.**

Next to voting, holding office is among the most critical and important
public privileges of citizenship. Individuals have many reasons for wishing to
gain public office. They may wish to serve out of a sense of obligation, civic
duty, ambition, or some mixture. Those who rely on leaders, be they in
elected or appointive office, have every reason to expect and demand that they
hold the community's interest as paramount. This does not mean they have
to be guided by majorities in opinion polls. Rather, it means that they must
take seriously the trust that they have been given. As an expected part of that
trust, leaders are often called upon to explain how their views are consistent
with community interest. A leader who represents a community is expected
to have that community's interest wholly at heart, even if he or she may not
agree with the constituents on a particular policy.

In the past, it went without saying that an elected or appointed official
would devote his or her full time and attention to the public matters that they
were elected or appointed to pursue. That is why public officials cannot serve
in the public and private service at the same time, except on boards and advisory positions. We would not expect a U.S. senator to hold another job. Nor
would we expect a member of the president's staff to do so. Even holders of
part-time legislative or executive positions are to avoid conflicts of interest.

Time, attention, and the community's best interests are the three key assumptions of public responsibilities. Yet all three are thrown into question by
the practices that are slowly arising with multiple citizenship. Over the years,
a number of Americans have gone to hold positions of power and importance
in other countries.

Muhamed Sacirbey, foreign minister of Bosnia in 1995–96, is an American
citizen and dual national. The chief of the Estonian army in 1991–95, Alek-
sander Einseln, also was an American. Valdas Adamkus, prior to becoming
president of Lithuania, was an administrator in Chicago for the Environmental Protection Agency.[38] In 2002, at least ten Americans of Nigerian descent
left the United States to campaign for office in Nigeria.[39] Many Americans
have served at the United Nations as ambassadors of their other country's
citizenship.[40] And a number of Mexican Americans have returned to Mexico
to run for office.[41] Former U.S. secretary of state Madeleine Albright was even
approached to seek the presidency of her native Czech Republic, but she declined.[42] In November 2004, the foreign minister of the Iraqi Governing

Council announced the appointment of Rend Rahim Francke as ambassador to the United States. She had become a U.S. citizen in 1987.[43]

Not all those Americans who return to their home countries necessarily add to democracy in the world. In 1998, the State Department said that as far as it could tell, Hussein Mohammed Aidid, a U.S. Marine Corps veteran, was a naturalized American citizen as well as Somalia's most powerful warlord before he died.[44] Still, most of those named above left the United States to serve in their country of origin in what would be considered a productive way.

There is no law against doing so, and on balance no real problem that they do so, as long as their civic and citizenship rights are not exercised in two places at the same time. It is quite acceptable for Adamkus to leave the United States to become president of Lithuania, but it would not be appropriate to vote in a U.S. election while serving. It would be acceptable for Einseln to become chief of the Estonian army, but not to be a member of the U.S. armed forces at the same time.

The basic issue here is to avoid a conflict of interest, in these cases a conflict between two different sets of national interests. It cannot be assumed that because two countries are democracies that they share the same interests. (France and the United States come readily to mind here.) Nor should the citizens of one or another country have to struggle with trying to figure out whether their national community interests are truly being represented.

The individuals noted above are clearly serving the country to which they returned and in that sense might be considered sojourners in the United States. Yet with the rise of transnationalism and the decision of many immigrant-sending countries to make political use of their nationals, a new development has arisen. Americans with dual citizenship are being asked, and are agreeing to serve, in foreign governments at the same time that they retain and exercise their American citizenship.

There are a number of examples. Jesus Galvis, a Colombian owner of a travel agency and elected official in Hackensack, New Jersey, recently ran a campaign for a seat in the Colombian senate.[45] He planned to hold both offices. He was asked in an interview whether he could represent his Hackensack constituents while splitting time in Colombia, and he said he would have been like a U.S. member of Congress with an office in his district and one in Washington. In each place, he said, "I would be representing the Colombians in the United States."[46] Galvis's non-Colombian constituents in Hackensack would no doubt be surprised and not pleased to learn that if they were not Colombian they would not be represented.

Others were not so sure. Saramaria Archila, head of a Latin American social services agency in the Borough of Queens, New York City, who had lobbied for the dual citizenship law in Colombia, nevertheless said Galvis had crossed the line. "If I am an elected official in a country, it is impossible to defend the interests of my community in another country," she said.[47]

Yet another development along these lines is carving up American territory as districts where foreign governments are represented by American citizens. A reporter noted, "In what experts call an extraordinary step, . . . three Mexicans living in the United States are running for seats in Mexico's Congress. If they win—and chances are good for at least two of them, in Chicago and Los Angeles—they will live in the United States and represent Mexicans here."[48] The report continued, "The National Action Party recently introduced a proposal in Congress to reserve 10 of the 500 seats for Mexicans abroad, and others talk of slates of United States candidates in the 2003 Congressional elections. . . . If they win, they plan to commute to Mexico at least part of the time Congress is in session—about six months a year, in two-month stretches."[49]

In 2001, Juan Hernandez, a former professor at the University of Texas at Dallas, was named the first American to serve in a Mexican president's cabinet.[50] When Mexican president Vicente Fox met with U.S. president George W. Bush, Hernandez was there as an adviser to Fox. And when a group of Democrats from the U.S. Congressional Hispanic Caucus met with President Fox, Hernandez was there.

Another version of this outreach is the setting up of a 120-member "advisory council" made up of American citizens of Mexican descent.[51] The report notes that the candidates must be at least age eighteen, Spanish speakers, Mexican citizens, and Illinois residents with no criminal record. They must also submit a petition with at least fifty signatures in support of their candidacy. That means there will be a campaign, as well as an election—yet another way to organize the attention and interests of Mexican Americans toward their "home country."

The major issue in many of these cases is, to repeat, the question of conflict of interest—in this case, the interests of two different countries represented by the same person. We enact conflict-of-interest laws in the United States precisely because individuals are not the best judges of what they will be able to place in separate spheres—and how well they will be able to do so. Individuals may well not see any disadvantages to multiple representations—but in many ways their views are the least reliable on these matters.

It is a fundamental principle of American republican government that representatives, whether in the legislature or executive, are expected to truly and faithfully represent the national community of which any local community is an integral part. Running for office in a foreign country and continuing to exercise the rights of American citizenship—especially holding office, but also voting and organizing one's fellow foreign nationals—seems incompatible with that expectation.

An expected response for persons serving as advisers to foreign governments is that they are representing the interests of their fellow Americans of whatever particular descent in their home countries. But one might ask whether that attention would not better be applied to improving the quality of life and citizenship within this country. The answer "I can do both" does not recognize the normal limits of time and attention that apply to most people. It also fundamentally neglects the psychological laws of attachment. That is why one lawyer cannot represent two opposing sides in a court case.

All these considerations underlie the United States' stake in these issues. This is not just a matter of exercising the personal freedom that American citizenship grants, but also the national community's stake in having it exercised for the benefit of the community. Of course, dual-national Americans may want to advise or serve their country of origin. But from the standpoint of the American national community, the question is why that desire should be given any standing or encouragement.

Serving in a Foreign Army

Recommendation 3: American citizens should be actively dissuaded from seeking to serve in a foreign military service of whatever kind unless specifically authorized by competent federal authorities. This discouragement should take the form of making such a prohibition a stated condition of visa applications, including an affirmation to this effect as part of the oath of naturalization, making it a finable offense while an American citizen and placing pressure on foreign governments not to make efforts to enroll American citizens in standing for or serving in foreign armies. American citizens who do should incur financial penalties.

The willingness to serve and protect one's country is one of the most solemn responsibilities of citizenship. The Naturalization Oath taken by new American citizens says in part, "I will bear arms on behalf of the United States when required by the law." That oath is an outgrowth of a long history of citizen-soldiers in the country. There is no more important ultimate stake that a citizen has than in the protection or preservation of his or her country.

Such willingness to serve represents a commitment and an acknowledgment that a citizen may be called upon to give up his or her comforts, livelihood, and even life if the circumstances warrant. It is the ultimate merger of responsibility and caring. The United States recognizes this fact, and immigrant green card holders who serve in the U.S. armed forces have the normal five-year waiting period before being able to apply for citizenship reduced.

Immigrants from countries in which ethnic military conflict is a fact of life can hardly be expected to leave their feelings behind when they arrive in the United States. For many years, Irish Americans contributed money to their ethnic brothers fighting the British in Ireland. Jews have contributed to Israel since that country's founding. And more recently, Muslim arrivals have contributed to their own ethnic-based charities (some of which have operated as fronts or helpmates for terrorist activities). The history of ethnic help for family homelands is an old American story.[52]

So, in a more limited sense, is the modern history of Americans fighting abroad. Americans on the left fought in the Spanish Civil War. In 1937 then-captain L. Chennault went to China at the request of Madame Chiang Kai-shek to help the Chinese develop an air force capable of confronting the attacking Japanese. This mission became the basis for the famous all-volunteer force, the Flying Tigers, which served with distinction both before and after Pearl Harbor. That volunteer group was sanctioned by the White House.[53]

In a well-publicized example in 2002, a Democratic candidate for Congress, and now a member of Congress from Illinois, Rahm Emanuel, was criticized by his opponent for being an Israeli dual citizen and having served in their armed forces while an American citizen.[54] That impression had been fueled by comments like those made by George Stephanopoulos, who told the television program *Nightline* that "Rahm had served in the Israeli army." The *Jerusalem Post* reported in July 1997 after an interview with Emanuel that "what has perhaps gained Emanuel the greatest admiration in Jerusalem was his coming to the country during the Gulf War to volunteer at a supply base near Kiryat Shmona. He said he did menial work at the base, separating tank brakes from jeep brakes from truck brakes, and downplayed the trip, saying it was not a sacrifice, merely 'something I wanted to do.'"

Some go further. During the savage ethnic fighting that flared in Yugoslavia in 2001, a group of about 400 Albanian Americans volunteered to join the rebel Kosovo Liberation Army.[55] Several died.

The problem of dual citizens, or even American citizens with strong homeland feelings, entering into combat in one form or another in their countries of origin is certainly not as large a problem numerically as the issue of foreign voting. The numbers are most likely very small. Nonetheless, it is worth paying attention to because it is part of a group of behaviors that tend to reinforce emotional ties to foreign countries—when every effort should be made to foster attachments to this country. The United States cannot easily cement immigrant ties to this country while encouraging immigrants to vote, serve, and fight abroad for other countries.

Dual Citizens and Public Life in the United States

RECOMMENDATION 4: **American citizens, whether naturalized or not, who desire to serve in elective or appointive office, or positions of**

governmental responsibility, should help establish the community norm of primary attachment to the American national community, or the local portion of it. In the specific case of dual citizenship, such persons should adhere to a standard that includes not holding or retaining dual citizenship while in American office and not taking part in foreign elections while so serving, detailing and severing all advisory positions with foreign governments.

The White House Fellowship is one of the most competitive prestigious fellowships in the country. Few are chosen and they go on to important positions in government, industry, education, and other key American institutions. On its website, the fellowship lists a number of frequently asked questions, among them is the following: Can I be a White House Fellow if I have dual citizenship?[56] The answer is no.

The questions that arise concerning the rights and responsibilities of American dual citizens in their own country are similar, but in some respects more complicated than the questions already addressed. Dual-citizen Americans are, after all, Americans. If they are not seeking to run for office in a foreign country, vote there, or serve as appointed advisers to foreign governments, they have avoided the actions that are most troubling to the integrity of the national community in which they live—or have they?

Here is the issue. The United States has within its population more and more immigrants from dual-national countries. They become citizens by naturalization or because they are born here to immigrant families. More Americans are, or can become, dual nationals.

Given American mobility patterns, it is just a matter of time before American dual nationals will begin to take their places in the halls of government, community, and civic organizations. In many ways, this will be a measure of successful integration. Dual nationals will begin to run for office. They will be appointed as judges. They have already begun to occupy advisory roles to those in power. And they will begin to staff U.S. decision-making institutions—for example, the Pentagon, Central Intelligence Agency (CIA), and State Department.

Indeed, they have already done so: Miguel Estrada, President Bush's choice for a federal judgeship, migrated to the United States as a teenager from Honduras. Michigan governor Jennifer M. Granholm was born in Vancouver, British Columbia. Zalmay M. Khalilzad, the former U.S. ambassador to Afghanistan who was recently confirmed as ambassador to Iraq, was born in Mazar-i-Sharif and is Pashtun by ethnicity. The commander of the U.S. Central Command is John Abizaid, a Lebanese American. And of course, almost everyone knows that California governor Arnold Schwarzenegger was born in Austria.

All these individuals, by virtue of their family's country of origin, are eligible for dual citizenship. Yet none of them has had the issue of dual attachments raised in connection with his or her leadership in such key institutional positions. It is worth asking why. As far as the record shows, none of these Americans has taken steps to cement himself or herself to their family's country of origin. None of them holds two passports. None has served in, or as an adviser to, a foreign government. None has served in the armed forces of another country. And none has a history of being a special advocate for his or her family's country of origin.

The question is this: Should Americans who hold dual citizenship serve in important public positions, and if so with what understanding? The United States now distinguishes between green card holders and citizens in only a few remaining areas, namely, the right to vote, the right to serve on juries, and the right to hold certain high-level elective offices and some state and all federal civil service positions.[57] These distinctions are based in part on understanding that it takes some time to learn the culture before you can adequately represent it. They are also based on the assumption that immigrants who have not taken the necessary steps to become citizens have demonstrated a lack of commitment that calls into question their interest in, and ability to, represent citizens. And two further issues are that such prohibitions encourage citizenship and also send a message that it is important.

But what of those who have already become citizens? They have certainly demonstrated a commitment by successfully going through the process. Should that mark the end of our concerns? This is a sensitive issue. However, it is a growing one.[58]

In 1998, a French Canadian with a U.S. passport ran for mayor of Plattsburgh, New York. He argued that the incumbent spoke French too poorly to be running a city so close to Quebec. He lost. Also that year, an Australian, Helen Cameron, who had traded her Australian citizenship for American nationality so she could do business, served on the school board and even sought the mayor's seat in Irvine, California. In the late 1990s, Adriano Espaillat, a naturalized American from the Dominican Republic and a member of the New York State Assembly, became the first Dominican elected to a U.S. state legislature. In 2002, an immigrant from India ran for the Iowa legislature.[59]

The major issue is one addressed above in the discussion of holding office in, or serving as an adviser to, a foreign government. A national community has the right to expect the highest standard of allegiance from those serving on its behalf. Indeed, because of the exercise of power involved in serving in decision-making roles, it could be argued that this standard is even higher that that of a citizen in general.

Spiro has suggested that this issue be addressed using a conflict-of-interest approach.[60] For example, a dual national in the State Department would excuse himself when dealing with an issue that affected his other country of attachment. Or to use Spiro's illustration, no American–Mexican dual citizens should serve on a U.S. trade delegation to Mexico.[61] Regretfully, the issue is not that easily resolved.

Spiro's solution depends on self-filtering—a person realizes that there is a conflict and removes himself or herself. But what if he or she does not think there is a conflict or feels they can handle it? The example Spiro gives— barring a Mexican American from a trade delegation to that country— assumes that a Mexican American cannot be trusted to champion American rather than Mexican interests. Should Alberto Gonzales disqualify himself from any issues that deal with Salvadoran nationals? That seems wholly unnecessary.

What if a dual-citizen American identifies with her Hispanic ethnicity? Will she then have to recuse herself from all dealings with Latin America and Spain? What about a dual-citizen American with strong feelings toward and identifications with his Muslim religion?

A national community can tolerate a certain number of its citizens who dislike the government. It can get along if some of its citizens have an attachment to other countries, so long as those are not strong enough to trump attachments to the national community. However, a community is much less able to tolerate those in position of power who divide their national loyalties between two countries.

A model for the dilemma is seen in recruiting patterns at the CIA. In the wake of September 11, a number of observers said, correctly, that intelligence agencies need to diversify. Senator Richard C. Shelby (R-Ala.) has said that "the government must do a better job at turning America's ethnic diversity and immigrant heritage into an intelligence asset by recruiting into its ranks Americans who speak Arabic and Farsi and can better meld into the byways of the terrorists."[62] They have been busy scrambling to add diverse nationalities to their rosters.[63]

Yet they have run into a problem. Many of the people they would like to recruit are naturalized citizens or children of immigrants from countries that have supplied many of the terrorists that they will be arrayed against. The issue that the CIA and other such agencies face is not so much the potential for disloyalty (although that is always a potential problem for intelligence or enforcement agencies) but rather the potential—one might say the likelihood—of conflicted loyalties or attachments.

How would it feel to be a first-generation Muslim whose parents came here from, say, Pakistan or Nigeria, and be sent there to recruit their nationals to spy for the United States? When doing background checks for the security clearances that must be given to top-level analysts, how is it possible to gauge the person's relative degree of commitment to his or her new country and country of recent origin? Which kinds of attachments are all right, and which are problematic? In the old days, all one needed to do was the historical research equivalent of looking into the person's wallet and seeing if he or she carried a membership card for the Communist Party. This will obviously no longer do. However, what does suffice is not yet clear. The danger is not treason but rather conflicted loyalties and the failure because of them to make this country's positions, policies, or interests sufficiently primary.

These same kinds of issues have already arisen for naturalized or dual citizens running for elective office. In the 2000 presidential race, the Nation of Islam leader Louis Farrakhan questioned the national loyalty of the vice presidential candidate Joseph Lieberman. In his remarks he said, "Mr. Lieberman, as an Orthodox Jew, is also a dual citizen of Israel. The state of Israel is not synonymous with the United States," he continued, "and the test he would probably have to pass is: Would he be more faithful to the Constitution of the United States than to the ties that any Jewish person would have to the state of Israel?"[64]

A similar circumstance arose in Iowa when a naturalized Indian American, Swati Dandekas, ran for office. Her opponent, Karen Balderston, sent an e-mail message asking, "Without having had the growing-up experience in Iowa, complete with the intrinsic basics of Midwest American life, how is this person adequately prepared to represent Midwest values and core beliefs, let alone understand and appreciate the constitutional rights guaranteed to us in writing by our Founding Fathers (note, her Founding Fathers)?"[65]

These accusations are farfetched. Joe Lieberman has spent his whole life here. He was no more Israel's Connecticut senator than John Kennedy was the pope's president. And Swati Dandekas, who was fifty-one at that time, had lived in Iowa for thirty-one years. Gonzales has never held two passports, and Schwarzenegger has never voted in a foreign election.

There are examples, however, that do underscore the nature of the potential issues. Josaphat Celestin came to the United States from Haiti. At first, he thought he would return as soon as possible. But then he decided to stay and organize his Haitian American community to support his bid for political office. After some losses, he was finally elected mayor of North Miami with the strong support of the Haitian community. This, in turn, has led to concerns of non-Haitians that their needs will be neglected.[66]

The issue of community history and experience is not a frivolous one. People generally want to be represented by persons who are like them. For some, this has a strictly racial or ethnic dimension. Yet more generally, people want to be sure that a leader knows the community, has spent time with it, and appreciates its values and generally agrees with them.

Ultimately, it is up to those doing the appointing or electing to make this decision. New Yorkers have twice elected senators who have little historical connection with the state. And a naturalized citizen who has been in the country only a few years will no doubt be judged differently than one who has lived in the United States for thirty-one years.

Having said this, however, does not wholly dispense with the issue. This is a period of pressure to be "black enough," or not to be a "coconut"—brown on the outside and white on the inside. Demands for ethnic and country of origin identification presents problems for all Americans. Even people who actively promote the idea of dual citizenship say there are limits to subdividing loyalties when it comes to political leadership positions. A New York City Council member, Guillermo Linares, the first Dominican American elected to any office in this country, made it a point not to vote in the 1996 Dominican election, the first in which Dominicans abroad could vote. "I am an elected official of the United States," Linares said.[67]

The question of how much identification a leader has with his new or old country is unlikely ever to be satisfactorily resolved. Internal identifications are, after all personal, sometimes shifting within a range, and often not wholly accessible to the person himself. There is no guaranteed measurement for the strength and nature of attachments.

Consider the case of Tony Garza, a longtime George W. Bush associate, who was recently appointed U.S. ambassador to Mexico. He is a second-generation American who speaks fluent Spanish and whose four grandparents were from Mexico. He graduated from the University of Texas; attended Southern Methodist University Law School; and was elected judge in Cameron County, the southernmost county in Texas.

After the Senate confirmed his nomination as U.S. ambassador to Mexico, he was asked in an interview about his views on U.S. policy and Mexican immigration. He replied, "I view it from the perspective of a Mexican and an American and I happen to think it's important to us that we move on immigration because I really do think it speaks to our character and our identity,"[68] I do not wish to make too much of a single sentence, but it is a professional habit to pay attention to what people say and how they do so. Garza mentions his Mexican identification first and his American one second, and he seems to weight them more or less equally, with the Mexican portion being first among equals.[69] Consider a possible alternative response: I view these problems as an American with a Mexican heritage. Perhaps the operational dividing line should be between those whose American identifications are naturally primary (e.g., American of Irish decent or Irish *American)* compared with those for whom it is not (e.g., *Irish* American, Hispanic).

Nonetheless, there are guidelines that could be followed. Signposts are possible to discern. Does the person currently hold, or have they ever held, dual citizenship? If so, what was the time frame and what were the circumstances? If naturalized, when did that happen, and how soon after it was possible to do so was the application made? Has the person ever voted in a foreign election? If so, when and how often? Has the person ever held elective or advisory office abroad? If so, when and under what circumstances?

These are the kinds of basic questions that might be asked of any person seeking to represent the national community or a local part of it. The issue is not so much a "loyalty test" as it is a form of legitimate quest for reassurance that the person has demonstrated by his or her behavior that attachments to any country of origin take a back seat to the primacy of identification with the American national community. Some positions, especially security and high-level advisory positions, will obviously require more.[70]

Writing in the Australian context, Castles notes there are already large numbers of dual citizens. He expects that in the future this will become even more widespread and expresses the hope this should not lead to exclusion from any rights, such as the right to stand for office.[71] It should not, of course.

Nor, because every citizen has the right to run for office once they are naturalized,[72] is any legislation possible in this matter, even if it were desirable—which it is not. The matter is best handled informally by the growth of a norm of demonstrated national attachment and integration in cases where persons run for political office or represent various communities in nongovernmental, but policy-relevant, positions.

Dual Citizenship Is Only Part of the Issue

All four of the above recommendations have one purpose in common: to help develop and strengthen the ties of immigrants to the American national community. Yet the issues of developing the American national community go well beyond whether U.S. citizens vote in foreign elections. If America is truly to be more welcoming to its immigrants, and true to its own citizens, it must do much more to foster attachments in the community as a whole. I turn to these issues in the next chapter.

Notes

1. Peter M. Schuck, *Citizens, Strangers, and In-Betweens: Essays on Immigration and Citizenship* (Boulder, Colo.: Westview Press, 1998), 227.

2. T. Alexander Aleinikoff and Douglas Klusmeyer, "Plural Citizenship: Facing the Future in a Migratory World," in *Citizenship Today: Global Perspectives*, ed. T. Alexander Aleinikoff and Douglas Klusmeyer (Washington, D.C.: Carnegie Endowment for International Peace, 2001), 28.

3. This example, and those that follow, are drawn from Thomas M. Franck, "Clan and Superclan: Law Identity and Community in Law and Practice," *American Journal of International Law* 90 (1996): 359–83.

4. Hammer notes that some dual nationals face the risk of having to serve in two different armed forces if they travel to the country in which they hold citizenship/ nationality but did not serve. He further notes that others countries, like Turkey, mandate in the Constitution that service in the army is a requirement for all Turks, period. Tomas Hammer, "Dual Citizenship and Political Integration," *International Migration Review* 19, no. 3 (1985): 438–50; the citation here is on 446. Later evidence, however, suggests that Turkey may have modified its position on this somewhat. Miller reports that at a conference organized by the Alien Commission of the West Berlin Senate in 1989, the Turkish counselor in Berlin said that his government permitted Turkish males living in Germany to pay 10,000 deutsche marks over a ten-year period to reduce their active time of service in Turkey to two months. Mark J. Miller, "Dual Citizenship: A European Norm?" *International Migration Review* 33, no. 4 (1991): 945–50; the citation here is on 948.

5. See Miller, "Dual Citizenship," 448.

6. Rodolfo O. de la Garza, Miguel David Baranoa, Tomas Pachon, Emily Edmunds, Fernando Acosta-Rodriguez, and Michelle Morales, *Dual Citizenship, Domestic Politics, and Naturalization Rates of Latino Immigrants in the U.S.* (Los Angeles: Tomas Rivera Center, 1996), 2–3. See also Michael Jones-Correa, *Under Two Flags: Dual Nationality in Latin America and Its Consequence for the United States*, Working Paper in Latin America 99/00–3 (Cambridge, Mass.: David Rockefeller Center for Latin American Studies, Harvard University, 2000), 3, 5.

7. Philip Martin, "U.S. and California Reactions to Dual Nationality and Absentee Voting, Foreign Ministry of Mexico," Foreign Ministry of Mexico, February 17, 2000. See also "Mexico: Dual Nationality," *Migration News* 7, no. 3 (March 2000); available at http://migration.ucdavis.edu.

8. Francis Sellers, "A World Wishing to Cast a Vote," *Washington Post*, November 21, 2004.

9. What does "affirmation intention" mean? On April 16, 1990, the State Department adopted a new set of guidelines for handling dual citizenship cases, which assumes that a U.S. citizen intends to retain his U.S. citizenship even if he or she (1) is naturalized in a foreign country; (2) takes a routine oath of allegiance to a foreign country; or (3) accepts foreign government employment that is of a "non-policy-level" nature. These assumptions do not apply to persons who (1) take a "policy-level" position in a foreign country; (2) are convicted of treason against the United States; or (3) engage in "conduct which is so inconsistent with retention of U.S. citizenship that it compels a conclusion that [they] intended to relinquish U.S. citizenship." For the law regarding this, see "State Department Explains New Evidentiary Standards for Expatriation," *Interpreter Releases*, October 1, 1990, 1092–95; and *Interpreter Releases*, July 23, 1990, 799–800.

10. Anticipating the Twenty-Fourth Amendment, in the case of *Harper v. Virginia Board of Education* (383 U.S. 663 (1966), the Supreme Court struck down poll taxes saying, holding that "the political franchise of voting" is "a fundamental political right because (it is) preservative of all rights." For a closer analysis of the constitutional foundation and importance of voting as a key element of American citizenship, see William N. Eskridge, "The Relationship between Obligations and Rights of Citizens," *Fordham Law Review* 69 (2001): 1721–51.

11. Bruce Fein, "Dual Citizenship Folly," *Washington Times*, March 1, 2005.

12. Schuck, *Citizens, Strangers, and In-Betweens*, 235.

13. E. J. Dionne Jr., "The Civics Deficit," *Washington Post*, November 30, 1999.

14. Cole Bruce, "Our American Amnesia," *Wall Street Journal*, June 11, 2002.

15. "What Makes a Citizen?" (editorial), *Washington Post*, June 5, 1998.

16. Benjamin Ginsberg and Robert Weissberg, "Elections and the Mobilization of Popular Support," *American Journal of Political Science* 22, no. 1 (1978): 31–54.

17. Ibid., 35–36.

18. Ibid., 52.

19. Alejandro Portes, "Toward a New World: The Origins and Effects of Transnational Activities," *Ethnic and Racial Studies* 22 (March 1999): 463–77.

20. Sam Dillon, "Mexico Weighs Voting by Its Emigrants in U.S.," *New York Times*, December 7, 1998.

21. John Ward Anderson, "Politicians without Borders: Mexico's Candidates Court Support of Migrants in U.S.," *Washington Post*, May 9, 2000.

22. Pam Belluck, "Mexican Presidential Candidates Campaign in the U.S.," *New York Times*, July 1, 2000.

23. Talk Back Live, "Las elecciones mexicanas con Francisco Labastida, el candidato del PRI" (English translation transcript), *Washington Post*, March 24, 2002.

24. A reciprocal process is under way as increasingly American politicians travel to foreign countries to campaign for the votes of that country's nationals in the United States. Democratic and Republican political leaders from New York and elsewhere routinely visited Vieques—a Puerto Rican island used for Defense Department war exercises, to protest that use. Amy Waldman, "New Yorkers Stand Out in Protests over Vieques," *New York Times*, May 5, 2000. In 2001, two top Democratic Party officials—Richard Gephardt, then the House minority leader, and Thomas Daschle, then the Senate majority leader—visited several areas in Mexico promising to do all they could to regularize the status of illegal alienation in the United States. Ginger Thompson, "Top Democrats Politick through Rural Mexico," *New York Times*, November 19, 2001; and Kevin Sullivan and Mary Jordan, "Daschle, Gephardt Visit Mexico; U.S. Leaders Hope to Return Attention to Immigration Issues," *Washington Post*, November 18, 2001. New York governor George Pataki visited the Dominican Republic to pay a condolence call on the relatives of those killed in the crash of Flight 857, which ran daily between New York and the Dominican Republic. This was shortly in advance of his try for a third term in office. "N.Y. Gov. Visits Dominican Republic," Associated Press, February 18, 2002. The then–mayor elect of New York City, Michael Bloomberg, made the same pilgrimage and included Puerto Rico, where he promised "closer ties." Jennifer Steinhauer, "Bloomberg, in Dominican Republic, Meets with Crash Victims' Relatives," *New York Times*, November 27, 2001; and Steinhauer, "In Puerto Rico, Bloomberg Promises Closer Ties," *New York Times*, November 28, 2001.

25. Leslie Crawford, "Mexican Politicians Cross the U.S. Border in Search of Votes," *Financial Times*, May 6, 1998.

26. Ibid.

27. Belluck, "Mexican Presidential Candidates Campaign in the U.S."

28. Adam Nagourney, "Jets Are Chartered for Israelis in U.S. to Get Out to Vote," *New York Times*, May 8, 1999.

29. Sellers, "World Wishing to Cast a Vote."

30. David A. Martin, "New Rules on Dual Nationality for a Democratizing Globe: between Rejection and Embrace," *Georgetown Immigration Law Journal* 14 (1999): 1–34.

31. Robert E. Pierre, "Poland's Big Debate Becomes Chicago's," *Washington Post*, June 7, 2003. Jonathan Eig, "Poland Must Decide on EU, but How Will Chicago Vote?" *Wall Street Journal*, June 2, 2003.

32. Pierre, "Poland's Big Debate." Nor is the Chicago E.U. vote devoid of Polish government self-interest. Eig reports that "in Poland where there are 29 million eligible voters, the referendum has widespread support, but government officials are worried about turnout. The results won't count unless more than 50% of eligible Poles vote. That helps explain why the Polish foreign ministry has instructed its staff in Chicago to get out the vote. Even 'no' votes will help push the eligibility figure toward 50%. 'It's an absolute priority to this office,' says Mariusz Brymora, deputy consul general. 'He has about 10 people in the consulate working full time to make sure the referendum passes.'" Eig, "Poland Must Decide."

33. Fein, "Dual Citizenship Folly."

34. Ibid.

35. T. Alexander Aleinikoff, *Between Principles and Politics: The Direction of U.S. Citizenship Policy* (Washington, D.C.: Carnegie Endowment for International Peace, 1998), 34–36.

36. Jeffrey R. O'Brien, "U.S. Dual Citizenship Voting Rights: A Critical Examination of Aleinikoff's Proposal," *Georgetown Immigration Journal* 13, no. 533 (1999): 573–95.

37. Ibid., 593–95.

38. Elizabeth Bumiller, "For Bush, a Big 'Aciu' from Eastern Europe," *New York Times*, November 25, 2002.

39. Christine Haughney, "Lecturing in New York, Campaigning in Nigeria; Professors in U.S. Seeking Office Back Home," *Washington Post*, May 28, 2002.

40. Franck, "Clan and Superclan."

41. Jennifer Mena, "3 Men, 2 Nations, 1 Dream," *Los Angeles Times*, June 30, 2001.

42. William C. Mann, "Albright Eyed as Czech President," Associated Press, February 28, 2000.

43. Anthony Shadid, "Attack in N. Iraq Kills 2 Americans," *Washington Post*, November 24, 2003.

44. Mark Fritz, "Pledging Multiple Allegiances: A Global Blurring of Boundaries Challenges Notions of Nationality—U.S. Analysts Worry about a Rise in Dual Citizenships of Convenience," *Los Angeles Times*, April 6, 1998.

45. Portes, "Toward a New World," 469.

46. Fritz, "Pledging Multiple Allegiances."

47. Quoted in Fritz, "Pledging Multiple Allegiances."

48. Belluck, "Mexican Presidential Candidates Campaign in the U.S."

49. Ibid.

50. Edward Hegstrom, "Straddling the Border; American in Fox Cabinet Aims to Protect Mexicans Here," *Houston Chronicle*, February 22, 2001.

51. Oscar Avila, "Mexican Nationals to Elect Advisors," *Chicago Tribune*, November 5, 2000.

52. Tony Smith, *Foreign Entanglements: The Power of Ethnic Groups in the Making of American Foreign Policy* (Cambridge, Mass.: Harvard University Press, 2001).

53. Claire Chennault, *Way of a Fighter* (Tucson: James Thorvardson & Sons, 1991; orig. pub. 1949).

54. An Internet web log site, SmarterTimes.com, carried the following background information, "A dispatch from Chicago in the national section of today's *New York Times* reports that the president of the Polish American Congress, Edward Moskal, 'suggested, erroneously, that' an Illinois congressional candidate, 'had dual citizenship with Israel and has served in its armed forces.'" The Associated Press reported in a 1996 biographical sketch of Emanuel that "in 1991, during the Persian Gulf War, he spent 2 and a half weeks rust proofing brakes for Israeli Army vehicles." And the *Washington Post* reported in 1992 that "Rahm retained dual citizenship until age 18, when he gave up his Israeli passport, but sometimes thinks 'ambivalently' about moving permanently to Israel. It is now part of his legend that during the Persian Gulf War in early 1991, when Iraqi scuds were falling on the country where he spent many a childhood summer, he volunteered for 2 1/2 weeks on an army base near the Lebanese border, rust-proofing brakes for military vehicles."

55. R. Jeffrey Smith and Peter Finn, "Three Americans Found in Serbian Mass Grave Site," *Washington Post*, July 15, 2001.

56. See http://www.whitehouse.gov/fellows/about/faq.html.

57. Peter Schuck, writing about the exclusion of noncitizens from federal civil service position and many state government jobs, writes: "I see no merit in denying voters or elected officials the opportunity to place aliens in the high elective office from which the law sometimes bar them." See Schuck, *Citizens, Strangers, and In-Betweens*, 6–7.

58. The examples in the paragraph that follows are all drawn from Fritz, "Pledging Multiple Allegiances."

59. Todd Dvorak, "GOP Pulls Support for Iowa Hopeful," *Washington Post*, October 29, 2002.

60. Peter J. Spiro, "Dual Nationality and the Meaning of Citizenship," *Emory Law Journal* 46, no. 4 (1997):1481–83.

61. Ibid., 1481.

62. Quoted in Allison Mitchell, "Senator Shelby Faults the Intelligence Agencies," *New York Times*, September 10, 2002.

63. Dana Priest, "The Slowly Changing Face of a CIA Spy," *Washington Post*, August 9, 2002.

64. Quoted by Teresa Watanabe, "Nation of Islam Leader Raises the Loyalty Issue," *Los Angeles Times*, August 12, 2000.

65. Dvorak, "GOP Pulls Support."

66. Dana Canedy, "Away from Haiti, Discovering the Politics of the Possible," *New York Times*, May 21, 2001.

67. Quoted in Fritz, "Pledging Multiple Allegiances."

68. Armando Villafranca, "Envoy Seeks Progress in Immigration Reform," *Houston Chronicle*, November 14, 2002.

69. I am aware that Garza's views on immigration closely follow the president's and that ambassadors are supposed to follow presidential policy.

70. Meredith Krause, "Divided National Loyalties: A Primer for Personnel Security Staff," Personnel Security Managers' Research Program, April 2002.

71. Stephen Castles, "Globalization, Multicultural Citizenship and Transnational Democracy," in *The Future of Australian Multiculturalism*, ed. Ghassan Hage and Rowanne Couch (Sydney: University of Sydney Press, 1999), 39.

72. The exception, of course, is the presidency of the United States. Article II, section 1, of the Constitution states, "No person except a natural born Citizen, or a Citizen of the United States, at the time of the Adoption of this Constitution, shall be eligible to the Office of President," Representative Barney Frank (D-Mass.) has introduced a constitutional amendment to overturn this provision. That bill (H.J. Res. 47) would require a naturalized citizen to live in the United States for twenty years before seeking the presidency.

CHAPTER 10

Becoming American: Some Proposals

A NEW REPORT ON IMMIGRATION POLICY FROM THE CHICAGO COUN-cil on Foreign Relations begins by saying that the only point of agreement among those who study, are affected by, or wish to change American immi-gration policy is that "the system is broken."[1] Just how it is broken is a matter of ongoing debate. Some point to the asylum system; others point to family reunification policy. Poor naturalization rates concern some; long waits con-cern others. Some critics complain that immigrants use more resources than they generate; others argue that they ought to have immediate access to the safety net. All these issues, and many others, have been strenuously debated in recent years.

What all these issues have in common is that they are important but not central. They fail to get at the heart of America's immigration dilemma. And though resolving each of these issues would no doubt improve American im-migration policy, by themselves they would do nothing to resolve its core dilemma.

And what is America's central, core immigration issue? It is this: *How is it possible to integrate more than a million new immigrants a year, on average, into the American national community? How do we help them feel more at home here while at the same time developing the attachments that will truly help them think of themselves as Americans first?*

This is, admittedly, a controversial and not widely held stance in a policy area that has been dominated by economic arguments and hypercharged po-litical rhetoric.[2] Some even question whether helping immigrants to become attached to their new country is not a form of racism and cultural condescen-sion. These are ugly accusations, ignorant of the psychology that underlies the very best aspects of American cultural, social, and political life.

The Emotional Underpinnings of American Life

Emotional attachment to the American national community is the foundation of U.S. citizenship and of this country's institutions and way of life. In the wake of the terrorist attacks of September 11, 2001, it is also a matter of national security. Liberals and conservatives alike believe that a commitment to the American ideals of democracy and justice are what unites us. However, the American Creed itself rests on a more basic psychological foundation, which includes a warmth and affection for, an appreciation of, a justifiable but not excessive pride in, a commitment and responsibility toward, and support of the United States—its institutions, its way of life and aspirations, and its fellow members.

These attachments define the basis of our identification as Americans. We do not often think about it except when events like those of September 11 remind us that our attachments to this country are profound and much deeper than believing that democracy is the best form of government. And they are much more extensive and nuanced than the caricature of lazy patriotism epitomized by the phrase "My country right or wrong."

The success of American democracy and its cultural and political institutions has always depended on these kinds of emotional connections. Yet as I have argued in this analysis, since the 1960s these attachments have been profoundly challenged and, in many ways, weakened by domestic and international developments. Within the United States, decades of cultural warfare over everything from the nature of families to civics curriculums have weakened America's primary social, political, and cultural institutions. At the same time, multiculturalism has successfully championed the primacy of racial and ethnic identities over more national attachments.

Internationally, easy global movements of information and people have allowed immigrants and citizens alike to be more closely in touch with their home countries and allowed their home countries to be more closely in touch with them, primarily for self-interested reasons. New and old immigrants have understandable attachments to their countries of origin. The question is: How can the United States facilitate attachments to *this* country?

The answers to this question do not concern new immigrants alone. They are national community issues. Both U.S.-born citizens and new immigrants have an important stake in increasing the extensiveness and depth of attachments to the American national community. And of course the government, representing all Americans, has a critical role to play in helping to foster American national identity and attachment. If national attachments are the psychological glue that holds this country together, how is it possible to help develop and consolidate these feelings? Certainly no laws can mandate them. Nor can we halt or reverse the march of technology and international connectedness.

Such feelings can only develop out of the experiences that foster them. The question is whether we can help put in place experiences that help to do that. In this chapter, I suggest six basic ways to do just that. These suggestions take the form of affirmative steps to do certain things and equally affirmative steps to make sure that we do not encourage certain things. Among the former are measures to facilitate cultural, economic, and political integration. Among the latter are measures blurring the political distinctions between citizens and legal resident aliens and undocumented illegal aliens. Addressing both sets of issues is critical to ensuring a fuller integration of immigrants and Americans into their national community.

It cannot be stated too strongly that the proposals made here are *not* put forward with the view that there is only one kind of American or one way to think about America to which everyone must or should adhere. Each immigrant and citizen will have to find his or her own ways to be and live life as an American. There are more than 260 million American stories in the naked city, to update the old television tag line. Finding points of attachment between Americans, both old and new, and this country's history, institutions, and traditions so that they can see how their lives and that of the country intersect provide one strong basis for connection and for the development of an American identity. Government, as well as private and civic organizations at all levels, have an important role to play in this process.

The Policies of Psychological Integration

There are many immigration policy reform proposals. One of them, the Center for Immigration Studies' report *Blueprint for an Ideal Immigration Policy*, draws recommendations from across the political spectrum.[3] For example, the report's authors suggest diversifying the immigrant stream, looking more closely at the issue of family preferences, and examining immigrant work programs as a method of increasing flexibility. These and similar proposals seem useful. However, they will not be my focus here. Instead, I focus on the particular question of how to integrate new immigrants and citizens alike into the American national community.

My concern is not new. In 1977, Barbara Jordan and the U.S. Commission on Immigration Reform (known as the Jordan Commission) used very strong and direct language to underscore the point that "Americanization" is not a dirty word but is in fact a key element of successfully integrating new immigrants into the American national community. The commission's report to Congress, *Becoming an American: Immigration and Immigrant Policy*, is an overlooked treasure of sensible ideas.[4] Yet the truth is that not much has been done to implement the Jordan Commission's important insights.

The 2004 study and policy proposals sponsored by the Chicago Council on Foreign Relations contain a few useful suggestions on this issue that parallel the Jordan Commission's suggestions in the 1970s to develop federal, state, local, and civic partnerships to help immigrants and to ensure that they learn English.[5] Yet these proposals also add some new ideas that are less central.

Streamlining and speeding up naturalization, disabusing American "misperceptions" about immigrants (whatever they are), and giving health insurance benefits to new immigrants do not seem to get at the heart of the issues here.[6]

In the years since the Jordan Commission's report, the United States has demonstrated that it is still not serious about helping immigrants become Americans. Nor has much thought been given to how we can help Americans consolidate their connections to their home country. The two are certainly related. If Americans have difficulty understanding and appreciating their country, how can we expect new immigrants to fare much better? In the post–September 11 age of catastrophic terrorism, this is a dangerous gap.

The failure to affirmatively act in this matter is not primarily the result of indifference. There is overwhelming support among Americans for integrating immigrants into American life. Indeed, what upsets Americans most about the issue—aside from the continuing surge of illegal immigrants—is the sense that the traditional expectation of immigrants becoming integrated into the American national community is no longer valued or expected by some, among them, as noted, our political leaders.

Not all the suggestions for immigration policy are helpful. Some feel that the burdens of becoming a citizen are already too heavy and they propose lightening them. Some want to lessen or do away with the requirement that immigrants learn English.[7] Some want to include illegal aliens in a new general amnesty.[8] And some want to do away with the renunciation clause in the Naturalization Oath, arguing that you cannot legislate feelings. These suggestions for the immigrant version of "EZ" citizenship, like allowing noncitizens to vote, do not seem designed to foster attachment. On the contrary, they promise to further fracture the American national community and the attachment that underlies it.

In this chapter, I make six general policy recommendations related to immigration and citizenship broadly conceived. They are, like the suggestions put forward in the previous chapter on reforming dual citizenship, ultimately aimed at the same goal: increasing the self-identification of immigrants and Americans alike with an American national identity and the attachments to the national community that flow from it. Specifically, the recommendations focus on cultural adaptation, language acquisition, civics integration, and the difficult problem of illegal immigration. Though there are numerous smaller and important ways in which our immigration policies can be improved, these four areas represent the foundation for integration into the American national community.

Integration into the American National Community

Like any new, tentative relationship, the one between an immigrant and his or her new community is an uneven experience. That process normally begins with an extensive application for a visa. Increasingly, there is a formal interview. Applicants may wait many months, even years, before a permanent visa is approved. Upon receiving the visa, immigrants may enter the United States, but they still must wait for a period of five years before they can stand for naturalization. At that time, they must present evidence that they are of good moral character, that they have a working knowledge of English, and that they know something of American politics. If immigrants are able to successfully present such knowledge, then they are asked to take an oath of allegiance in which they "renounce" their former attachments.

The process is long, though not necessarily difficult. The length of the process, while frustrating, is a natural result of enormous numbers, national security concerns, and the workings of a large bureaucracy. Critics call all these difficulties "unwelcoming" and propose doing away with, or lessening, the number of requirements. The easier, the better, in their view.

However, as long as the United States is serious about retaining some judgment about the enormous numbers of people who wish to live within its borders, the process will not be short. As long as the United States wishes to protect those already here, the process of inquiry cannot be shallow. Of course, the process should be transparent and easily understood. But a transparent and explained process is only the first, introductory stage of what the government can do to help immigrants become Americans.

Cultural Adaptation: A Real Welcome for Immigrants

A real welcome begins before immigrants arrive in this country. The U.S. government maintains a *Welcome to America Pamphlet* on its immigration website. But it could and should be translated and distributed overseas to all foreigners applying for green cards. Videotapes could supplement this introductory material either on websites or at libraries. More and more in-depth orientation to America needs to happen before immigrants arrive here.

What do many immigrants need most immediately upon their arrival? Those who arrive with high-education job placements waiting, or to take up advanced education, generally need less help with orientation. Others, the majority, need help finding a job, housing, and their way around. Generally this has been the domain of civic organizations—churches, advocacy groups, and ethnic communities. But these organizations are often too few and too poor, and often not sufficiently attentive to the broader community interest in fostering attachment to the American national community.

RECOMMENDATION 1: **Federal, state, and local governments, in partnership with business, education, and civic leaders, should develop and help maintain welcome centers throughout the United States**

whose sole purpose would be to help immigrants and their families adjust to the culture of this country and its institutional practices.

It would be useful for government to join with a range of immigrant-oriented groups, on a nonpartisan basis, to develop a nationwide network of hosting institutions in major cities and geographical hubs that could act as orientation centers and as clearinghouses for jobs, training, and housing. This would be an excellent place to develop an "Immigration Corps"—young and old people who give of their time and effort to help new immigrants become oriented.

Businesses could also be tapped to help their new immigrant employees. This would include not simply the important role of workplace socialization but also voluntary, after-hours orientation to the wider society in which the immigrants now live. Government–business partnerships could be forged for this effort, and extra costs to businesses redressed with tax credits or rebates. This will hardly be possible if businesses continue to employ illegal immigrants, with few questions asked, and the government turns a mostly blind eye to the practice.

High schools and junior colleges could also be enlisted. Evening and weekend classes could be developed for immigrants and their families covering a number of aspects of American life, to help educate them on how our culture works.

Consider one such effort, the newcomer centers in Chicago—where, in addition to academic subjects, students "also learn the ropes of U.S. schools: when to raise their hands, how to react to freshman hazing, what to expect on the lunch menu. . . . Students learn the basics about a school culture, from lunchroom to locker room, that is alien to them. It isn't unusual for a student from rural Mexico to go directly from a one-room schoolhouse to a 1,500-student high school that holds more people than his hometown. Cold milk at lunch might be new. So might coeducational classrooms. Perhaps students have never used a locker. Maybe they are used to being lectured for an entire class and feel uncomfortable working in small groups."[9] American students hardly think twice about these matters, and most do not have to. They grew up here. In this respect, immigrants cannot take very much for granted, and this requires a level of adjustment that few Americans appreciate.

These centers are focused on students and helping to develop success in schools. Yet there are adults—fathers, mothers, sisters, and brothers—who would also benefit from learning the ins and outs of American society as they gradually find their place within it. Macomb Junior College in Michigan runs a free, twice-a-week class titled "Living in America,"[10] which teaches such things as how to get a driver's license, how to apply for insurance, how to fill out a job application, how to shop in an American store, and how to make an appointment at a doctor's office.

We take these things for granted—but immigrants cannot. Yet learning about them would make immigrant transition much easier. The result would generate immigrants' feelings of becoming more a part of this society and culture, which would serve as a building block for an attachment to the community. The additional possibility of setting up such centers abroad for immigrants whose applications for a permanent visa have been approved should also be examined.

English, English, English

RECOMMENDATION 2: **Federal, state, and local governments should take steps to ensure that any immigrant who wishes to acquire or improve his or her English skills can do so without charge.**

It is difficult to imagine a more basic ingredient for feeling at home and doing well in a new society than knowing the language. Knowledge of English is so central to life in the United States and thus so obvious a key element in "feeling at home" that one hesitates to make it. Walk down the street in Hong Kong or in a city in Germany or India. If you do not speak the language, the street signs, stores signs, ads, announcements, building functions, and so on are lost to your understanding. This is even before you attempt any written or spoken transitions. Could you apply for a job in Italy without speaking Italian? Could you read a lease in Germany if you wanted to rent an apartment? A working knowledge of English—that means reading, speaking, and writing—is a critical element in easing what will always be to some extent a difficult transition.

The United States began, of course, as an English-speaking country, and it has remained so in spite of having no official language policy. America has, over the centuries, welcomed speakers of many foreign languages.[11] Between 1840 and 1924, two-thirds of the immigrants to this country spoke a language other than English. Yet as the sociologist Stanley Lieberson notes, "Despite efforts on the part of all immigrants groups to maintain their ancestral languages, their descendants soon contributed to the growing number of English monoglots in the United States. The shift was rapid . . . and in most cases it was final."[12]

There are a number of reasons for this. Schools taught English, and occupations required it.[13] Yet, in the end, Schiffman agrees with his colleague Kloss that the ultimate reasons are not to be found in nationality laws that were not unfavorable to other languages, nor in government policy or coercion,[14] but rather in "the absorbing power of the highly developed American society . . . the manifold opportunities for personal advancement and individual achievements which this society offered were so attractive that the descendants of the 'aliens' sooner or later voluntarily integrated themselves into this society."[15]

The same remains true today. English facility does function as a common bond, and in turn facilitates the connections to the country and its people. It underlies an understanding of, and therefore facilitates connection to, the shared social and political values of the country and an understanding of them. A working knowledge of English is the foundation of a basic understanding of republican democracy. Indeed, it is hard to see how the exalted American Creed can play much of a unifying role if people do not understand the language upon which it is built and operates.

At one time, government, civic organizations, and industry took this responsibility seriously. They no longer do. As I discussed in chapter 5, the original legislation for the Bilingual Education Act of 1967–68 developed by Texas senator Ralph Yarborough was specifically designed to increase English facility. The English learning provisions were gutted by ethnic advocates and their allies with results that retarded the integration of generations of immigrants into the American national culture. Given the large number of immigrants that arrive in this country, both legally and illegally every year, and the diversity of their backgrounds, there are probably more foreign languages spoken here than ever before. In these circumstances, a common standard language is even more important to developing and maintaining a national community.

Historically America conducted its national political, economic, and social business in English. The same is true today. Therefore, it is a matter of central importance on community, economic, political, and psychological grounds to encourage English language skills. The government could, and should, take the lead in fostering partnerships with colleges, schools, businesses, churches, and civic organizations to ensure that there are enough free or low-cost English language classes for those who want them.

English language classes should be available to all who want them, and scheduled for evenings mornings, weekends, or whenever people can get to them. They should not be directly tied to passing the English portion of the nationalization test, except in the sense that better speakers pass. Nor, as should be the case with welcoming centers, should they be anything but strictly nonpartisan. The point of these initiatives is to ease immigrant transition, not political recruiting.

Furthermore, there is no reason to wait until the person arrives in the United States to begin this process. Some countries base their immigration decisions on a point system—with so many points awarded for a number of the things, knowing the language of the country in question among them. Perhaps such a point system would be worth considering. However, such a system need not be in place in order to encourage the development of English language skills before immigrants arrive.

English language schools could be set up abroad for those who have been given provisional visa clearance and await final approval. That same group could have their language classes act as a form of anticipatory orientation for life in America. Those who wish to emigrate to the United States and are in the process of applying, or who might do so in the future, could receive a plus factor of some sort on evidence that they have or are taking English language courses.

In helping immigrants master English, Americans offer a welcoming hand in a manner that give immigrants the tools for a productive and independent life in the United States. It is an investment in the well-being of the immigrants who come here and could not be more welcoming. Language acquisition and mastery is also a vehicle for helping to develop attachments—to fellow Americans, to what the country stands for, to its institutions, to its way of life, and to the national community more generally.

It is not that immigrants will necessarily be grateful for such help, although they might certainly be appreciative. Rather, one develops attachments through experiences that are shared to some degree and commonality is established. This is very difficult if two people do not speak or understand the same language.

Given these compelling reasons for reaching out to help immigrants in this way, it is surprising that more has not been done. Perhaps some worry about being criticizing for trying to "Americanize"—as if that were an act of cultural imperialism and not a vehicle for the realization of immigrants' hopes and aspirations. Perhaps the lessons of the Bilingual Education Act are still a haunting memory for some. Yet, whatever the reason, a laissez-faire approach to helping immigrants learn English damages immigrant mobility and attachment.

It is important to be very clear here. This is *not* a suggestion for a national law making English the language of the land. It is *not* a suggestion that we have an *English only* policy in the country. It is *not* a brief in favor of doing away with bilingual education. Immigrants and others are, in my proposal, welcome to their languages.

This *is* a suggestion that it is very important for immigrants to master English, as well as possible and as quickly as possible. It is a suggestion that this country pursue an *English first* policy. However, if forced to choose between an immigrant learning English to facilitate their entry into, and their ability to thrive in, the American national community, and a commitment to maintain their native language, I would opt for the former.

Hairdressers in Nevada: Spanish Sunsets?

RECOMMENDATION 3: **To the extent possible, English should be facilitated as the language of professional and public affairs in the United**

States. Other languages should be welcomed in those areas on a *temporary* basis, with a view toward encouraging persons to make the transition to a fuller English language facility.

Almost all private- and public-sector jobs require knowledge of English, except if a person is specifically hired for outreach to specific language communities. So, generally, those who would like to maximize their occupational access and mobility would be well advised to know English. Yet there is another arena of access and integration in the American national community. This involves government licenses, permits, and ultimately participation in America's civic system. Consider the case of Hispanic hairdressers in Nevada.[16]

A number of immigrants were practicing professional hairdressers in their home countries. Naturally, when they arrived here they hoped to take up the work they already knew. Yet, the state of Nevada, like other states, licensed hairdressers because of the chemicals and dyes involved in the work, and many immigrants failed a 125-question examination written in English. The issue had also come up with licensing used car salesmen and plumbers in California, and increasingly has and is likely to further find its way into a number of state licensing examinations—as, for example, with driver's licenses.

In the past, Nevada had allowed interpreters until accusations were made of cheating. The new debate in Nevada centered on public safety and fairness. One concern was that workers would be using chemicals and dyes labeled in English but be unable to read what they were using. Another was the unfairness of not offering the test in other languages. In fact, it turned out that there were more Asian than Hispanic hairdressers. In the end, the licensing body allowed persons to take the exam in a language other than English with advanced (six months) notice and allowed an interpreter to be present—paid for by the applicant.

The issue was framed as a clash among three values—encouraging and facilitating work, public safety, and fairness to all groups. We want immigrants who come to this country to become part of it by working, making a living, and becoming integrated into the productive community. But many immigrants who want to practice their trade as hairdressers and other licensed professions do not speak English well enough to take and pass a test of subject competency in English.

The Nevada solution was pragmatic and flexible. Yes, you could work. Yes, you needed to take the exam. Yes, a member of any language group could take the exam in their language if they provided a translator at their own cost.

So, is this a perfect resolution? Not quite. Lost in the debate were questions about doing more than encouraging economic self-sufficiency, about cultural and psychological integration as well.

What if, instead of granting persons a license in field X gained with the language aid of an interpreter, the licensing board introduced a language "sunset" provision? The licensing board would grant a provisional license gained with the aid of a language interpreter, with the understanding that the person would have to retake the exam in English in two, three, or however many years seemed appropriate. Exemptions could be made for those older immigrants, as they are in the English portion of the citizenship test.

Such an approach could be used in almost all cases for which language facility, not substantive competence, is an issue. It could also be easily accommodated in circumstances where competency must be retested after a period of time.[17] Such a proposal has much to recommend it. It would honor America's interest in and facilitation of the immigrant work ethic. It would be fair to all language groups. It would stimulate the acquisition of a competency that would advance mobility. Of particularly importance, by being time limited, it would encourage people to master the language in which they will conduct most of their lives in America's work and civic culture. And finally, in adapting such a measure, the competent governmental licensing agencies would send a message in support of learning English.

The same approach could be used in the political system. The Supreme Court has ruled that people cannot be discriminated against on the basis of their language ability. As a result, bilingual voting machines, voters' guides, and ballots are now features of American civic life.[18] This is paradoxical, because to vote you must be a citizen and to become a citizen you must demonstrate a competency in the English language. How it is possible to demonstrate enough English proficiency to become a citizen but not know enough English to understand the issues before you is one of the hazy mysteries of unexamined practice. Yet, what if a sunset provision were put in place for bilingual voting? New citizens must have a five-year residency (generally) before taking the citizenship and becoming naturalized.[19] What if, thereafter, they were allowed bilingual ballots for a limited period of time, say, eight or even ten years, with a suitable exception for older immigrants? Surely a decade gives immigrants ample opportunity to learn. No foreign-language ballots should be given to persons born in this country and reaching voting age.

Critics will argue that this deprives immigrants of their political rights. Yet, as a matter of public policy it could well be argued that the state has an investment in encouraging all its citizens to understand the language in which civic and political discourses are conducted. With rights come responsibilities as well.

Critics might argue that the message being sent by such a policy is disrespect for an immigrant's native language. This might be an appealing argument to some, but it fails to draw a distinction between disrespect and preference for good reason. I can prefer A to B without any necessary disrespect or dislike of B. Inherent in the disrespect argument is a demand for primacy that would result in foreign languages being put on an equal governmental basis with the language of the country.

The argument is disingenuous given the degree of diversity in many areas. It would essentially require the United States to be a multilingual country. It is clear that many advocates of ethnic language rights want others to learn theirs. It is not as clear that they are willing to learn others'. At any rate, if the integration of a national community is an important goal, splintering the country into multiple, government-sanctioned language groups seems a poor vehicle for accomplishing this important purpose.

Civic Integration

RECOMMENDATION 4: **Schools remain the most critical institution for helping young people to develop knowledge of America, a realistic appreciation of their country, and an understanding of the common cords that link each of us to each other and those who have gone before us. Affection for one's country and a commitment to it grow out of realistic knowledge and pride in what has been accomplished, alongside the acknowledgment of what remains to be done. Support of this country, its way of life, its institutions, and its people relies on realistic knowledge about all these things. It means attention to the things that have united us, as well as those that have divided us. It means attention to the ways in which our institutions have developed, along with their growing pains. And it means attention to the many things that America provides, as well as those it does not yet offer. This is a central responsibility of public education.**

Becoming part of the American national community is not only a matter of cultural adaptation or language acquisition. It is not only coming over here with the psychological elements—like ambition, determination, resilience, and optimism—that help lift new and older Americans alike through the trails and opportunities of freedom and capitalism.

New immigrants and Americans alike need to become more integrated into the American national civic community. For many new adult immigrants, it will be hard enough for them to culturally adapt, become familiar with the language, and earn a living. That is the commitment they made in coming here as working-age adults. Yet, cultural centers and language classes can provide some orientation to the country and its operation, including its political life.

But the real focus of American policy here should be on the immigrant children, and this means a focus on schools. Few readers of this book will need to be reminded that the civics curriculum in American public schools has been a battleground for thirty years and remains so. Education, like other fields, has its enthusiasms and fads, but here the failures result in lifelong disabilities.

The battle over civic books and classroom content has been, and remains, intense. Well-meaning and some not-so-well-meaning advocates have insisted that ethnic contributions, real and sometimes imagined, be given prominence, even primacy, in learning American history. Others, wanting to ensure that children never forget each and every wrong committed by this country and its leaders historically, insist that material be repeatedly emphasized. Still others are equally insistent that Americans are insular and insufficiently tolerant and demand that Americans learn more about other cultures. As a result of these centrifugal pulls, students gain very little appreciation of their common heritage or why it remains a beacon for the millions who come here and many millions more who would like to do so.

Going back to my discussion of patriotism in chapter 3, immigrants find, or are given, little basis for *appreciating* what this country has accomplished, and why it might be worth supporting, not in every single instance, but in general. Having little appreciation of its virtues, along with its stumbles, there is less of a basis for feeling that the country merits a commitment toward it, its institutions, and its way of life. After all, if our history, institutions, and way of life are essentially corrupt in some fundamental way, whether because of consumerism, racism, or other failures, how could we possibly develop a commitment and responsibility for it? And if our identities are primarily tied to our particular racial, ethnic, or religious group, how can we develop a warmth and affection for our fellow Americans, those who do not share our skin color, country of origin, or the other categories that can be used to set us apart from each other?

In fact, one of the primary lessons that American education needs to keep in focus is that we are all, or should be, more American than otherwise. We need a curriculum that comes to grip with our failures, to be sure. But more than that, children need to be reminded that no country is perfect, no group an identity island, and aspiration, effort, and perseverance are the quintessential American narratives of which every immigrant and citizen has his or her own version. We truly are more American than otherwise.

Along with the themes that help immigrants and citizens alike to understand the ways in which we share a common heritage of aspirations and experiences, Americans need to know more about their own country. I have already reviewed the dismal state of civic knowledge in our public schools in chapter 7. To give just one reminder of that data, more than half of high school seniors thought that Italy, Germany, or Japan was a U.S. ally in World War II.[20]

Lest this be seen as an issue affecting only public schools with their mixed record of academic performance, the results of a survey conducted at America's most elite colleges is instructive. A recent report by the American Council of Trustees and Alumni and groups that support liberal arts education recently asked a series of high-school-level multiple-choice questions to a randomly selected group of graduating seniors at the nation's most elite colleges, including Harvard, Princeton, and Brown. The results were dismal: A total of 71 percent of our nation's best students did not know the purpose of the Emancipation Proclamation; 78 percent were not able to identify the author of the phrase "Of the people, for the people, by the people"; and 70 percent could not link Lyndon Johnson with the passage of the historic Voting Rights Act. Yet 99 percent correctly identified Beavis and Butthead, and 98 percent could correctly identify Snoop Doggy Dog.[21] One study of students at fifty-five elite universities found that over a third were unable to identify the Constitution as establishing the division of powers in our government, only 29 percent could identify the term "Reconstruction," and 40 percent could not place the Civil War in the correct half century. A survey carried out by the Columbia University School of Law found that almost two-thirds of Americans think Karl Marx's maxim "From each according to his ability, to each according to his needs" was or could have been written by the Framers and included in the Constitution.[22] Of the fifty top colleges and universities in the country, none require the study of American history, and only 10 percent require students to study any history at all.[23]

There can be little or no warmth or affection for, appreciation of, or pride in this country if citizens do not have much beyond erroneous ideas of the facts of its existence. There can be little informed support of the country, or its way of life, its institutions, and its fellow members if the country is covered over by a vast swath of historical amnesia.

Affection for one's country, and a commitment to it, grow out of realistic knowledge and pride in what has been accomplished, and of what remains to be done. These matters will provide U.S. residents with a fuller, more balanced appreciation of their country and hence for the basis for an attachment that may honor it, do it justice, and improve it.

Noncitizen Voting

RECOMMENDATION 5: **Noncitizens should not be allowed to vote in national, state, or local elections. Consideration, however, should be given to allowing legal residents with children the ability to vote in local school board elections. Immigrants should be encouraged to work within the political and civic organizations of their choice as**

soon as they wish to do so. This includes campaigning, contributing money, and other general features outside voting that inform American civic life.

New York City's Charter Revision Commission recently met to consider a resolution calling on Governor George Pataki to give the city the right to allow noncitizens to vote in local elections. A bill to that effect has already been introduced in the State Assembly. Many may be surprised to learn that noncitizen voting is already on the books in several localities in the United States and is being pushed in many more.

Advocates advance many arguments for this change.[24] It is only fair, they say, because noncitizens already pay taxes and can serve in the military. It provides an ideal way for new immigrants to learn about citizenship. It helps new immigrants feel more welcomed and included. It ensures that those who are not yet citizens will be represented. And it will help to increase declining rates of political participation. These arguments seem reasonable. To advocates they are compelling. Yet, a closer look at each suggests they are neither.

Voting has always been a critical element of full citizenship. One can trace America's moral and political development through the expansion of suffrage—to the poor, different religions, races, or ethnic groups. It is true that over our 229 years of existence, a few localities allowed resident noncitizens to vote. However, this was always a minuscule exception to a general rule that reserved voting to citizens. By the late 1800s, this practice, limited as it was, had almost wholly died out, and with good reason.

Voting is one of the few, and doubtlessly the major, difference between citizens and noncitizens. Citizenship itself, and open access to it, is one of the major unifying mechanisms of "E pluribus unum." When citizenship loses its value—and it would if voting were not an earned privilege—a critical tie that helps bind this diverse country together will be lost. Given the challenges that face us, this ought not be done lightly. Some will ask about fairness. It is often overlooked that immigrants from most countries enjoy an immediate rise in their standard of living because of this country's advanced infrastructure, for example, hospitals, electricity, communications. They also get many services for their taxes, such as public transportation, police, and trash collection. As for serving in the armed forces, noncitizens earn this country's gratitude and, by presidential order, a shortening of the period before they can become citizens.

Moreover, no law bars noncitizens from learning democracy in civic organizations or political parties. No law keeps them from joining unions or speaking out in public forums. Indeed, no law bars them from holding positions of responsibility in all these groups. In all these many ways, legal residents can learn about their new country and its civic traditions. Voting is not the only means to do so, and it may not even be the best; it can be done from start to finish with the pull of a lever.

Some will ask how noncitizens are represented. The very fact that advocates push noncitizen voting undercuts the argument that this group's interests are not represented. This country is a republic, not a democracy. We depend on our representatives to consider diverse views. The views of legal noncitizen residents are no exception. The more such persons take advantage of the many opportunities to participate in our civic and political life, the more their voices will be heard.

As to those who argue that allowing noncitizens to vote will encourage more participation, the record of noncitizen voters should lead advocates to pause and reflect. Takoma Park, Maryland, often cited as a model by advocates, refuses to ascertain whether noncitizen voters are in the country legally. Even so, their participation went from a high point of 25 percent in 1997 to 12 percent in the next election and to 9 percent in the election thereafter.

There are many things this country could do to make new immigrants feel welcomed. We could provide free English classes to all those who want them—and that desire is great. We could set up classes to help immigrants learn about the nuts and bolts of our country's life. How do you get insurance? Why do you raise your hand in class? We take these things for granted, but new immigrants cannot.

Every effort ought to be made to integrate legal immigrants into our national community. Yet, is it not fair to ask that they know something about it before they fully take up the responsibilities, and not just the advantages, of what has been the core of citizenship?

Advocates of noncitizen voting do not discuss whether these new voters would need to demonstrate language proficiency or knowledge of this country, as they must now do for naturalization. Would that requirement be waived? Nor have they said what they would do if many noncitizens decided that there was no longer a need to become a citizen—because they already can vote. We do immigrants no favor by giving in to demands for ever thinner forms of citizenship.

Illegal Immigration: A Misplaced Welcome

RECOMMENDATION 6: **Every effort should be made to discourage illegal immigration, including—but not limited to—placing pressure on foreign governments to help stem the flow of such immigrants, making business and other institutions responsible for providing correct legal information about persons working for them, and taking steps to remove them if they are not. This should also include removing the incentives like driver's licenses and in-state tuition rates, and making "no amnesties" national immigration policy—with excep-**

tions for specialized circumstances such as natural disasters or personal tragedies.

"Welcoming," as noted, is a word that appeals to American national psychology. Americans are by nature open and generous. They are also, as a rule, pragmatic and generally orientated toward productive results. As already noted, they are also increasingly disinclined to make adverse judgments about others' tough choices.

It is hard for many Americans to seem harsh or even to be tough-minded when it comes to politics and life. We can see these characteristics in operation concerning illegal immigration. Americans do not like it. Yet, there is some ambivalence associated with those feelings.

For example, an international survey conducted by the Chicago Council on Foreign Relations asked Americans to name and assess a number of possible threats to the United States and some possible responses to them. Seventy percent expressed the desire to "control and reduce illegal immigration." Interestingly, only 48 percent of an "opinion leader" sample felt this way.[25] Along similar lines, a poll conducted by the Roper Organization found that 85 percent of Americans believe that illegal immigration is a "problem"; 47 percent of these thought it was a "serious" problem, and 68 percent would support the goal of completely halting it.[26]

How could that be accomplished? A large majority, 64 percent, are willing to support strict enforcement of laws against illegal immigrants that would make that status inhospitable. More specifically, 88 percent agree that Congress should pass laws requiring state and local officials to notify immigration officials when they determine that someone is here illegally or has presented a false document. Additionally, a majority of Americans would support Congress passing laws requiring verification of legal immigration status for persons applying for a driver's license (82 percent), opening a bank account (75 percent), or enrolling in a school or college (73 percent). A total of 87 percent want current laws against employers who hire illegal immigrants to be strictly enforced. Seventy-nine percent would like employers to be required to verify the immigration status of those they hire.

Still, there is an undercurrent of sympathy for those who endure those hardships for a better life. Most illegal immigrants are drawn by the wish for a better life and the hope that once they are here they will be able, somehow, to stay. The second is not a farfetched hope, as many past exceptions and amnesties suggest. Moreover, the view that illegal immigrants perform jobs that "Americans don't want to do" adds understanding and appreciation framed by self-interest to sympathy.

Is Illegal Immigration Victimless?

Some, like Peter Schuck, go so far as to call illegal immigration a "victimless crime."[27] It is not. Some people believe that illegal immigrants provide a pool of willing and cheap workers for jobs that no American wants. That is not quite true. Not all jobs that illegal immigrants hold are jobs that no American would do. Nor has that conventional wisdom been tested by raising wages. And as long as wages are artificially depressed by illegal immigrants—for whom extremely low pay represents a comparative improvement over what they could earn in their home countries—that wisdom will not be tested.

The idea that illegal immigration is nothing to be concerned about appears in many places and institutions. Peter Beinhart, who complained about the Bush administration's detentions of possible or suspected terrorists after September 11, 2001, says that most were held "mostly for *minor* immigration offenses."[28] Apparently, lying on a visa application, overstaying the visa period, holding a job when you are not legally entitled to do so, and using false documentation constitute "minor" offenses.

When federal agents began background checks of 750,000 airline employees in the wake of September 11, they found false identification papers in wide use by workers at airports as well as criminal backgrounds that had been concealed. A substantial number were arrested. There were complaints about these actions. Eliseo Medina, executive vice president of the Service Employees International Union, said the raids were not focused on terrorism but on immigrants. Medina said, "It's a disgrace. President Bush is punishing hardworking immigrants for the crimes committed last September by terrorists."[29] Apparently, Medina feels that it is perfectly permissible for people to break the immigration laws, lie on their government documents, and conceal their criminal backgrounds.

Illegal immigration is most certainly not a victimless crime. It fuels criminal transport gangs. It makes some immigrants into the modern version of indentured servants. It subjects them to death in passage. It results in bribes to officials, which in turn corrupts the government. It breeds an underground of illegal activity, including document forgery. It allows the exploitation of workers by their employers. It promotes disrespect for the country's laws. It creates enormous costs for the United States in terms of hospital and other service uses. It breeds a sense of insecurity among Americans that their borders are unsafe and insecure. And it is dangerous.

In an age of catastrophic terrorism, unverified identities are a source of potential disaster. Mohammed Atriss, a businessman who sold fake identification cards to two of the September 11 terrorists, was convicted on a lesser charge simply because he sold tens of thousands of fake IDs to immigrants and had no idea of the background or intentions of these two clients.[30] Illegal immigration spawns crime and underground criminal activities. Some of these, like transporting illegal immigrants, may or may not be more dangerous to the immigrants than to the country. Other illegal activities, like the vast underground of illegal identification and rootless lives, provide a pool of potential danger for the country itself.

The inquiry into September 11 revealed many disturbing facts about the state of the U.S. immigration system. The terrorists were smart and focused, and they exploited every loophole they could find. One of these was the ability to get a driver's license in Virginia by having someone vouch for you in an affidavit, without having to present proof of residency in person. Several men were charged and convicted for helping some of the terrorists obtain identity documents. One of them was Martinez-Flores, a native of El Salvador who entered the United States illegally in 1994 and worked as a day laborer in northern Virginia. His lawyer said that Flores was in need of money, so he helped the two terrorists obtain their Virginia driver's license documents.[31] Living and taking part in a culture of illegality fosters illegality, with results that can be catastrophic to this country.

Institutional Interests versus Community Interests

Many American institutions have been unhelpful in addressing the issues of illegal aliens. Some churches have set up refreshment stands along the paths that illegal immigrants crossing the Mexican border take to get into the United States. They view their primary mission as helping people. Yet they are also helping people to contribute to the general set of problems noted above and below.

In the wake of the first World Trade Towers bombing in 1993, the U.S. Immigration and Naturalization Service (INS) and other federal officials realized that the terrorists had made use of student visas to enter the United States. When they set out to try and tighten this potential source of danger, schools were reluctant to get involved.

When the federal government asked schools with large foreign student populations to report the collection of the fees they charge these students in electronic form, making and keeping track of such students easier, a number of universities demurred.[32] Their job, they said, was as students' advocates, not regulators. Dixon C. Johnson, executive director of the office of international services at the University of Southern California, was quoted as saying, "We don't want to be a bill collector or policeman for the government." The idea that university administrations do not regulate students seems counterintuitive.

Two years before September 11, the INS asked schools to help them upgrade their background checks on the many foreign students who come to the United States each year. The schools complained that it was a privacy violation to conduct in-depth checks of applicants whose backgrounds raised red flags of possible terrorist involvement. They objected to scrutinizing bank accounts of students, their parentage, birthplaces, and travel histories. The vice president of the American Council on Education was quoted as saying, "We, like most Americans, are very uncomfortable with any form of profiling. We are not law enforcement officers."[33]

Even law enforcement officers, however, cannot be wholly counted upon in this matter because of conflicting views and felt professional obligations. In Austin, the assistant police chief said, "Our job is to protect and serve the residents of Austin, legal and illegal. It's not our job to deport anyone, or report them to INS."[34] That report continues: "This year, police joined Mexican consular officials to publicize the department's "we won't tell" pact with immigrants. The police are caught between two conflicting obligations: to protect every person regardless of their immigration status, and not to turn a blind eye to the breaking of the law.

The issue, however, became much more complicated after September 11. Among the many failures of the INS was an inability to track people who had been before a judge in an administrative hearing and been ordered to leave the country. At least 314,000 simply then disappeared, as absconders. The period after September 11 brought into sharper relief the holes in the immigration system that had been exploited. Congress mandated a tightening of controls. A list of all absconders was put in a nationwide database that local police use to check on individual status when they are following through on an infraction. "In theory, this law should only worry absconders, but critics complained that doing so would give rise to the very fears that "we won't tell" pacts were meant to dispel. Critics did not explain how having police ignore law and court orders would give Americans and legal immigrants confidence in their integrity."

Defining Lawbreaking as Legal

These are familiar issues to those in the immigration field. However, there is another issue that gets less attention. Speaking to immigrants at a ceremony at Ellis Island, President George W. Bush reminded those assembled to take the naturalization oath that "our democracy's sustained by the moral commitments we share: reverence for justice, and obedience to the law." One could ask whether illegal immigrants who begin their lives here by not respecting the immigration laws of the country are good candidates for citizenship.[35]

The view that illegal immigration is a victimless crime rests on a basic error. The premise is wrong. Illegal immigration is deeply corrosive and corrupting—of the national community, of trust in government to secure the country and enforce the laws, of institutions that turn away or flout such laws, in allowing large anomic pools of unconnected individuals to be loose in the United States, in the primary and secondary crimes that such circumstances spawn, and in other ways as well. An examination of these issues suggests there are many rather than no victims.

As noted above, borders and boundaries have deep psychological as well as cultural and political significance. Aside from helping to demarcate here from there, a country's boundaries and borders represent the range of home in whose boundaries citizens expect to be safe, and they expect their government to take appropriate and necessary steps to ensure that. Millions and millions of illegal immigrants breach that understanding. As a result, citizens care about this issue, and more and more of them since September 11, rightly conclude that the government either cannot or will not effectively address and resolve this issue. It is not a good development for the national community to view its government as either helpless or hopeless in matters that affect people's basic sense of territorial and personal security.

Nor are matters helped when public officials substitute their personal views for national law and public policies. There are federal laws that require illegal aliens convicted of crimes to have their immigration status reported to the federal government. At least five major American cities—Chicago, Houston, San Francisco, Seattle, and New York—refused to comply with this requirement, making themselves so-called sanctuary cities.

In New York, Mayor Edward I. Koch had signed an executive order in 1990 prohibiting city officials from reporting illegal immigrants to the federal authorities.[36] In 2002, a large number of Dominicans living in New York were killed in the crash of an airplane taking them to a homeland visit. Grieving families expressed concern that if they traveled abroad to the funerals, they would have difficulty returning to the United States. Then-mayor Rudolph Giuliani said he would issue a temporary waiver of the enforcement of immigration laws given the circumstances.

Then–New York City mayor-elect Michael Bloomberg then said that he would make permanent his predecessor Giuliani's temporary waiver of immigration enforcement and extend it to all undocumented aliens in the city. He said in an interview with WABC Radio's John Gambling, "Whether they're Dominicans or not, those people who are undocumented do not have to worry about city government going to the federal government."[37]

New York repealed its statutory resolution in 2003 after a woman was raped by five men, four of whom were illegal immigrants with past records that, if reported, could have led to deportation. Immigration advocates argued that the new executive order would "erode any trust immigrants had in local policy."[38] How the selective enforcement of laws would raise immigrant trust in the policy was not made clear.

In Boulder, Colorado, one city council member said he thought undocumented workers should be allowed an opportunity to earn a living locally.[39] In one sanctuary city, a county worker was fired for turning over to the INS authorities the name of an illegal alien. This person had been found to be out of compliance with the state's support laws and was a convicted heroin dealer.[40] The fired worker had alerted the authorities who were seeking that illegal alien to his presence in her office. The administrative officer in the hearing said, "It is difficult for the average person to comprehend that the chief law enforcement officer in the county instructs his employees to ignore criminal behavior they observe."[41]

Several important issues are raised by these facts. Let us assume that the city mayors and other leaders who support a de facto amnesty for illegal aliens do so out of sympathy and a wish not to make life harder than it already is for those who come here illegally. On the other side of the ledger, those leaders are sending a signal of acceptance and encouragement to illegal aliens— not only in New York but also in the many places abroad where people pay attention to these issues. One message is that if you make it to New York, San Francisco, or other sanctuary cities, you are safe from deportation.

Another signal is being sent as well: that although the United States has laws against illegal immigration, some of the country's highest elected officials do not really plan to enforce them. I am referring here not only to mayors of big cities but also to Congress itself. When Congress was considering allocating money to cities to help with homeland security, a resolution to financially penalize cities that retained their "sanctuary status" was turned back 322 to 104.[42] Understandably, many no doubt felt that homeland security was too important an issue to hold up while seeking to force cities to adhere to the law on illegal immigration. Yet, there is unlikely to be much federal pressure against such state or local stances in the future because there has been little in the past. This sends the clear message that major players in the American political system disregard the law and thereby encourage others to do the same.

Or consider the debate over driver's licenses. In New York, two State Assembly members introduced legislation to make it easier for illegal immigrants to get driver's licenses.[43] The sponsors argued that allowing illegal immigrants to obtain a license would allow them to have a documented identity and to lead less isolated lives. One of the sponsors is quoted as saying, "Current laws do not recognize that undocumented immigrants routinely operate motor vehicles on state roads as part of their livelihood." The logic here seems to be that because illegal immigrants are already in the country illegally, are already working illegally, and are already driving illegally, the state should not enforce its laws but rather should legalize their breaking of the laws. These sets of arguments seem a somewhat novel interpretation of the American Creed as expressed by President Bush at the Ellis Island naturalization ceremony, in which he pointed out that we are bound together as a nation by obedience to laws.

In California, a similar measure was touted as a way to help police identify drivers who are stopped for infractions and encourage illegal immigrants to get insurance.[44] Traditionally, the police response to stopping a driver for cause and finding that he or she was driving without a license or insurance would be to not let the driver continue driving and to issue appropriate violation tickets. In the past, removing such drivers from their vehicle and the vehicle from the road was also considered a way to increase the safety of the community.

The United States has passed laws making it a crime to knowingly hire illegal immigrants. Yet these laws are not routinely enforced. Investigations take time and labor power, and enforcement agencies argue plausibly that they have more immediate important concerns in the wake of September 11. Employers, hungry for cheap, reliable labor, do not expend much time or energy checking documents and argue that they are also victims of false documentation.

Yet even when both the federal government and business employers have direct, easily obtainable evidence of immigration wrongdoing, they back off. In the wake of September 11, federal officials began to send employers lists of workers' social security numbers that did not match—nearly a million of them—indicating that false information had been given.[45] However, the government decided to scale back the program because so few employers responded and there were thus too few corrections to its numbers.[46]

This is why so-called grand bargains do not work. They are neither grand nor bargains—at least for Americans. The 1986 Immigration and Control Act (IRCA) was supposed to be one of the grand bargains, a "one-time" amnesty for illegal immigrants in return for sanctions against employers who subsequently hired them. Illegal immigrants got their amnesty, but businesses were allowed a large loophole that allowed them to only show that the people they hired had identification. The fact that this loophole contributed to a vast empire of fraudulent identifications was of no concern to employers; after all, they had done their part by asking.

Moreover, the IRCA amnesty was hardly a one-time amnesty. Various forms of "adjustments" and "regularizations" have been proposed and enacted since then, including the most recent batch of proposals for the massive legalization of illegal immigrants—one from President Bush and a separate one from Senators Edward M. Kennedy (D-Mass.) and John McCain (R-Ariz.). Under these schemes, illegal immigrants will "earn" their legality by paying a fee. In return, they will have access to all the benefits that U.S. citizenship can and does confer on them, their families, and their relatives. These benefits are immense, and all you have to do to receive them is break the law. Surely this will not dissuade other illegal immigrants from the prospect of achieving an unimaginable increase in their standard of living and those of their family by simply paying a relatively small fine.

Amnesty advocates argue that this new grand bargain will be "tough as nails."[47] Past experiences with such calming reassurances leave anyone with one ounce of realism skeptical. The bilingual education bill, which is at the center of much controversy over teaching to immigrants English in school, started out as a bill to further the teaching of English not home languages but was derailed and hijacked as it was implemented after congressional passage. IRCA stimulated more illegal immigration, as amnesties do, because the anticipation of future adjustments is historically realistic and the incentives are high.[48]

Illegal Incentives

Few people realize that the Social Security Administration holds the Social Security payments of persons with invalid Social Security numbers in separate accounts that can be adjusted if the person gets a legitimate Social Security card—that is, becomes legalized.[49] Mexican president Vicente Fox has asked that Mexicans who have worked in the United States, including illegal aliens, be credited with the money they paid in holding accounts. Aside from the difficulties of ascertaining whether the person claiming a false Social Security number was the person who used it, there is another large issue involved. The ability to come to the United States using forged documents, including Social Security cards, and then to receive this money would create an enormous incentive for illegal immigrants to come to the United States.[50]

In truth, those incentives are already well stacked in favor of coming, and the incentives are growing. True, immigrants who cross the borders, especially the southern ones, undertake an arduous and dangerous journey. Yet once here, their economic lives take a turn for the better. Yes, it is true that they are often offered low-paying jobs and not able to rely on many of the protections available to legal workers. Yet, at the same time, even comparatively low wages and hard work may be better than the dismally low wages for hard work that is their lot in their home countries. In one three-month period, illegal immigrants deposited $50 million in California banks.[51]

Every immigrant who comes to the United States, whether legally or not, has the advantage of this country's infrastructure, which includes many things that Americans take for granted but the persons who live in many other countries cannot. Among other things, they include such basics as running water, sanitation, electricity, modern hospitals with well-trained doctors, and free public education. These "basics" are provided by a tax infrastructure to which illegal immigrants have difficulty contributing because they often work off the books.

Even a college education is increasingly becoming an incentive for illegal immigrants and their families throughout the country.[52] One of the controversies that has sprung up in a number of states is whether illegal immigrants' children should be college educated at "in-state" rates—which are appreciably lower than out-of-state tuition. In some respects, the former are subsidized by the latter, and additionally by state taxpayers.

A 1988 federal law required such students to pay the out-of-state rate. Yet California, Texas, Utah, Oregon, Washington, and most recently New York have adopted legislation that would circumvent that federal law by granting in-state tuition to any graduate of a high school within the state, regardless of immigration status.[53] New York had not complied with the law until it conducted a review after September 11. It then raised the tuition of illegal immigrants attending colleges in the City University system to be in conformity with federal law.

One response to these changed circumstances came from the president of one of these colleges, who wrote to the *New York Times* as follows: "Hunter College was one of the first City University of New York schools to ensure that no students' studies would be adversely affected by an increase in tuition charged to CUNY students who are illegal immigrants. When the tuition changes were announced, Hunter College immediately made available a generous package of grants, interest-free loans, and other payment plan assistance according to the individual needs of the students." In other words, illegal immigrants were now guaranteed a generous package of grants and other financial incentives. Because the pot for such aid is limited, illegal immigrants became in effect a preferred group for the distribution of financial support.[54]

Welcoming Illegal Immigrants—Revisited

Americans are a generous people. They are also people, as Alan Wolfe found, who dislike making judgments about others' choices.[55] Illegal immigrants and their families force Americans at all levels to make tough choices that most would prefer not to make.

There is little support in the United States for illegal immigration—and less so since September 11. Yet Americans retain an image of immigration that has much to do with its iconic place in American history. It is easy to imagine that the future will resemble the past—that immigrants will become part of the American community.

Yet it is hard to imagine that the issues raised by illegal immigration will disappear. Long-term solutions like making the many countries that fuel illegal immigration to America more attractive to their own citizens is a long-term proposition. In the meantime, illegal immigrants keep arriving at a minimum of about 500,000 a year.

Illegal immigration is not a victimless crime. The victims are American institutions and the sense of a safe, rule-abiding community. Americans, and many of their leaders, do not wish to be or appear ungenerous or intolerant. So, at a time when the country's sense of physical and psychological security has been shaken, it is not reassuring that some political leaders have turned a blind eye toward illegal immigration. At a time when there are major questions about how well the massive influx of post-1965 immigrants is being integrated into American society, several democratic presidential candidates in 2004 called for blanket amnesties for more than 8 million illegal immigrants.[56] At a time when the physical safety of tens, perhaps hundreds, of thousands of Americans is dependent on better knowledge of who is coming into the country and why, some institutions demur against doing things that they have defined as outside their traditional roles.

Yet these issues will have to be addressed, because these are not traditional times. Should there be another round of amnesties to "regularize" illegal immigrants? Should illegal immigrants be given driver's licenses? Should they pay less tuition? What do all these issues suggest about the stance of Americans toward these issues in the future?

If the United States and its leaders fail to act, has the country not essentially just become a new home to all those who can come and overstay or slip across the borders? What are the implications of that stance for the American national community and attachments to it?

These are all difficult questions. However, they are made more so by a failure to ask and answer a prior one: Why has this country not done more to stem the flow of illegal immigrants and to make it less attractive to not follow our immigration laws? Why are businesses not required to check the Social Security numbers of their employees and require verification of correct information? Why is more pressure not placed on the top sending countries of illegal immigrants to help stop the flow? Why do we not have better tracking information so that we know who is in the country and whether or not they have overstayed their visas?

These questions lead to difficult, and perhaps tough, policies. Some people will not be able to come to the United States. That is unfortunate. Yet we cannot have open borders—regardless of the editorial views of the *Wall Street Journal* and liberal theorists. Open borders are unsustainable. So long as we have a fair, balanced system of immigration, the United States can go a long way toward being able to claim legitimacy in protecting its borders and the well-being of its citizens and their communities from being victims of what is assuredly not a victimless crime.

Notes

1. Jim Edgar, Doris Meissner, and Alejandro Silva, *Keeping the Promise: Immigration Proposals from the Heartland* (Chicago: Chicago Council on Foreign Relations, 2004), 34–35; available at http://www.ccfr.org/publications/immigration/ccfr%20immigration%20task%20force%202004%2020report.pdf.

2. For another against-the-current kernel of conventional wisdom, see Charles Krauthammer, "Assimilation Nation," *Washington Post*, June 17, 2005.

3. Richard D. Lamm and Alan Simpson, eds., *Blueprint for an Ideal Legal Immigration Policy*, Center Paper 17 (Washington, D.C.: Center for Immigration Studies, 2001).

4. U.S. Commission on Immigration Reform, *Becoming an American: Immigration and Immigrant Policy—Final Report to Congress* (Washington, D.C.: U.S. Government Printing Office, 1977); see also Robert Pear, "Panel Urges that Immigrants Become Further Americanized," *New York Times*, October 1, 1979; Barbara Jordan, "The Americanization Ideal," *New York Times*, September 11, 1995.

5. Edgar, Meissner, and Silva, *Keeping the Promise*, 34–35.

6. Ibid., 35–36.

7. Peter J. Spiro, "Questioning Barriers to Naturalization," *Georgetown Immigration Law Journal* 13 (1999):479–517.

8. Edgar, Meissner, and Silva, *Keeping the Promise*, 54; Darryl Fears, "Immigration Measure Introduced," *Washington Post*, May 13, 2005.

9. Oscar Avila, "New Centers Try to Soften Immigrants' School Shock," *Chicago Tribune*, February 26, 2002.

10. Mike Wowk, "Class Offers Immigrants Tips on American Culture," *Detroit News*, February 21, 2002.

11. Harold F. Schiffman, *Linguistic Culture and Language Policy* (New York: Routledge, 1996), 21–24; Juan F. Perea, "Am I an American or Not? Reflections on Citizenship, Americanization and Race," in *Immigration and Citizenship in the 21st Century*, ed. Noah M. J. Pickus (Lanham, Md.: Rowman & Littlefield, 1998), 66. James Crawford, *Language Loyalty: A Source Book on the Official English Controversy* (Chicago: University of Chicago Press, 1992).

12. Stanley Lieberson with Timothy J. Curry, "Language Shift in the United States: Some Demographic Clues," *International Migration Review* 5 no. 2 (1971): 125–37; the citation here is on 125.

13. Schiffman, *Linguistic Culture*, 210–47. Other languages—most notably German—were widely spoken by waves of immigrants in the 1820s and especially in the 1870s. Sections of Pennsylvania and the Midwest had thriving German language communities, but by 1842 German was one more subject of academic instruction among many others and not the language of school instruction itself (p. 224).

14. Heinz Kloss, *The American Bilingual Tradition* (Rowley, Mass.: Newbury House, 1997), 284.

15. Schiffman, *Linguistic Culture*, 227.

16. Timothy Pratt, "Bilingual Voting Will Alter Local Politics," *Las Vegas Sun*, December 17, 2001.

17. A student in my immigration seminar, Marie Camacho, suggested wisely that language classes could be offered free of charge as a condition for a temporary waiver of the requirement for the examination in English.

18. Pratt, "Bilingual Voting."

19. This number may be reduced for legal immigrants who serve in the American armed forces.

20. These and other civics finds can be found at http://www.nces.ed.gov/nations reportcard/ushistory/results.

21. S. Veale, "History 101: Snoop Doggy Roosevelt," *New York Times*, July 2, 2000.

22. The Columbia Law School survey may be found at http://www2.law.columbia .edu/news/surveys/survey_constitution/index.shtml.

23. This is an American Council of Trustees and Alumni report, available at http:// www.goacta.org.

24. Ron Hayduk, "Democracy for All: Restoring Immigrants Voting Rights in the U.S.," *New Political Science* 26, no. 4 (2004): 499–523. Hayduk's concern turns out to be less about democracy than forging a "progressive" (read: left-wing) political agenda, which he believes can be brought about in part by allowing noncitizens to vote. A similar perspective is found in Lisa Garcia Bedolla, "Rethinking Citizenship: Noncitizen Voting and Immigrant Political Engagement," paper presented at the Nation of Immigrants Conference, Berkeley, Calif., May 2–3, 2003. More scholarly views on this issue and its history can be found in Jamin B. Raskin, "Legal Aliens, Local Citizens: The Historical, Constitutional, and Theoretical Meanings of Alien Suffrage," *University of Pennsylvania Law Review* 141 (1993): 1391–1470; Gerald M. Rosenberg, "Aliens and Equal Protection: Why Not the Right to Vote?" *Michigan Law Review* (April–May 1977): 1092–1136; and Ko-Chih R. Tung, "Voting Rights for Alien Residents—Who Wants It?" *International Migration Review* 19, no. 3 (1985): 451, 467.

25. Chicago Council on Foreign Relations, "U.S. Leaders: Top Line Report," October 2002, available at http://www.worldviews.org/index.html.

26. Roper Organization, "Americans Talk about Illegal Immigration," March 2003, available at http://www.roper.com.

27. Peter M. Schuck, *Citizens, Strangers, and In-Betweens: Essays on Immigration and Citizenship* (Boulder, Colo.: Westview Press, 1998).

28. Peter Beinhart, "Duty Free," *New Republic*, December 17, 2001; my emphasis.

29. Quoted in Associated Press, "Airport Sweep Nabs Airport Workers," August 23, 2002.

30. "Nation in Brief," *Washington Post*, June 4, 2003.

31. Josh White, "21 Months in Jail for Man Who Helped Terrorists Get Ids," *Washington Post*, February 16, 2002.

32. "Colleges Oppose Collecting Fee to Assist INS," *Los Angeles Times*, March 22, 2000.

33. James V. Grimaldi, "Planned INS Probes of Students Blocked: Schools Opposed In-Depth Checks," *Washington Post*, March 16, 2002.

34. Quoted by Deborah Tedford, "Police Say 'Protect and Serve' Extends to Illegal Immigrants," *Boston Globe*, December 30, 2001.

35. George W. Bush, "Remarks at an Immigration and Naturalization Service Ceremony on Ellis Island" (July 10), *Weekly Compilation of Presidential Documents* 37, no. 28 (2001): 1019–41; the citation here is on 1025.

36. Mae M. Cheng, "Koch Changes Immigration Tune," *New York Newsday*, June 3, 2003.

37. Quoted by Carl Limbacher, "Bloomberg: I Won't Enforce Immigration Laws," *NewsMax.Com*, November 19, 2001.

38. Cheng, "Koch."

39. Adam Ewing, "Aliens: Like a Virus,' Man Says," *Colorado Daily*, December 23, 2002.

40. Patrick J. McDonnell, "Calif. Worker Fired for Turning in Illegal Immigrant Is Reinstated," *Los Angeles Times*, August 16, 1998.

41. Adam Ewing, "'Aliens—Like a Virus,' Man Says," *Colorado Daily*, December 23, 2002.

42. Steve Miller, "Effort to Punish 'Sanctuary Cities' on Immigration Fails," *Washington Times*, June 26, 2003.

43. John Gonzales, "Measure to Help Illegal Immigrants: Lawmakers Push Bill to Ease Driver's Licensing," *New York Newsday*, April 21, 2003.

44. Rick Orlov, "City, Business Leaders Back License Measure: Cedillo Says Immigrant I.D. Card Bill Will Increase Safety," *Los Angeles Daily News*, May 30, 2003.

45. Eduardo Porter, "U.S. Crackdown on Immigration Hits Illegal Workers, Employers," *Wall Street Journal*, May 12, 2003.

46. Mary Beth Sheridan, "Social Security Scales Back Worker Inquires," *Washington Post*, June 18, 2003.

47. Tamar Jacoby, "Getting beyond the 'A-Word,'" *Wall Street Journal*, June 20, 2005.

48. A comprehensive empirical analysis of IRCA's effects concluded: "We find little evidence that IRCA has significantly deterred undocumented Mexicans from entering the United States." See Katharine M. Donato, Jorge Durand, and Douglas S. Massey, "Stemming the Tide? Assessing the Deterrent effects of the Immigration Reform and Control Act," *Demography* 29, no. 2 (1992): 155.

49. The following question and answer are taken from the Social Security Administration (SSA) website (http://www.ssa.gov):

Question: When I came to this country, I purchased a Social Security card from someone on the street. I used it when I obtained employment. What happens to all those earnings?

Answer: Each year employers send their W-2 forms to SSA and a match is performed against the name and Social Security number on the forms and SSA's records. If the information does not match, the earnings are held in a suspense file until we can determine to whom they belong. Once you have obtained authorization to work in this country from INS, and you have applied for and received your Social Security number [SSN], you should contact Social Security to have all your earnings posted to your correct SSN.

50. Jonathan Weisman, "U.S. Social Security May Reach to Mexico," *Washington Post*, December 19, 2002; "No Social Security for Illegal Immigrants" (editorial), *Intelligencer Wheeling New Register*, December 22, 2002.

51. Jacob Stevenson, "Mexican Migrants Saving Record Amounts in U.S. Banks," *TheNewsMexico.com*, February 7, 2002. Some further indications of the figures involved are covered in the remittance data in chapter 6.

52. Lori Montgomery, "Ehrlich Vetoes Tax, Tuition Bills," *Washington Post*, May 22, 2003; Ricardo Sanchez, "Immigrant Scholars Deserve a Break," *Seattle Post-Intelligencer*, November 8, 2000.

53. Joyce Purnick, "Ads Can Show Two Faces of a Candidate," *New York Times*, November 14, 2002.

54. Jennifer Raab, "Letter to the Editor," *New York Times*, February 18, 2002.

55. Alan Wolfe, *One Nation After All: What Middle-Class Americans Really Think About: God, Country, Family, Racism, Welfare, Immigration, Homosexuality, Work, the Right, the Left, and Each Other* (New York: Penguin Books, 1998).

56. Oscar Avila, "Legalization for Migrants Proposed," *Chicago Tribune*, October 11, 2002; Ruben Navarrette, "Bush Drops Mexico Initiative-and Leiberman Picks It Up," *Dallas Morning News*, June 11, 2003.

EPILOGUE

Americans do not often think about what it means to be an American. Lawrence Fuchs, whose magisterial work *The American Kaleidoscope* is a landmark in immigration research,[1] writes in another context: "I recently read an essay written by a Massachusetts woman, who said: 'I was well into adulthood before I realized that I was an American. Of course, I had been born in America and had lived here all my life, but somehow it never occurred to me that just being an American citizen meant that I was an American. Americans were people who ate peanut butter and jelly on mushy white bread that came out of plastic bags. Me, I was an Italian.'"[2]

This woman came to her realization late in life. She had first confused acculturation to products with identity. She then substituted that mistake with another: that being an American was "just being an American citizen."

We live in a time when there is a conflict between cultural and national affinities. Yet it has always been important to the health and well-being of the United States to help its immigrant citizens integrate their ethnic and cultural histories with a psychological attachment to the American national community.

National attachments do not happen primarily by accident. And a laissez-faire approach is not effective. This is especially true given the variety of powerful incentives both within and outside the United States that can weaken those attachments.

Perhaps in the past the United States could afford to have a number of its citizens be simply unaware of their connection to this country. Perhaps it could afford to have some of its citizens confuse their national identities with culinary preferences or other forms of "symbolic ethnicity."[3] But that is no longer the case—if it ever was.

The United States faces determined enemies both at home and abroad, and it will do so for the foreseeable future. In this truly dangerous climate, it is increasingly important that citizens become aware of their country—what it is, how it works, and most important, their relationship to it.

Patriotism is not, to use that hackneyed and shallow aphorism, "the last resort of scoundrels." It is the emotional glue of the American national com-

251

munity. A warmth and affection for, an appreciation of, a justifiable but not excessive pride in, a commitment and responsibility toward, and support of the United States—its institutions, its way of life and aspirations, and its fellow members—are the most basic bedrock attachments to this republic. Nurturing and developing those connections among citizens and immigrants alike is a legitimate and necessary undertaking by our government, our institutions, and our families.

To do so will not be easy. Citizens will be swimming against the tide domestically, where many argue that multiculturalism and the primacy of ethnic group attachment is the preferred identification. And they will also be swimming against the tide internationally, where liberal cosmopolitans of all types encourage them to look beyond their supposedly parochial national attachments.

Along the way, they will have to endure the opinion that they are insufficiently sensitive or tolerant. They will be told they are not skeptical enough about America's professed ideals or sufficiently cynical about their realization. And they will be reassured that as long as they affirm their general belief in democracy, nothing further is needed.

Immigrants and their families, not understanding that these perspectives are recent developments and who have little relationship with the country's real history and development, will surely be perplexed. Their former home countries will entice them. Their new country will generally stand mute rather than help and guide them to become more integrated and attached in their new home. If that happens, it will be hard if not impossible for new or even older Americans to connect their personal histories with this country's long tradition of freedom and opportunity.

America's institutions have a strong and necessary role in helping these critical attachments develop. That is why President George W. Bush's "We the People" program is one of the most important but underappreciated domestic initiatives his administration has undertaken.[4] Few people have ever heard of this program, and President Bush has rarely discussed it. He should do so more often. The president helped legitimize love of country after September 11, 2001. Yet he must urge us to remember that real patriotism includes not simply love of country but also respect for and attachment to its institutions and way of life and our fellow citizens.

Most Americans long to be united, to have a sense of community and attachment that transcends political, ethnic, racial, gender, and other differences. Americans want a president who will protect them in a world they now understand is very dangerous. But they also want a president who will reunite the frayed strands of the American national community. President Bush has proved he is willing to protect America's citizens. But he must understand that the most fundamental vision that unites Americans is not a new policy paradigm but a clear and strong sense of ourselves, all of us, as Americans.

Consider the president's proposed immigration program. It entails allowing workers who now come here illegally to do so legally for a limited time if they have work. The program has some attractive features. It certainly is compassionate, and it recognizes that people who come to this country want to better their circumstances and those of their families. The program would match participating workers with work. Yet President Bush has not yet addressed what will happen to those who bypass it, or those who want to stay.

President Bush wants to make the United States a more welcoming society for immigrants—and he is surely right to do so. He offers opportunity. Yet he has been silent about the responsibilities of immigrants. Of course, Americans have a right to expect immigrants to abide by U.S. laws. But should they not also learn English? Of course we want to honor the heritage of immigrants. But does this mean we should encourage them to retain their allegiance to their home country by voting there or advocating here on its behalf?

As I have tried to make clear, attachment to the American national community is not simply an immigrant problem. A lack of knowledge, understanding, and heartfelt attachment also affects many longtime American citizens and their children.

Some dismiss concern with national attachments to this country as being based on "outdated theories."[5] Along similar lines, Spiro urges Americans to accept other possible platforms for national personal emotional attachment like "new diasporas, transnational civil society, and other identity groups" and the "thinning out of national ties." He says that "it is time to accept an America . . . whose bonds are secondary to other forms of association . . . that appears to be an increasing accurate description of what America means and what it means to be an American: less."[6] For the sake of the viability of this republic, its people, and its institutions, let us hope not.

The question of American national identity and the strength of our attachments to the American national community are, given our diversity, critically important. In an age of terrorism that knows no bounds, it has become perhaps *the* most important domestic national issue facing this country.

Notes

1. Lawrence H. Fuchs, *The American Kaleidoscope: Race, Ethnicity, and the Civic Culture* (Hanover, N.H.: University Press of England, 1990).

2. Lawrence H. Fuchs, "Citizenship, Identity, and Loyalty," keynote address to the Conference on Dual Citizenship and Identity in the Global Context, Boston University, Boston, May 6, 2000.

3. Herbert Gans, "Symbolic Ethnicity: The Future of Ethnic Groups and Cultures in America," *Ethnic and Racial Studies* 2 (1979): 1020.

4. The program can be accessed at http://www.wethepeople.gov/.

5. Jeffrey R. O'Brien, "U.S. Dual Citizenship Voting Rights: A Critical Examination of Aleinikoff's Proposal," *Georgetown Immigration Journal* 13, no. 533 (1999): 573–95; the citation here is on 578.

6. Peter J. Spiro, "The Citizenship Dilemma," *Stanford Law Review* 51 (1999): 597–639; the citation here is on 601.

Appendix

Countries and Territories Allowing Dual Citizenship in Some Form

1. Albania
2. Antigua and Barbuda
3. Angola**
4. Argentina[1]
5. Australia[2]
6. Bahamas**
7. Bangladesh[3]
8. Barbados
9. Belarus
10. Belgium**
11. Belize
12. Benin
13. Bolivia[4]
14. Botswana**
15. Brazil**
16. Brunei Darussalam**
17. Bulgaria
18. Burkina Faso
19. Cambodia[5]
20. Cameroon**
21. Canada
22. Cape Verde
23. Central African Republic
24. Chile[6]
25. Colombia
26. Congo (formerly Zaire)**
27. Costa Rica
28. Côte d'Ivoire (formerly Ivory Coast)
29. Croatia**
30. Cyprus
31. Cyprus (North)
32. Denmark**
33. Dominica
34. Dominican Republic
35. Ecuador
36. Egypt
37. Eritrea[7]
38. El Salvador
39. Fiji
40. Finland[8]
41. France
42. Gambia[9]
43. Germany[10]
44. Ghana
45. Greece[11]
46. Grenada
47. Guatemala
48. Guyana
49. Guinea-Bissau**
50. Haiti
51. Honduras**
52. Hungary
53. Iceland[12]
54. India[13]
55. Iran
56. Iraq**
57. Ireland

255

58. Israel
59. Italy
60. Jamaica
61. Japan[14]
62. Jordan
63. Latvia[15]
64. Lebanon
65. Lesotho
66. Liberia**
67. Liechtenstein
68. Lithuania[16]
69. Luxembourg**
70. Macao (with Portugal)
71. Macedonia
72. Madagascar
73. Malawi**
74. Maldives
75. Mali
76. Mauritania**
77. Mauritius
78. Moldova**
79. Mongolia **
80. Mozambique**
81. Myanmar **
82. Malta
83. Mexico
84. Montenegro (Yugoslavia)
85. Morocco
86. Namibia**
87. Nepal**
88. Netherlands**
89. New Zealand
90. Nicaragua**
91. Niger**
92. Nigeria
93. Northern Ireland*
94. North Korea[17]
95. South Korea**
96. Oman**
97. Pakistan**
98. Palau**
99. Panama

100. Papua New Guinea**
101. Paraguay
102. Peru
103. Pitcairn +
104. Philippines
105. Poland[18]
106. Portugal
107. Qatar**
108. Romania
109. Russia
110. Rwanda**
111. Saint Kitts (Saint Christopher) and Nevis
112. Saint Lucia
113. Saint Vincent
114. Senegal**
115. Serbia (Yugoslavia)
116. Sierra Leone**
117. Singapore**
118. Slovak Republic
119. Slovenia[19]
120. Samoa**
121. South Africa
122. Spain
123. Sri Lanka[20]
124. Sudan**
125. Swaziland**
126. Sweden**
127. Switzerland
128. Syria
129. Taiwan**
130. Tanzania**
131. Thailand**
132. Tibet
133. Togo
134. Tonga**
135. Trinidad and Tobago
136. Tunisia
137. Turkey
138. Tuvalu
139. Uganda**
140. Ukraine**

141. United Arab Emirates**
142. United Kingdom
143. United States
144. Uruguay
145. Uzbekistan**
146. Vanuatu**

147. Venezuela**
148. Vietnam **
149. Yemen**
150. Zambia**
151. Zimbabwe**

*Limited sovereignty, under U.K. law.
**Denotes a state that has no provision for dual citizenship but allows children of nationals born abroad to retain their home-country citizenship.

Notes

1. Citizens of Argentina can also hold dual citizenship with Spain as per bilateral agreement. See Investigations Service, U.S. Office of Personnel Management, *Citizenship Laws of the World* (Washington, D.C.: U.S. Government Printing Office, 2001), 19.

2. For information on Australia, see Gianni Zappala and Stephan Castles, "Citizenship and Immigration in Australia," *Georgetown Immigration Law Journal* 13 (1999): 273, n. 137. Also see Stephen Castles, "Multiculturalism Citizenship: A Response to the Dilemma of Globalization and National Identity?" *Journal of Intercultural Studies* 18, no. 5 (1997): 238, who quotes the Australian Citizenship Act of 1948 as follows: "People must have deliberately sought and acquired the citizenship of another country in order to lose their Australian citizenship; if they acquire it automatically rather than by taking some action to acquire it they do not lose their Australian citizenship."

3. The U.S. government reserves the right to recognize dual citizenship in certain cases. See Investigations Service, U.S. Office of Personnel Management, *Citizenship Laws*, 28.

4. A Bolivian woman, married to a foreigner, is not required to relinquish her Bolivian citizenship even if she acquires her husband's citizenship through their marriage. Former citizens of Spain and other Latin American countries, who become naturalized Bolivians, are not required to relinquish their previous citizenship as long as Bolivia has a reciprocal agreement with their former countries. See Investigations Service, U.S. Office of Personnel Management, *Citizenship Laws*, 36.

5. A Cambodian wife of a foreign national is permitted to retain her Cambodian citizenship unless required to renounce it by the laws of the husband's home country. Investigations Service, U.S. Office of Personnel Management, *Citizenship Laws*, 44.

6. Chile has a dual-citizenship agreement with Spain. A child born abroad to Chilean parents, who obtains citizenship of country of birth, may retain dual citizenship until the age of majority (twenty-one years). Upon reaching the age of majority, a person must choose which citizenship to retain. Persons, working or living abroad, who must acquire a foreign citizenship as a condition of remaining legally in that

country. See Investigations Service, U.S. Office of Personnel Management, *Citizenship Laws*, 50.

7. Special arrangements may be made for Eritrean citizens by birth who wish to retain a foreign citizenship they have since acquired. See Investigations Service, U.S. Office of Personnel Management, *Citizenship Laws*, 73.

8. Dual citizenship is accepted under these circumstances: Child acquires Finnish citizenship from one parent and another citizenship from the other parent. A Finnish citizen who marries a foreigner and automatically acquires the nationality of the foreign spouse without formal request. A child born to Finnish parents who becomes a foreign citizen by birth in another country. A child born abroad (as a dual citizen) must return to live in Finland before the age of twenty-two and upon reaching twenty-two must choose one nationality in order to retain Finnish citizenship. See Investigations Service, U.S. Office of Personnel Management, *Citizenship Laws*, 77.

9. A Gambian citizen, who acquires new citizenship through marriage, is not required to renounce Gambian citizenship. See Investigations Service, U.S. Office of Personnel Management, *Citizenship Laws*, 80.

10. In July 1999, the Citizenship Law Reform Act was published in the German official gazette. This act entered into force on January 1, 2000. Under the new law, German citizenship has always been and will continue to be passed on by parents to the children. Any child of a German national (mother or father, married or not married) will be considered a German citizen by birth, whether born inside or outside Germany. The Reform Act introduces an aspect of "Äuterritorial acquisition": any child born inside Germany to parents of foreign nationality will acquire German nationality by birth if at least one parent has been lawfully resident in Germany for at least eight years and has for at least three years been the holder of a certain higher form of residence permit. This new provision will apply to most children of migrant workers who have been living in Germany for at least eight years. Those children, however, once they have grown up will have to decide between keeping German citizenship and renouncing their other citizenship (i.e., that of their parents) or keeping the foreign nationality and losing the German nationality. Under the existing German Citizenship Law (which in this respect corresponds to that of many other countries) German nationals lose their German citizenship if and when they acquire a foreign nationality upon their own application, i.e., by naturalization. It has always been possible in theory to be granted a waiver by German authorities for keeping German citizenship when acquiring a foreign nationality. Under the new law this waiver will be granted more easily.

The relevant section of the act reads: "When deciding upon an application in accordance with sentence 1 (waiver), the public and private interests will have to be balanced. In the case of an applicant with residence abroad, it will have to be taken into consideration whether he/she can make the case for continuing links to Germany." That means, in effect, that in terms of the naturalization of foreigners as well as the acquisition of foreign citizenship by Germans, the threshold of tolerance of dual citizenship (which has never been a problem in the case of acquisition of several nationalities by birth) will be made much more flexible. While there is a provision requiring renunciation, Stephan Senders says that in the past there has been no requirement to prove that it was done. He reports that according to unofficial government estimates 8 percent of naturalizing Turks retain their Turkish citizenship. Ethnic Germans who have other citizenships were allowed, even under the old law, to retain their German citizenship even when they were naturalized in other countries. A 1993 government study estimated that 1.2. million Germans legally held a second foreign citizenship. See Stephan Senders, "National Inclusion in Germany," *New German Critique* 67 (1996): 147–75; the citation here is on 158–59. The fact that the United States makes no effort to follow through on the renunciation clause in its own oath of allegiance essentially renders any such provisions in the laws of other countries a moot point.

11. Greek law does not automatically remove citizenship upon a person acquiring a foreign citizenship. When a Greek citizen acquires another nationality, he or she is technically a dual citizen until the Greek government has given permission for the removal of Greek citizenship. See Investigations Service, U.S. Office of Personnel Management, *Citizenship Laws*, 84.

12. Dual citizenship not recognized. Exception: a child born to married parents of different nationalities, one being Icelandic and the other a foreigner. See Investigations Service, U.S. Office of Personnel Management, *Citizenship Laws*, 93.

13. See Peter M. Schuck, "The Re-Evaluation of American Citizenship," *Georgetown Immigration Law Journal* 12, no. 1 (1997): 1–34 (the citation here is on 11); and Schuck, *Citizens, Strangers, and In-Betweens: Essays on Immigration and Citizenship* (Boulder, Colo.: Westview Press, 1998), 222. On December 22, 2003, legislation was passed by the Indian Parliament to grant dual citizenship (a.k.a. overseas citizenship) to persons of Indian origin who are citizens of certain countries. The legislation will also grant overseas citizenship to Indian citizens who may take up the citizenship of these countries in the future. At present, this benefit is being extended to persons of Indian origin of the following sixteen specified countries: Australia, Canada, Finland, France, Greece, Ireland, Israel, Italy, Netherlands, New Zealand, Portugal, Republic of Cyprus, Sweden, Switzerland, United Kingdom, and the United States of America. See Cyrus D. Mehta, "Impact of Dual Citizenship for Persons of Indian Origin in the U.S.," *Immigration Daily*, February 19, 2004.

14. If a child is born abroad to Japanese parents, the child can acquire dual nationality if citizenship is also acquired in the country of birth. A person with dual nationality has to choose one nationality by the age of twenty-two years. If dual nationality is acquired between the ages of twenty and twenty-two, the person must choose one nationality within two years. If one does not choose Japanese nationality within these periods, the minister of justice can require one to choose a nationality. Failure to comply within one month of this requirement will result in loss of Japanese citizenship. See Investigations Service, U.S. Office of Personnel Management, *Citizenship Laws*, 103.

15. If a citizen of Latvia simultaneously can be considered a citizen or subject of a foreign country in accordance with the laws of that country, the citizen shall be considered solely a citizen of Latvia in relations with the Republic of Latvia. See Investigations Service, U.S. Office of Personnel Management, *Citizenship Laws*, 115.

16. Ruta M. Kalvaitis, "Citizenship and National Identity in the Baltic States," *Boston University International Law Journal* 16 (1998): 238; the citations here are to nn. 184 and 227. Note 184 reads: "Members of the Latvian diaspora, however, are allowed

to hold dual citizenship. See Law on Citizenship (Lat.), supra note 175, transitional provisions 1, 2." Note 227 reads: "Lithuania, however, allows members of its Western emigre community to hold dual nationality, despite the fact there is no established law to this fact."

17. It is difficult to renounce North Korean citizenship. Most citizens of North Korea who become naturalized citizens of another country will remain unofficial dual citizens, still considered North Korean citizens by the North Korean government. See Investigations Service, U.S. Office of Personnel Management, *Citizenship Laws*, 109.

18. Poland does not recognize dual citizenship of its citizens. Polish law does not forbid a Polish citizen from becoming the citizen of a foreign state but Polish authorities will only recognize the Polish citizenship. See Investigations Service, U.S. Office of Personnel Management, *Citizenship Laws*, 160.

19. To be granted citizenship: Both parents must be citizens of Slovenia. One parent is unknown or has no citizenship, but the other parent is a citizen of Slovenia. The child must either be registered with appropriate authorities or return home to Slovenia as a permanent resident before the age of eighteen. After the age of eighteen, a person who was not registered and is now considered a legal adult can still obtain Slovenian citizenship by personally declaring for Slovenian citizenship before the age of twenty-three. See Investigations Service, U.S. Office of Personnel Management, *Citizenship Laws*, 178.

20. Exception to the dual-citizenship laws is made if it is felt to be of benefit to Sri Lanka. See Investigations Service, U.S. Office of Personnel Management, *Citizenship Laws*, 185.

INDEX